The Secrets of Silk

From Textiles to Fashion

Priscilla Lowry

St John's Press
2004

First published in the United Kingdom in 2004 by
St John's Press

UK Agents and Distributors
St Johns Press
Prescott House
Old Hill, Longhope,
Gloucestershire, GL17 OPF
Email: silkbooks@the-workshop.org

New Zealand
Priscilla Lowry
39 Kawerau Avenue, Devonport,
Auckland, New Zealand
Email:silkroad16@aol.com
Website: www.priscillalowrysilks.co.uk

USA
Kristine Brooks
Curious Creek Fibres
3070 Palm Street, San Diego
Ca 92104, USA
Email: kbrooks@boncer.com

ISBN 09544140-1-2

British Library Catalogue-in-Publication Data
A catalogue record for this book is available at the British Library.

Cover illustration: Lady with a Parasol, from an engraving by J D de Saint-John, c1770

Contents

Introduction and Acknowledgements

Chapter One: Byzantium   1

Chapter Two: The Europeans   17

Chapter Three: Trade, Fairs and Banking   33

Chapter Four: Gold and Dyes   51

Chapter Five: The Huguenots and Other Strangers   65

Chapter Six: Knitting   81

Chapter Seven: Lace   99

Chapter Eight: Buttons and Bows   115

Chapter Nine: Home and Fashion   131

Practical: Designing and Knitting with Silk   151

Appendix: Silk Glossary   168

     Bibliography   187

     Index   193

Introduction and Acknowledgments

In this, the second book in the series on the Secrets of Silk, the fascinating story moves first to Byzantium. Silk was highly valued and promoted, and as the Byzantine Empire expanded, it left the knowledge of silk and sericulture in its wake. Silk continued to spread into many parts of Europe, with the development of the exquisite woven silks and the incorporation of valuable gold and dyes. For sericulture to survive the silk needed to be sold, so trade, fairs and banking all expanded to meet the need. Conflict with life styles, economic realities and religious principles forced many silkworkers to flee their homes and countries and a chapter is devoted to the flight of the Huguenots and others from France and the Low Countries. Many brought their skills with them to England and contributed to the development of the English silk industry. The later chapters concentrate on specialized areas, on the use of silk in knitting and how the lacemakers utilized the knitting machine to produce silk machine nets and laces. Silk contributed to the growth of many English counties, but was not without conflict. The final chapters are on the use of silk in fashion and the home, and the practical aspects of designing and knitting with silk. Once again there is an extensive silk glossary and suggestions for further reading.

It is an exciting challenge to try and piece together the story of silk. The words 'silk' or 'sericulture' rarely appear on the cover of any book. Mostly the information is found in monographs, a particular piece of research, a brief mention in a chapter on another topic entirely, a paragraph in a book on travel, economics, fashion, art, world history and biographies. Precious items are recorded in wills, shipping lists, sales invoices, inventories and prohibited items. In recent years many stories have been scrutinized by modern scholarship and the details continue to be fleshed out. This second volume attempts to piece it all together into the bigger picture.

Once again I am deeply indebted to so many overseas experts, scholars, librarians, friends and colleagues for their help and support. One of the richest areas of any research is the exchange of ideas and passionately held views, but in the end, the story needs to be told. Scholars disagree on many points but I have been helped, advised and encouraged by many who are experts in their field including Marie Lasenby, Jenny Dean, Margaret Stove, Kathleen Harris, Fiona Nisbet, Eve Alexander, Simon Parish and Cynthia Brownall. I would also like to thank my family and in particular, my daughter Stephanie Sheehan and my sister Leone Paget whose help and support has been incalculable and to whom this volume is dedicated with love.

Byzantine woman. She was described as a dancer but her halo and hands in an open position suggest, despite the beautiful clothes, that she is an early saint.

Chapter One
Byzantium

Silk in Byzantium

The little town of Byzantium was believed to have been named after Byzas, a Greek colonizer and adventurer and it grew to be the capital of the mighty Byzantine Empire that lasted for over eleven hundred years. The boundaries were in a constant state of flux. In its Golden Age in the sixth century, at the time of the Emperor Justinian I, the Empire extended from Mesopotamia in the east to Spain in the west, from the Black Sea to the Danube and to the coastal fringes of Africa. By the fifteenth century it had shrunk to little more than the city of Constantinople and parts of southern Greece.

It was Justinian's desire to halt the outflow of gold that prompted him to find out the real secret of the origin of silk and to establish sericulture in Byzantium. At that time, all silk came from the East, from Persia and far distant China and had to be paid for in gold. Beautiful silks were coveted by ambitious nobles and royal courtiers, but they did not know how it was made. The leisured, noble women of

Constantinople flaunted their wealth and style, swathed in lustrous glowing silks, their men magnificent in rich brocades, but the outpouring of gold was crippling the Empire. Justinian knew that if sericulture could be established under his control, he would have a source of great power and prestige. Silk was not only an economic asset, but was also a political tool, a symbol of wealth and luxury that could raise envy in other foreign rulers and nobles, and tax wealth and trade revenues for the Empire.

Procopius of Caesarea (500-65) writing in the mid-sixth century, maintained that Indian monks brought Justinian the secrets of silk in 552, and that they came from 'Serinda'. Theophanes of Byzantium, writing a few decades later, said the monks came from Persia, from 'the land of the Seres where silk comes from.' Procopius further insisted that the eggs were covered with dung to warm them and start them hatching, and this is still a method used in northern India.

Justinian gave orders that the monks were to be given every assistance and sericulture was to be established, mulberry trees planted, buildings constructed for the egg hatcheries and feeding rooms and skilled people brought in. Generous finance was made available to ensure the success of the venture. Closest to his heart was the Imperial Silk Workshop, within the precincts of the Great Palace in Constantinople. He took care to keep absolute control over all silk, from the raw silk to the finished product, to guarantee that the highest standards of quality, weaving and design were maintained. Its manufacture remained a secret, only imparted to the imperial family and senior members of the court who were entitled to wear silk. The workers, both slaves and skilled craftsmen lived their whole lives within the palace walls to ensure that they were not able to spread these precious secrets. Glorious imperial silks were a symbol of refinement and sophistication, and reflected the power and might of the Byzantine Empire, so no expense was spared. The finest silk and gold textiles could cost a king's ransom, and years could be spent making one exquisite hanging.

The Emperor personally appointed the Prefect of the City the *eparch,* to have complete control over all twenty-three imperial guilds in the capital. The Prefect combined the roles

Coin depicting Justinian I in armour, with a lance, riding regally on his charger

of chief of police, justice and regulator of all the commercial and human activity there. He also took personal charge over the Imperial Silk Workshop. The silk workshop's sole purpose was to supply the Emperor and court with all the luxuries they desired. Profit was not the main motive in the early days, but it became increasingly so for the five non-imperial and private silk guilds. They were also under the control of the Prefect and they produced a limited range of silk fabrics for the wealthy middle class and foreign secular patrons and made silk vestments and furnishings for churches in Byzantium and the west. In Justinian's time, silk was so tightly controlled that even if a lady was entitled to wear silk, she could not just buy it at the market, or even through a silk merchant. Silk could only be purchased from 'The House of Lamps', the royal emporium in the Great Palace. There the lamps were kept lit even through the night, and their glow reflected enticingly on the shimmering silks glimpsed through the windows.

In the sixth century, the population of Constantinople was around 600,000. It was a very cosmopolitan city, with people coming from all corners of the Empire. They paraded, resplendent in their exotic clothes and furs. There were court dignitaries on horseback wearing brilliantly coloured brocaded silks, in sharp contrast to the half-naked slaves doing the menial tasks of the city. Noble women rode by in their

Map showing the extent of Justinian's Empire by the time of his death in 565 AD

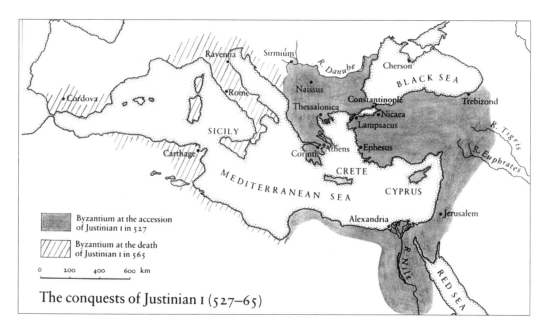

Byzantium at the accession of Justinian I in 527

Byzantium at the death of Justinian I in 565

0   200   400   600 km

The conquests of Justinian I (527–65)

Noble woman carried on a camel

decorated carriages, or were carried on a litter, reclining on gold embroidered cushions. All the major processions, religious and state, flowed through the main thoroughfare, a broad boulevard known as the Mese or Middle Street. It was lined with statues and fine shops displaying the wealth of Byzantium, especially the silks and gems. In the imperial gardens near the sea, there were shaded walks and fountains where peacocks strutted. Among the flowering shrubs and fruit trees was the porphyry or purple chamber, reserved for the birth of royal children, 'born in the purple'.

All the minutiae of imperial life, along with the correct procedures were explained in graphic detail in the 'Book of Ceremonies'. It also described the magnificent silk drapes and furnishings decorated with griffins and eagles, bulls and flowers, and the elaborate court costumes, purple, green, gold, blue and red. From the ninth century, silk textiles from the Imperial Workshops had the emperor's name or monogram, or that of the Prefect woven into the selvedge. This clearly identified fabrics designated as illegal silks or *kekolymena*. These could not be legally sold or exported. Some like the hunter silk now at St Austremoine at Mozac and the two silks in the Sens Cathedral Treasury depicting the Life of Joseph turned up in the west.

The Guilds

The general manufacture and distribution of the silk was handled by the five non-imperial silk guilds. The elite were the silk merchants, guildsmen who had sufficient capital and standing in the city to import large quantities of raw silk from abroad. Next were the guildsmen who imported silk garments and fabric in woven lengths. Another guild was made up of merchants who sold all grades of raw silk to the local craftsmen. The two practical guilds were the master spinners and weavers who had private workshops, and the highly skilled silk dyers who imported most of their dyes from the East, any colour other than purple, because that was reserved for the Imperial Workshops.

There were also private workshops in the homes of wealthy Byzantine citizens and these domestic studios supplied the affluent people, and sometimes fulfilled the specific requirements of the court. Possibly some silk work was carried out in monasteries, but there is no proof. The silk guilds had harsh rules with strict divisions of labour. They spelt out exactly the limitations on who could handle the silk, and what styles and quality of silk could be worked. Usually the membership of the guild was hereditary so it was almost impossible for a guildsman's son to pursue another craft. Intermarriage between members of different guilds was discouraged, so the guildsmen were free, but not free.

The silk dealers also had a guild with a code of practice, detailed in the Book of the Prefect, written in Constantinople in 911 or 912. These rules were unique, and pre-date by two or three hundred years, similar rules set out in Western guilds. Each guild could appoint their own senior master who had to be endorsed by the Prefect, and each man had to supply a character reference before he could be considered for guild membership. Charity and care for each member was a fundamental part of a guildsman's honour. He was obliged to make a contribution to a holding fund to be available to other members and their families, should they fall on hard times, become ill or die. There were rules for engaging and paying their journeymen and restrictions on selling silk to other members of the guild. He could only take a profit of 8 ½ %, to limit any desire he may have to do business independently on his own account, to work for another silk dealer, to embezzle or travel to buy silk. It was acknowledged that a merchant's slave or assistant could act for him, provided that the merchant himself took full responsibility for any of his assistant's dealings. He could not secretly spin or sell raw silk from his own home, only at the market, and any infringement attracted harsh penalties, including being beaten and having his head shaved.

Government Administration

Even with imperial silk, there was some surplus and so a government agency was set up called the *kommerciarioi*, to supervise and sell the silks not required by the state. The officials also tracked down and confiscated any illegal silk goods and handed them over to the state.

Soon the officers were functioning as private businessmen and selling surplus silks and taking a profit. By the ninth century, they were collecting a tax called the *kommerkion,* on all these sales. Restrictions were imposed to ensure that only the cheaper silks could be sold to foreigners and only for their own use, not for resale. Baggage was checked, and if a person was caught smuggling the prohibited cloths, the penalty was a severe flogging as well as confiscation. Even such harsh restrictions did not deter some ambassadors and high churchmen from attempting to smuggle out some of the gorgeous textiles, and one those caught was the Bishop of Cremona (950-972).

Lead or tin alloy seals were also used to identify the silks. They were attached in strapped pairs to the selvedge, proving the authenticity of the goods and that the tax had been paid. These seals varied over the years, with numbers or portraits of the emperor stamped on them. Occasionally foreign dignitaries were presented with fine damasks and gold brocade, which had conspicuous lead seals as an export permit. Seals also indicated ownership if the cargo was lost at sea, and some manufactures applied their own seals, but there were severe penalties for misrepresentation or counterfeit tags.

In the early days, when sericulture was being established in the Byzantine Empire, there was no way it could supply all the silk required for the workshops. Most of the of silkworm crop was raised near the southern shores of both the Caspian and Black Seas. The cocoons were then transported to Constantinople or further afield to Tyre and Alexandria, Egypt or Syria for reeling, throwing and weaving. Many of these provincial factories produced beautiful, sophisticated silks. Damascus, the capital of Syria had an outstanding reputation for its striped silk robes, banded with inscriptions and wonderful silky carpets. Egyptian and Mesopotamian weavers produced a variety of sophisticated textiles including velvets with both cut and looped pile, some with gold thread. Yet, despite the high value of the silk, the workers, both town and country folk, had no great status and were poorly paid. Fancy silk weavers received around 40 *denarii* per day, on a par with other minor but skilled craftsmen, blacksmiths, wall mosaicists and bakers. The most highly skilled of the gold embroiderers were paid up to 500 *denarii* per ounce of gold and it was rumoured that one master weaver had once earned 1000 *denarii* per ounce for weaving one exquisite and extremely complex silk and gold textile.

Silk in the Empire

Sericulture was established in Greece, although the indigenous silkworm produced a rather inferior silk. The *Vita Basilii* was one of the few sources of information about silk production in the Peloponnese and it recorded gifts given to Basil I around 880 by a fabulously wealthy, beautiful young widow called Danielis. She controlled

Danielis being carried by a relay of 300 young men on a litter to visit Basil I

vast lands near Patras, which included eighty estates and a number of towns, with workshops where women wove fine silk and gold textiles. The local people believed that Danielis had rooms full of treasure chests, bulging with sumptuous textiles, clothes and jewels.

Basil had been born in Macedonia of poor parents but high ambition, and rose to power through feats of honour and valor and some rather questionable acts of skullduggery. One version of his story was written by John Scylites, an eleventh century Byzantine official and illustrated with tiny miniatures by Sicilian monks. It is now in Spain's National Library in Madrid. Danielis had taken a vow of 'spiritual sisterhood', but with great foresight, told Basil that one day he would be Emperor. Some years later Danielis came to visit Basil, who had now eliminated all the other claimants, and had been crowned Emperor. She was carried to Constantinople reclining on a litter, borne in relay by three hundred youths. She brought gifts, including five hundred slaves, one hundred eunuchs and one hundred female silk weavers. She also brought precious silk rugs and textiles including *sidonia*, a silk fabric similar to sendal, manufactured in the Muslim East. Basil, in gratitude and honouring their long friendship and her wisdom, gave her the title of 'Mother of the Emperor'. He died some years later after being mauled by a boar while on a hunt, and Danielis, now very elderly, made the long journey to pay homage to Basil's successor Leo, making him heir to her own vast fortune.

The Peloponnese was formerly called Morea, and probably named after the local, wild mulberry tree, the *Morus*. It was a prominent feature of the landscape in the late ninth century. There was an extensive silk industry, and large regional markets like the Thessalonican fair of St Demetrios, where the beautiful silk fabrics of Thebes were sold. Rabbi Benjamin of Tudela was a traveller who visited Thebes and Corinth in the 1160s. On his return to Constantinople, he wrote admiringly of the luxurious silk fabrics, worn by the nobles. The dazzling textiles included garments and accessories, vestments, furnishings, cushions, bed-hangings and horse trappings. Benjamin also reported that a new palace built by Emperor Manuel I at Blachernae had '…towers filled with silk and purple garments and gold'. Emperor Romanos IV Diogenes (1068-71) must have seen his storehouses of silk as 'money in the bank' because at a time of a severe cash shortage, he offered bolts of iridescent silk instead of gold coins. The imperial court had probably ordered and paid for these rich silks, but some of the lesser quality textiles would have been collected from small workshops as taxes. Most small farmers would handle very little cash. They paid their taxes and dues in skeins of reeled silk, raw silk or cocoons.

In the twelfth century, the island of Andros in the western province of the Empire, was renowned for its splendid silk textiles, especially the light weight tabby weave called sendal, and a heavier glossy twill weave called samite. They were both highly valued, especially as worthy items to include in a daughter's dowry. Andros was situated on the navigation route linking Constantinople with Southern Greece, the Cyclades, Chios and the Italian ports. Andros was mentioned in a letter written around 1130 by a Genoese woman to her merchant husband, asking him to bring back some silk fabric. This is not conclusive proof that silk was grown at Andros because it may have just been woven there. Another kind of rough silk was mentioned as being stored in Naples and as coming from the Peloponnese. It was used to make an inferior grade of silk fabric known as *cocculario*. Leonardo de Veroli, a chancellor of Frankish Morea had a bedcover of *cocculario* and it was sufficiently important for it to be mentioned in his will of 1281.

Thebes in the eleventh century had a highly qualified and flourishing Jewish community of silk workers. Some had come from other Byzantine cities, even beyond the boundaries of the Empire. Large numbers of Jewish weavers and dyers left Syria and Palestine in the twelfth century to settle in Egypt. Some writers maintain that there were some high ranking Jewish women among the captured weavers, tailors and silk workers, abducted and taken to the Royal Workshops in Palermo by King Roger II of Sicily. This was after his military campaigns and raids on Thebes, Athens and Corinth in 1147-8. Silk is noted in military documents, with the finest silk fabrics carried in leather containers, while lesser quality items were packed in sacks and baskets. Rough spun silk is mentioned too, as being made into leggings and other garments. The insulation and comfort qualities of silk were obviously recognized by the military. Some items would have been half silks, a mixture of fibres woven with silk, partly to keep the cost down. The Jewish Karaite Bible warns against wearing *sha'atnez*, a hybrid cloth containing two or more different fibres. This cloth was seen as ritually impure, because it combined a vegetable and an animal product, such as cotton with silk.

By the fall of Constantinople in 1453, the Ottoman Turks had taken over the Byzantine silk trade. The Sephardic Jews, expelled from Spain in 1492 were now under the protection of the Ottoman government. They settled in the Adriatic ports, especially Avlona, and promoted trade with Venice until 1520. The Jewish merchants bought silk cocoons in the villages and arranged for their export. They were also the local bankers and exerted considerable power. They arranged loans and raised much of the credit, with the result that Ottoman Christians, merchants and shopkeepers were often in their debt.

The Ottoman Government policy was based on limited production for a limited market. It appointed a state market controller a *muhtesib*, to ensure regulations were kept, and there was consistency in price and quality of goods. Regrettably, at times the *muhtesib* accepted bribes, so when the bales were weighed, the sale tax was somehow overlooked. The silk was then supposed to be handed over to the brokers to be sold at a fair price. Periodically the government issued a list of the silks that were prohibited from export. It also raised taxes, as it did at the port of Izmir, the chief outlet for the Anatolian and Iranian silk trade. The inflated taxes made the traders furious. They thought that the taxes were against Islamic Law, because they were farmed out to private people who made a profit collecting them. Of course there was smuggling and if caught, the merchant was arrested, punished and the goods confiscated. Various kinds of subterfuge were employed, including using unofficial entry points. Some provincial merchants went out to meet the caravans at Tokat, on their way to Bursa from Iran. They procured all the silk and took it straight to Bursa, thus paying the tax only once, not at each customs point. Some traders wet the silk to make it heavier so that the broker paid more for it. It was a highly developed commercial world, market orientated and increasingly geared towards profit. The most powerful merchants lent money on interest and chartered their own ships to transport their goods. They were probably not actually involved in sericulture, and got their agents to deal with the workers. The agents would have seen that the peasants paid taxes on their mulberry trees, and cash or kind to their landlords for the rent of premises.

Trade and Routes

Bursa and Tabriz were both prime centres for Asian trade, more important than Baghdad. They were on major trade routes, with caravanserai where the traders could meet, conduct business and rest their animals. These crossroad cities became very wealthy, until the mid-fourteenth century, when the period of cooperation with the Mongols of China, known as *Pax Mongolica*, ended.

Much effort was made to establish Tabriz as the greatest trade centre for raw silk and textiles. Some Latin merchants, coming via Hormuz and Baghdad settled there, exchanging fine woollen cloth for Iranian silk and Indian spices. The Genoese preferred Bursa and that city became the economic foundation of Ottoman power from this time. The Italian merchants had a privileged position trading precious velvets and brocades and they established a 'colony', or trading centre at Pera, opposite Constantinople and were influential and prosperous. With Ottoman control of the principal silk centres on the route to Bursa, silk caravans could travel relatively safely. The best quality silks all sold at the Bursa market which handled record quantities of raw silk between 1487 and 1512. The price and supply fluctuated, with the peak season in spring when the silk caravans arrived, each carrying an average of 200 fardels, or bundles of silk. There were around 1000 looms in Bursa and they absorbed five loads of silk a day, so vast amounts were required annually. Customs bills show that much of this silk was re-exported to the Balkans, and central and northern Europe.

Chintamarni representing 'the lips of Buddha' and the leopard's spots and tiger stripes. 17th century Turkey, woven from silk and gold threads.

The struggle for control of the silk routes between Tabriz and Bursa persisted in the fifteenth and sixteenth centuries, under a number of rulers. Mehmet II (1451-81), known as the Conqueror, incorporated the war-like tiger stripes and three leopard spots, called the *chintamani* design as his personal emblem on silk twills, lampas, and velvets. In 1514, during what came to be known as the 'Silk Wars', Sultan Selim I used embargoes to try and control smuggling and to destroy Iran economically and financially. It made the traders angry, and they claimed it was unacceptable and illegal to confiscate their merchandize for political reasons. They protested that seizing their goods deprived them of their livelihood, not the enemy of a source of revenue. In reality, the Italian silk industry lost its main source of raw material, which resulted in panic and as feared, poverty for the poorest people. The Italians tried to revive old trade routes through the Caspian Sea and Astrakhan, even through Moscow, and later the English sought a route from India. The silk trade with Iran was in a pitiful condition and was not restored until Selim's son Suleyman I (1520-66) released detained merchants, returned their silk and offered compensation.

Silk in the community

The silk spinners were often among the poorest in the community and had the least protection when there was a downturn in the industry, or there was war or civil

Traders on camels. From Pliny the Elder's Historia Naturalis, Book XIII. In the background are ships and a town.

disturbance. In Bursa, the silk women worked for the silk merchants, bleaching and spinning silk. Around half of them owned their own spindles and so were not totally beholden to the merchants. The women had not formed a silk spinners' guild so they did not have the obligations or expense of guild fees, but they did not have the protection afforded by guild rules either. Some worked in their homes, sold their spun silk in the street, or at special markets.

Some successful trades-women supplied the harems of the wealthy with silk fabrics and other fancy goods. A trader could not enter the harem so the sale of silk was negotiated through an intermediary, the highest ranking eunuch in charge of the women's quarters. When the new silks arrived the women clustered around, feeling the luscious fabrics, holding them up to their faces, and draping them around their bodies. Allure was their business. Some wealthy women administered their own property or used their capital, investing it by commissioning a merchant to import Iranian silk on their behalf. On her death one woman left an estate of almost a million *akce*. Many of the merchants, both men and women owned slaves, and after they had worked for their owners for many years, some were freed and given money to continue working with silk on their own account. The decline of the silk industry in Bursa saw a gradual disappearance of slaves in silk merchant's households. By the 1640s, Bursa was no longer a major manufacturing centre and many of the looms had ceased operation, although by 1649 there had been some recovery.

Aleppo in north-western Syria was also a major centre for slaves. It minted coins, had a sheep market and had become the most important silk exporting city in the Levant, with over half of the silk going to Italy, especially Venice. The silk had a value of more than a half million ducats, and brought wealth to the treasury in Aleppo in duties and taxes. The reeling factories of northern Italy had become more mechanized and were producing a more consistent quality yarn. They were now using Iranian raw silk for the weft, with a fine machine reeled Italian silk for the warp. Aleppo's decline was attributed to harvest failures and the civil wars. The silk caravans were unable to get through, so the foreign merchants avoided Aleppo and commerce declined. The Armenian traders continued to transport Iranian silk via Erzurum and Tokat, and raw silk was re-exported via Izmir.

By 1620 some Armenian merchants were forging links directly with Marseilles. This was strongly opposed by the French merchants who feared the foreign imported silk would ruin the local market. Armenians were more successful marketing both raw silk and silk fabrics in Russia, while other Arab merchants focused on Holland, importing silk and exporting other Dutch merchandise. Alternative routes were sought by the Levant and East India Companies, but for the Armenian merchants, Aleppo had the advantage of being a market they knew well, and where traditionally, both French and Venetian merchants had met.

In the seventeenth century it was Smyrna's turn to be the pre-eminent market for Iranian silk for the Europeans. Smyrna had a large population, a natural harbour, and was a major terminus of the overland caravan trade. Although Aleppo was closer to the source of Persian silk, this route through Smyrna was more secure and attracted fewer taxes. Syria was

Fete given for Valide Sultan '...in the palace in the presence of Madame de Giraudin, Ambassadress of France who had it painted immediately after she had attended, and then brought to Paris in 1689'. On the far left is a black eunuch, with women and dwarfs dancing and playing music.

heavily planted with mulberry trees and had an extensive sericulture industry. In April the silkworm houses were set up in the woods, and the whole family moved there for three months. There was a holiday atmosphere until the eggs started hatching and the real production got underway. Everyone was involved, although the landlords and merchants were more interested in profit than family holidays.

The world market for silk continued to expand. Silks from the Mongol Empire, made their way to all parts of Muscovy and as far north as Archangel and the North Sea. Here the French and English bought directly and the Dutch shipped their silks via Stockholm to Holland. Frederick the Great built Frederickstad in Holstein especially as a silk port, but it silted up and was not particularly successful. In the increasingly sophisticated European markets, the wealthy were looking for exotic and unusual silks, and it was essential that the right silks in the right colours were selected if they were to be the fashion choice, and sell in the west.

Pamphile collecting cocoons from mulberry trees on the Island of Cos.
French, from Boccaccio's Des Claris et nobles femmes, c1470.

Chapter 2
The Europeans

Spanish Silk

In the eighth century, the Arabs conquered Spain and spread the secrets of sericulture from the east to the west. Spain became part of the Oriental world, and developed a culture and politics that was isolated from the rest of Europe. The Moors brought their skills and knowledge of silk, and soon mulberry trees were planted and silk weaving established. Gradually, less raw silk had to be imported to keep the weavers supplied, and by the tenth century the production of silk was firmly established in Spain. Silk was the common thread, and from the Iberian Peninsula, it soon spread to Sicily, France, Italy and across Europe.

The Moors brought with them the tradition of tiraz. That was the name for both the weaving pavilion and the Persian word for a particularly rich and valuable textile. The cloth had script woven or embroidered into a band, giving the name of the ruler in whose reign it was made. It sometimes had a Koranic verse or dedication and the date and place of

Tiraz, 8th-9th cebtury, a fragment of silk tapestry. The animal appears to be a feline.

manufacture. This gave the most important tiraz fabrics almost mystical and spiritual powers. Its manufacture and export was strictly controlled by a government appointed official, the *sahib al-tiraz,* and its fibres and dyes subject to annual levies. It could not be sold officially, although pieces were frequently sent abroad as diplomatic gifts. Caliph Hisham II sent a gift of tiraz to North Africa in 993, and a *panno tirazes* was donated to a Portuguese church in 994. By now there were independent tiraz workshops, and gradually it began to be traded like any other luxury textile.

Spanish raw silk and textiles became highly sought after, and are mentioned in some tenth and eleventh century charters. One commercial order, sent from Egypt to Tunisia in the mid-eleventh century, wanted fine Andalusian *iltiqat,* a thread spun from scraps of waste silk, or *lasin* another waste silk. Waste silk did not necessarily mean poor quality but just that it was other than filament silk, wound off the cocoon. Other styles included *ibrism,* a high quality raw silk, *harir,* another raw silk thread, and *khazz,* a lower quality floss silk.

Sericulture was a village industry and to ensure that the right style and quantity of silk was available, the merchants would often control the trade by putting the peasants under contract, and then pay them in advance for the spun silk. Many isolated country areas became snow bound in winter and the passes blocked, so most of the silk was delivered to the cities and ports between June and September, to fit in with the summer sailings of the Mediterranean galley fleets. Almeria was the principal port for silk being exported to both Arab and Christian countries around Europe, and the Near East. It had hundreds of looms for weaving tiraz and brocades, striped silks and furnishings.

By the twelfth century, Andalusian silk textiles were no longer so important, although Ibn Sa'id, who died in 1286, still maintained that he had seen 'gilded brocades that amaze people in the east with the beauty of their workmanship.' Spanish silks were widely available, and French romances were full of exotic descriptions of *siglatons d'Espagne* and *soie d'Aumarie.* It was not just fabrics that were exported from Andalusia. An inventory of goods belonging to Abd al-Rahman III included silken rugs and carpets. In an effort to expand its production, the Andalusi silk industry copied other renowned silk textiles. It is not clear whether they were a sincere imitation or made to deceive the consumer. Possibly the names had just become generic types, like *baghdadi* and *attabi*, both known to be made in Minorca. Contemporary merchants were very astute, and they would know if it was a *jurjanis* from Jurjan or an imitation cloth from Almeria.

The Moriscos, or mudejares were Spanish Muslims who had chosen, or had been forced to convert to Catholicism. They had always been involved with sericulture and those who were successful, enjoyed a relatively good standard of living. Many secretly tried to keep up their Muslim faith and although silk was always expensive, it was part of their tradition to wear silk undergarments. The Christian re-conquest of Spain initially changed very little in the silk industry and the Morisco weavers continued to work under a policy of *convivencia,* and cooperation with the Christians in authority. In 1492 Granada, the last Muslim stronghold was conquered, and at the instigation of Ferdinand (1452-1516) and Isabella (1451-1504) the powerful joint rulers, the Inquisition was begun, to make Spain an entirely Catholic country. The last of the Moriscos' rights were removed and families were subjected to harassment and harsh punishments to make them comply with all aspects of Catholic beliefs and rituals. Many fled to Africa and Sicily and other parts of Europe to escape persecution, taking their skills with them.

As Seville became more prosperous and the master weavers more powerful, the guild felt sufficiently emboldened to impose strict conditions on the members and families. Yet, whenever there was an economic slump, it was the Spanish women whose opportunity to work was controlled and curtailed. The rules were very harsh. Directly after the funeral, the widow was informed that she could only continue weaving silk for one year after her husband's death. The guild took the moral high ground, maintaining that their concern was to sustain the highest standards. Her work had to be repeatedly inspected, although she had probably been weaving for most of her life, certainly her married life. If the work was acceptable, she could continue with the help of her own children, but no other apprentices. The guild

Prostitute in Sicily, accepting money from a young merchant.
From Albert Schramm Der Bilderschmuck fer Frubdrucke, Vol. IV, Leipzig, ill. 2908 woodcut.

restricted her ability to earn money even further, by insisting that she reduce her output to one loom only, just enough to keep her from poverty and not become a charge on the city or guild. This dramatically reduced her income, and often she could not afford to buy materials, and ended up being little more than an out-worker, weaving the plainest cloth. In one stroke she had lost the companionship and support of her husband, and she now had the full financial burden of her home and family. She had no job protection or support from the guild, and all too often she became just one of the 3000 women known to have been exploited by the master weavers. With an income at subsistence level, some women were reduced to renting their looms from the master weavers thus adding to their debt. Many young widows with children to support were brought before the ecclesiastical courts on prostitution charges. As young women, many worked for years to save for a dowry. Their husband used this money when they married to purchase a mastership and now that, and her livelihood was all gone.

Seville was now one of the largest and most important and prosperous cities in Europe, with a virtual monopoly of trade to the Americas and the bullion it generated. The elite merchants started living like princes, even attempting to break down the class barriers and to marry their daughters into the aristocracy. The promise of riches attracted some of the oldest families in Spain to become involved in trade, as bankers, brokers and bullion dealers. The men of the rich and idle hidalgo class, who lived on state annuities and rents from their estates, were not interested in either the source of their continued wealth or to promote the silk industry. They saw themselves as gentlemen and Catholics, conquerors of the Moors, superior and above trade or getting their hands dirty. As a result they were not prepared to back the Parliament, known as the Cortés when the lack of investment contributed to stagnation and despair in the silk industry.

Toledo had different problems. In the sixteenth century, it was handling around 435,000 pounds of raw silk annually. Pedro de Medina, writing in 1543 tells of the great surge of activity and higher prices for silk during the reign of Charles V, and that sometimes the merchants had to wait for years for their special orders of fine woven silks to be fulfilled. Employment in the silk industry had increased between the years 1525 and 1550 from 10,000 to 50,000 workers, but there was still the ever-present problem of insufficient labour, both skilled and unskilled in many parts of Castille. In desperation, the streets of Valladolid, Salamanca and Zamora were combed for beggars and vagabonds. The Cortés of Madrid in 1551 appointed an officer to round up all the lay-abouts and idlers, and they were forcibly and unceremoniously marched off, and made to work in the silk factories.

The master weavers of Barcelona were extremely conservative. Their guild had barred the silk women, known as *sederes*, from an apprenticeship and formal training, and had used this to justify a policy of denying them their own workshops. In 1636, against the opposition of the guildsmen, the City passed an 'Ordinance in Favour of Women' saying they had a right to earn a modest living through their own work. They could continue making small silk items and sell them in the public market, but not weave, as that was illegal. The guildsmen saw the *sederes* as competitors, but the Council valued the tax revenue they brought in. They were less concerned about equality of rights, but acknowledged that without the opportunity to work, the *sederes* might become destitute and be a charge on the city. The guildsmen reluctantly agreed that the women could do low status work, such as spinning and carding silk, even producing plain weave taffetas, but once they started to become financially successful, they felt it threatened their position as masters. They objected to them owning looms and hiring workers, or selling their work outside their houses and in particular, making any items similar to those produced by the master weavers. The weavers maintained that the goods would not be of the same high standard that they produced. This was the basis of the complaint brought by Joseph Ponsico, that the women were making and selling silk hairnets just like the ones he made, but at a lower price.

Silk In Sicily

The Sicilian silk industry was based in Palermo and was greatly influenced by Spain. Mulberry trees were planted in the tenth century and by 1050AD 20,000 trees were reported. The industry gained a real boost from the enthusiasm of the Norman ruler Roger II and by the addition of the captured Greek silk weavers, brought to Palermo after his lightening raids on silk towns in the Peloponnese. Roger II's famous Coronation mantle or pluvial, was made of red kermes-dyed silk samite. It was richly embroidered with gold and featured a pair of lions attacking camels. It has a Kufik inscription, '(Made) in the royal workshop of the capital of Sicily in the year 528 H' (1133/34 AD). The lining is an exquisite red and green silk tapestry weave with small figures and animals, with a geometric trellis on a gold ground. The whole design is more Arabic than Christian and it was in fact, made fifteen years before the Greek silk weavers arrived in Palermo. William I, who succeeded Roger II, was most reluctant to release the abducted, highly skilled Greek artisans, and only freed the less valuable prisoners after the treaty of 1158 was signed between himself and Emperor Manuel I Comnenus.

Manuel Comnenus I (1143-1180), an Emperor who wanted to be a brilliant ruler but his exploits left Byzantium weaker, not stronger

Messina was another major silk producing centre and port in Sicily. A Genoese merchant arranged to export 94 pounds of raw silk from there to North Africa in 1161. In 1271 Messina was still exporting thousands of bales of silk fabrics and raw silk to Ancona, but by 1310, sericulture had almost disappeared from the records, and so most of the raw silk for the weaving industry was imported from Calabria and parts of Spain. Some skilled craftsmen found the political situation too difficult and left Sicily for Genoa, but things must have picked up again in Messina, because the major fairs were moved to April and August, to fit in better with the silk cocoon and raw silk production. In the 1430s, the silkweavers had become sufficiently established for a street to be named after them, and Antonio de Troia of Messina was given the right to nominate a person to officially weigh the silk, a *ponderator serici*. Much of the silk was shipped out on Venetian galleys to Flanders and Northern Europe. The light-weight woven silks and silken garments were packaged into bales, but their quality apparently, was not very good, which limited their export price. The Sicilians rejoiced in their silks. They loved festivities and carnivals and they dyed their silk vibrant colours and hung silk flags and bunting all around the open spaces. Any excuse was an opportunity to dress up in their most festive silk garments and sing and dance.

Silk in Italy

Sicilian Jews are said to have introduced silk to the Tuscan town of Lucca. Weaving workshops, based on Arab and Byzantine techniques were set up, and by the 1250s, Lucca had become the capital of the Italian silk industry. It specialized in the richest silks, the baldachin, samite brocades and velvets. The lighter silks like sendal, were popular for banners, gowns and dress linings.

Weaver, using a treadle loom, with the warp angled upwards, probably to save space. From Rodericus Zamorensis, Spiegel des menschlichen lebens, Augsburg, 1479, woodcut.

It was the merchants who controlled the enterprise. They obtained the raw silk and gave it to the throwsters, spinners, dyers and weavers, then paid the worker and organized the distribution of the silk and its sale. The silk was highly valued and most dowries listed silk scarves, veils and other decorative items. While that did not prove that the articles had actually been made in Lucca, there was a growing demand for Lucchesse luxury goods in Rome, Genoa, Florence, and at the international Champagne Fairs. Before the wars and civil disturbances, records note 240 highly skilled silk weavers in Lucca, but many left and sought refuge in other northern Italian towns, including Milan, Bologna, Venice and Florence. These towns welcomed the immigrants, and the secret techniques they brought with them. Their knowledge of weaving the valuable silk damasks and taffetas, helped increase production throughout Italy and the bed hangings, drapes and church vestments became highly sought after.

Industrialization of the silk industry meant change. The development of the water-powered throwing mill, introduced into Italy during the late thirteenth century, was an exciting new technology, as was the pedal operated loom and the spinning wheel. There were always problems procuring raw materials and finding and holding skilled workers, so it was essential to be outward looking, to expand and export, rather than focusing on home needs and older methods. Industrial subterfuge was rife. Unfinished cloth, known as 'raw goods', was purchased in Bologna but the finishing processes were completed elsewhere in remote country districts. It was labeled 'Bologna Silk', and the name of the Bolognese weaver was even forged on the outside wrapping.

Italian ciselé velvet, 16th century red satin ground featuring fighting cocks.

The silk industry was always subject to fluctuations and in the fourteenth century it was the turn of Milan and Genoa to prosper. They had technical skills and sophisticated financial and commercial networks. For a long time the Chinese velvet weavers had kept the secret of how velvet was manufactured. Then the Italians had a lucky break. They unwrapped a bale of Chinese velvet and found the rods still inserted, ready to cut the pile. The clever Italian engineers adapted their drawlooms to produce velvets, with floral patterns, palmettes, Gothic arches and pomegranates. Velvets were highly valued by church and state and were the most expensive of all the heavy luxury silks. They required a major capital investment in raw silk and skilled weavers, dyers and gold beaters. As the patterns got larger, richer and more complicated, the cost went up. There were infinite varieties of smooth and tufted silks, including the *velluti ad inferriata*, named because the curling pattern was reminiscent of wrought iron. *Alto-e-basso* had pile woven in two or more heights, while *Allucciolature* had massed or individual small gold or silver loops set in areas of pile. A fifteenth century Florentine treaty mentions a voided satin velvet woven in Florence *alla vinciziana,* meaning that it had been woven in the Venetian manner. Half-silk velvets had a pile of silk above the linen tabby base, and could be cut, left uncut or partly cut as in ciselé velvet. The Oriental and Persian motifs had been based on the lotus flower and were regarded as symbols of immortality and fertility. They continued to dominate the fine Italian damasks, brocades and velvets into the sixteenth century. Many of the Italian silk cities produced velvet, but Genoa was supreme.

The earliest recorded date for the Silk Guild of Florence, the *L'Arte della seta* was 1193 and by 1224 it was incorporated as the *'Ars et Universitas della Seta Civitatis Florentinae'*. It was also known as the *'Por Santa Maria'* the Guild of Saint Mary's Gate.' It was named after the splendid palace next door, used by the silk guild and the Parte Guelfa, a powerful political association supportive of the guild. A Neopolitan called Napoleone, was the first silk master named in the register. He is described as 'a merchant in silk cloth' and by 1233 there were 360 names. In 1472 Benedetto Dei recorded that there were now 84 workshops belonging to the guild of the *'Por Santa Maria'*, and that cloth of gold, silver brocades and silk tissue were woven in a rainbow of colours and textures. There was another group of lesser silk makers, the *Setaiuoli Minuti* who owned their own tools and equipment, but had less capital and in truth, lower standing in the guild. They were a much larger group, making and selling a variety of items, but requiring a licence from the Consul to actually spin or weave silk. This group included the bobbin winders, carders and coarse silk workers. Some members dealt in raw

Francesco di Marco Datini, merchant who died in Prato on the 16th August 1410. He left a marvelous record of his life and business.

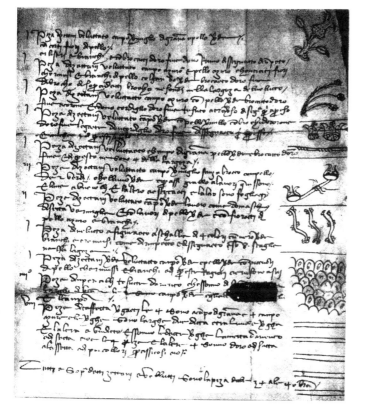

Invoice for velvet and brocade. It begins... "1 cloth of silk embossed in velvet, the ground vermilion embossed in green, with flowers in relief, pale blue and white with gold brocade, one branch drawn here' (in the margin)..."
From The Merchant of Prato by Iris Origo.

25

silk, or oversaw the export of goods, while others were printers and dyers of silk and satin, and weavers of the plainer styles of cloth of gold. The finishers and embroiderers made church vestments, vests and doublets and the hosiers and tailors were included if they mostly worked in silk. Within the city, over 16,000 silkworkers were employed. Florence now had a vast export trade to Provence, Antwerp, Lyon, Rome, the Levant and Morocco.

There was fierce competition between the major Italian cities as well as the provincial centres like Bergamo, Vicenza, Lombardy, Verona, and Padua. Each tried to outdo the other in technological supremacy, quality and novelty of these extremely valuable textiles. There was some specialization; for example Venice made ribbons and Naples, decorative trimmings. Although Genoa claimed supremacy in the weaving of velvets, the Velluti family of Florence was credited with its early development. The family had outgrown their premises when in 1285 they set up an even larger warehouse and factory at Oltrarno, in a street that came to be named the Via de' Velluti. Other wealthy and influential families joined them and it soon became an elite and thriving quarter of the city. Right from the start, the guild celebrated feasts and festivals, especially the Feast of San Giovanni. All along the streets where the wealthy silk merchants had their villa's, workshops, shops and offices, they hung the magnificent silk brocades. These rich silks and cloth of gold were emblazoned with the arms of the ten kingdoms, and the courtiers and elite of the city paraded there, in the finest products of the Florentine silk looms.

The Mulberry Orchards

There were two guilds of men involved with mulberry growing, the *Padroni di Terreni*, the owners of land suitable for growing mulberry trees, and the *Maestri di Mori e di Foglie*, the Mulberry Growers and the Purveyors of Mulberry Leaves. Their professional approach improved the quality of the leaves, and Florence gained a reputation for its healthy silkworms, and top quality cocoons and eggs, and buyers and merchants began arriving in droves. By 1442 a *Provisioni* had to be passed in an attempt to keep control of the situation. It forbade the export of everything associated with the actual manufacture of silk; worms, cocoons, raw silk and mulberry leaves.

Sir Richard Dallington, an English traveller to Tuscany in the middle of the sixteenth century was most impressed by all he saw. He mentioned the lushness of the mulberry leaves, sold at '*foure quattrini* the pound'. In May and June the silkworms were hatched by warming them in the sun, or by putting them in a little bag, strung around the neck of the woman so that the warmth of her body caused the eggs to hatch. He noted that after the cocoons had been spun, they were collected and immersed in hot water by the *Calderai* to release the silk thread. What was more unusual was that both men and women, the *Filatori* and the *Filatore* drew this thread out onto large reels. After that the *Torcitori* the silk throwsters, wound several strands together into hanks of raw silk.

In Pescia near Lucca, silk had become more important than either wine or olive oil. In 1546, the mulberry trees provided food for the 13 million silkworms that produced 6600 pounds of silk per year. The trees were kept low to make it easier for the women to pick the leaves without a ladder and they harvested and got paid for it, rather than the farmers. Silkworm eggs, known as silk seed were produced locally, but some was imported from international seed merchants in Lahidjan and Talich by the Caspian Sea, or Chios, Turkey or Asia Minor. A local man, Bendinello di Jacopo Cheli of Pescia saw an opportunity. He was not even an important local businessman but a shoemaker, and he imported seventy ounces of silkworm seed from Palermo in 1549 and sold it to the local growers. Water power had already been used by the commercial oil presses, so it was a small step to install it in the reeling and throwing

4th Instar, Silkworms on mulberry leaves, the feeding period just before they spin their cocoons.

Silkworms spinning their cocoons

mills, built on the swiftly flowing streams. The council had been worried about the young people leaving the district and the mills offered work locally. By 1603 there were twenty-three silk mills providing work for between 700-800 people from the country districts in Tuscany.

France

In the thirteenth and fourteenth centuries, both Italy and France had been involved intermittently in confrontations within the Catholic Church. It all came to a head during the schism, when a second papal court was set up in Avignon. Many accounts contain requests to supply rich silks to the Papacy in residence there, as each successive Pope was determined it would be the most glorious ecclesiastical court, even in exile. When the Black Death raged through Europe in 1347-8, the Church gained unexpected benefits. There was a flood of donations of land, glorious vestments and silk textiles, gifts from the fearful and legacies from the estates of the dead.

Mediterranean France had long had a culture of silk, whether it was sericulture in the Cevennes at Arles, Nimes or Avignon, or the luscious textiles of the troubadour court of Aquitaine. Many silks have survived because they were valuable religious vestments, both Moslem and Christian, like the chasuble of St Regnobert in Bayeux. There are Islamic

Map of Avignon, showing the Papal Palace during the Pontificates of John XII and Benedict XII (1334-42).

silks with leopards and Arabic inscription at Chinon, and the beautiful shroud of St Germain in Auxerre has fine Byzantine eagles. The Spaniards came to Montpellier in the late 1330s, bringing their mixed Christo-Islamic heritage and Montpellier became a major market town rather than a producer of raw silk. The bankers and merchants supplied many of the different silks; red silks dyed with kermes, silk shirts and gold and black silks from Lucca. It became famous for its silk corduroy *condurarie de serico* and the manufacture of gold threads.

Louis XI (1423-83) was deeply involved in all the legislation involving the crafts, correcting, improving statutes and by-laws, setting work hours and public holidays, advising on types of manufacturing and pronouncing on quality. He estimated that France lost 400,000 to 500,000 gold crowns to Italy every year for the purchase of luxurious silks and cloth of gold, so in 1466 he offered Lyon 2,000 *livres tournois* to establish the silk industry there. The Lyonnaise were very conservative and thought the whole scheme foolhardy and expensive, and were most reluctant to cooperate. In exasperation, Louis made the same offer to the silkmen of Tours who were much more enthusiastic and within four years, silk was firmly established there. Charles VIII (1470-98) continued to give Tours assistance in the making of '*draperie de luxe*'. In 1485 he forbade the importation into France of damasks, satins, velours and gold or silver cloth. Chronic political troubles in Italy led some silk weavers to leave, and the French king welcomed them, and granted them exemption from taxes. Mulberry trees were planted by royal decree, and in 1520 Francis I (1515-47) brought silkworm eggs from Milan and had them reared in the Rhone Valley. The area around Lyon, Avignon and Nimes, soon became the centre of the French silk industry.

In Lyon, silk was a family enterprise. When a woman married, she was expected to support her husband in his trade. Young girls were taught by their mothers to spin or assist at the loom, while the boys were more likely to be educated, in the hope of adding status to the family. The wife could be a skilled silk thrower, taffeta or velvet maker,

Hinc vermium permulta sæpe millia   *Simul legunt, parantq; telas feminæ .*

French women soaking the cocoons in basins of hot water to dissolve the sericin.

or she might unwind cocoons and prepare the thread for bobbins. Many young women came, not from the town of Lyon but from the mountainous villages of Forez, Besse, Bugey and parts of the Dauphin. They were known as 'silkmaker's servants', living in and often sleeping under the looms. Like domestic servants they were paid annually or when they left the employment of the master. They started as teenagers, and it could be fifteen years before they had earned and saved enough to marry. Estienette Leonarde was the wife of a silk master on the rue Grolee and she hired girls in 1557 to unwind the cocoons, paying them between one *livre* ten *sous* and four *livre* two *sous* per year. Wages for women and girls tended to be between half to one third that of men.

There were a few women who were artisans in their own right. The wives of two silk merchants in Lyon formed a partnership in 1559 and all agreed that the women should run it, but instead of taking a salary, the business would support them. In 1571, two experienced silkwomen were mentioned in the tax lists of Lyon. Francoise la Regnarde was a silk thrower and Germanine Clement, a silk weaver. Silkworkers, along with seamstresses, pin makers, knitters and spinners tended to be poverty-stricken, and it was not unusual for some women to become prostitutes, just to make ends meet. They openly admitted to the judges when they were picked up, that they could not make a living at their craft, and keep their families fed.

Cologne

In Cologne the situation was rather different, as a high percentage of the silk women were educated and came from middle class families. They formed a Silkwomen's Guild, and many of the apprentices were daughters of the raw silk merchants or the children of members of the silk guild. Their families had achieved financial success and status in the community. Tryngen Ime Hove was the daughter of a merchant, and an exceptional silkmaker and business woman. She completed her apprenticeship around 1450 and over the next 39 years, had an apprentice training with her every year. In her business she used over 5000 pounds of silk per annum, a total of around 20,000 pounds of raw silk between 1491 and 1495. This was a massive amount, representing a third of all the raw silk that came into Cologne. Her husband Mertyn Ime Hove, was a highly regarded merchant with vast trading experience, a guildsman who had been honoured as a citizen of Cologne. Many other major silkwomen were involved with their guild, trained their apprentices and handled substantial amounts of silk. Styngen Kremers and Mettel an dem Huhnermarkt were both merchants as were Fygen and her unmarried sister Sewis van Berchem. They paid tax on the substantial amounts of silk and wine they imported in the 1470s. They accumulated a great deal of property, and at their deaths were very wealthy indeed.

By the beginning of the sixteenth century an increasing number of silk families in Cologne were relying on putting out work, rather than silk production with apprentices. Guild statutes were being flaunted, guild controls breaking down and the situation declined. Despite the introduction of new statutes, by 1506 the situation for the women's silk guild was very poor indeed. There were social abuses and typically it was the silk spinners and throwsters, the semi-skilled who suffered. They were outworkers, powerless and the most vulnerable. They were paid for their labour but had to compete with the convents where the work was done *gratis*. All too often, the spinners and throwsters were paid by the truck system, with silk or cloth rather than cash. To raise the cash for everyday items, the goods had to be sold and the amount of silk they were given was frequently worth less than their comparable wages. This truck system was condemned in the guild's statutes and from the pulpit, but was never stamped out.

Fleet of ships with Crusader tents at Constantinople during the period of the Fourth Crusade.

Chapter 3
Fairs, Trade and Banking

Trade

Silk continued to travel long distances, the traders taking the safest and most appropriate route from the Far East to the West. Some caravans were a thousand strong and heavily loaded with silk. The traders paid customs duties at border stations and because the exquisite silken fabrics were always in demand, took every opportunity to barter and trade all along the route. Shipping also thrived and anchored at the ports were the big dromonds of the Imperial Byzantine fleet, Dalmatian barks, galleys from Genoa, Venice and Amalfi, light feluccas from the east and caiques from the Greek Islands. For much of the time there was an imbalance of trade. The west coveted the exotic eastern goods, especially the gorgeous silks, but they had very little that the east wanted in return, except possibly slaves, dyes and hunting dogs, with the result that the silks had to be paid for in gold.

The Iranian merchants were mostly Muslims from Azerbaijan and later Azeris. The Prophet Muhammad had been a merchant, and trading was honoured. After he died in 632 AD leaving no sons to inherit, his son-in-law and husband of his daughter Fatima, founded the separatist Shi'ia movement. The Fatimid court loved luxury and gloried in displaying the colourful silk garments, richly embroidered in gold. Initially the Koran offered no limitations to depicting animal and natural forms, but restrictions were introduced in the Hadith and they became another of the Traditions. By the eleventh century the Fatimid treasury included fifty thousand silk damasks, and some were a new compound weave with a smooth ground and a slightly raised twill design, known as lampas or diasprum. In Cairo, the Street of the Silk Worker and the Street of Brocade became centres of silk production.

When the Byzantine economy started to breakdown, it was the Latin traders who seized the opportunities. They rarely had direct contact with the original suppliers but worked through agents, because of restrictions imposed by the Muslim leaders, both physical and commercial on European contact with the Far East. Nevertheless, the Italians enjoyed many privileges, including tax exemptions. By the twelfth century, the Venetians had a virtual monopoly, with trading headquarters in Tyre, Cherson and later Sudak and also on many of the islands of the Cyclades, including Andros, Mykonos, Paros, and Milos. A Genoese merchant noted the tight controls put on the export of prized silks and that even the Venetians failed to obtain permission to buy silk in Corinth before 1171. A Genoese cargo at Abydos, probably on its way to Constantinople in 1201 had its silks confiscated. The records note both an inexpensive lightweight silk, as well as two pieces of very valuable samite, worth altogether 80 bezants. In addition there were some raw silks and kermes dyes.

The Italian Merchants

After Pope Urban II's clarion call to the Crusades, the Pisan merchants were the first Italians to secure concessions and set up trading posts in the captured

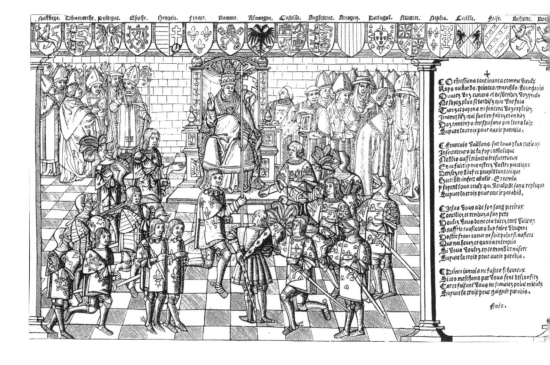

Syrian towns and to profit by providing transport to the first and second Crusades. Then Genoa secured a trading concession in Antioch where the new ruler Bohenund reluctantly granted the merchants a trading base consisting of thirty houses and a bazaar.

Pope Urban II at the Council of Clermont (1095) where he called for all Christians to respond to the first Crusade

Venice was rather late in claiming its concessions. It was unwilling to further antagonize the Byzantine Emperor who was rather sensitive to the way the Italians had ruthlessly established Latin kingdoms all over his former territory. The fiasco and mismanagement of the fourth Crusade enabled the astute and rapacious Venetians to step in and control trade, reaping vast profits, and supplying most of the goods and transport it was said, to both sides. The Venetians set harsh terms that included a premium of up to fifty percent on all gains and seizures. The wealth of Byzantium was a revelation to many crusaders. They had never seen such glorious textiles. They stripped the homes and churches and claimed the silks as booty and the spoils of war.

After the Latin conquest of Constantinople in 1204, the Italians established themselves in the Crusader ports of the Levant, and gradually ousted the Byzantine merchants and controlled the trade, skillfully marketing all silks to many destinations in Europe and the Muslim East. Geoffrey I of Villhardouin in 1209 was forced to pledge that he would deliver two valuable pieces of silk to the church of San Marco in Venice and one to the Doge each year. The Archbishop of Patras, near where Danielis had had her silk workshops many years before, also promised that he would give Cluny Abbey an exquisite piece of finely woven silk each year. Silk in Italy was highly developed, in stark contrast to the upheaval in the silk industry in Constantinople after it fell, first to the Latins and then to the Ottomans.

Venice had developed into a great maritime nation with its own convoys of galleys. One convoy usually went to Constantinople and the Black Sea, another to Beirut and a third to Alexandria. The largest galley was around 500 tons, and had a crew of 60 oarsmen and 20 crossbow men. Some galleys carried pilgrims as well as cargo, and all the vessels needed sufficient food and water for the whole trip. About 2,000 tons of eastern merchandise went to Venice each year and about the same amount to Genoa. Pirates and thieves caused the greatest anxiety and in January 1273 a Venetian ship going from Nauplia where silk was produced, to Apaulia, was robbed of its cargo of raw silk, kermes dyes, rough silk fabric and cocoons. By 1277 the routes had greatly expanded, protection improved and Genoese galleys now called at Cadiz, Seville, France, Flanders and on to England.

Francesco Balducci Pegolotti, an agent of the Bardi of Florence wrote a commercial manual, *La Practica della Mercatura* around 1340, with advice for the merchants. It listed over 300 items that were traded, including twenty-three different sorts of silk, velvet and gold brocade produced in Baghdad, Damascus, Teheran and the Far East. He was anxious about the way silk was transported, and advised that it should be firmly packed and neither too damp nor too dry. He was concerned that the canvas bales were protected from rough handling and not 'rubbed' or the corners scuffed when they dragged on the ground or scraped along the hedges, because the silk got spoiled, severely reducing its retail price.

Until the devastation in 1347-8 when the Black Death swept through Europe, the west experienced enormous growth in both industry and commerce with the introduction

of speedier galleys, the compass, astrolabe and improved roads making travel easier and faster. The Italians' objective was to set up a network and acquire a virtual monopoly on valuable oriental goods from the east, and transport and then sell them at a profit in Northern and Western Europe. With the proceeds, they imported raw silk from the Caspian provinces of Gilan, Shamakhi and Karabagh providing the growing Italian silk weaving industry with the raw silk it needed. The Latins also had a hand in re-exporting some of these manufactured silk textiles and embroideries all over Europe, the Empire and the Moslem countries of the Near East, frequently making a further resounding profit on all these transactions.

Italian bankers were involved in financing the large amounts of silk for sale and export. The silk needed to reach the ports in autumn in time to be loaded onto the galleys going westward to the Mediterranean with the seasonal convoys returning from Cyprus, Romania and the Levant. A missed sailing meant the silk had to wait until the spring when the ships returned, a problem Lorenzo Acciaiuoli had in 1379 when a package of 53 pounds of his silk had to be stored at Modon over the winter. John Laskaris Kalopheros also had to arrange storage for silk at Modon in 1381. He was an adventurer who had won the heart and married one of the daughters of Erard III Le Maure. Erard was one of the most powerful barons of Frankish Morea, Lord of Arcadia, Saint-Sauveur and Aetos in Messinia. The silk could have been from Erard's estates, and collected as part of the dues or payment in kind from his peasants who were compelled to sell a portion to him at a nominal price. John Laskaris Kalopheros sold two consignments, a total of 2,773 'light pounds' to several foreign merchants who shipped it to Provence and Majorca. He was an energetic entrepreneur and conducted his business on a large scale, acting as agent or independent merchant, backed with considerable capital.

Fairs

While ports like Venice, Genoa and Marseille were expanding, so were towns geographically at the crossroads of land and river routes. Major cities like Paris, Cologne and London had fairs, as did smaller cities like Lucca that specialized in silk manufacturing. The celebration of a major saint's day would draw people from miles around, and a fair would evolve within the precincts of the church or in the town square. After the processions and high drama of the religious celebrations, all the local people, including the homeless adventurers, itinerant traders, peddlers and chapmen with their packs and trays of haberdashery would mingle in the crowd. It was an excellent opportunity to do some business and build up contacts, settle debts, make new arrangements and trade. Some churches or local lords were very accommodating and supportive, offering security for money and goods, warehouses and hostels. It became the custom for groups of men dealing in similar products to congregate informally in a particular area of the fair. Later, some groups coalesced into a more formal structure of minor merchants dealing in a specific commodity, like silk veils or caps. The wealthier merchants with capital and often with family backing, took a more professional approach to the expansion of trade, and formed themselves into a merchant's guild or hanse, establishing a network to protect themselves and facilitate commerce over longer distances.

The fairs took over the whole town, some large national guilds owned permanent halls, stables and hostels, connected by underground walkways, a veritable subterranean city. The guards of the fair were there to maintain law and order and the integrity of all the commercial dealings. Some were on a fixed wage, unique at the time. The fair attracted a cosmopolitan mix of people and discipline could be a problem, especially in the evenings. The people gathered to drink, gamble, fight, tell yarns and chat up the available ladies. In 1377 one fair had 140 guards, 20 of them mounted and around 40 notaries to draw up contracts and keep records of transport arrangements and affidavits of merchandise arriving too late or in poor condition.

The diamond dealers, possibly Genoa. 14th century woodcut

The Champagne Fairs

The fairs were a major opportunity to trade in the exotic luxurious silks and merchants came from far afield. The fairs were a phenomenon of the Middle Ages and the earliest was reputed to be the Paris fair of St Denis founded by Dagobert I in 630. The autumn fair began on October 3rd and continued for four weeks and in 1124 a summer fair was added. Louis VI (1078-1137) set aside land north of Montmartre for a new fair called the *Foire du Lendit*, which began on the second Wednesday in June and ended on St Johns day, the 24th of June. The fair was opened with religious formalities led by the bishop of Paris, and this fair included silk, dyes and alum.

The six fairs of Champagne were the most highly developed. They were controlled by the counts of Champagne who were eager to promote their territory and reap the rewards. Champagne is situated on a fertile plain in central France, with an extensive river system, ideal for transporting the goods. It includes the Seine to Normandy and the Channel coast, the Meuse to the Low Countries and North Sea and the Moselle and Soane to the Rhone Valley and the Mediterranean. The Marne connected the Rhine with Germany and the high passes through the Alps to Italy.

Gradually, internationally accepted rules and regulations were agreed. Under the care of the illustrious Count of Champagne known as Henry I, 'the Liberal' (1152-81) the fairs reached their apogee. He united the counties of Brie and Champagne and the fairs continued under the families of the Etiennes, Henris and Thibaults. Some of these Counts had strong, able wives who also ruled and presided at the fairs. When the heiress of Champagne married the King of France in 1285, control of the fairs passed to the king. Now the state levied new taxes on the booths, residences of merchants, sales and purchases, weights and measures. Extra payments were required from Jews and Italians for safe conduct, and additional wardens were appointed to be responsible for order and the settlement of disputes.

The six Champagne fairs were held annually in four towns. The first, and one of the earliest was the St Ayoul fair at Provins that began on the Tuesday before Ascension Day in September and lasted until All Saints Day on the 1st of November. Records show that in 963 it was held in the lower city, while the summer fair was held in May in the upper city. Another early fair was at Bar-sur-Aube, where it is known that cloth was purchased and taken to Italy in 1114. This fair started each year on Shrove Tuesday and in 1160 only lasted fifteen days, but by 1250 it had grown to the more usual five weeks. By now the fair was truly international, bringing silks from many towns especially Lucca and Florence. Merchants' records show that the traders came from as far afield as Flanders, Brabant, Spain, England, Cremona, Milan, Asti, Piacenza, Germany and Savoy. Italians brought their Eastern silks and goods from outside Europe, including dyes, alum, lacquer and exotic spices. There was also a winter fair that started on the 2nd of January at Lagny on the Marne. There were two fairs at Troyes on the Seine, a 'hot fair' in the summer that began on the 24th of June, and a 'cold fair' in winter on the 2nd of November. In 1267 a Genoese merchant made arrangements to receive payment of 392 *livres provinois* at the Troyes fair for silk bought at Montpellier.

There were many smaller additional fairs, but the major fairs lasted five or six weeks and they all followed a similar

Cloth market, Italy, where cloth was traded and clothes were made and sold

pattern. During the first eight days there was a sense of excitement and anticipation as the traders set up the booths and stalls. Then the bell was rung to start the first section, the serious business of the fair, the sale of woollen cloth. At the end of ten days the bell was rung again by the fair sergeants who called 'Haro! Haro!' to show that first part of fair was now closed. The next eight to ten days dealt with a wide variety of goods including leather and grain, and the last part was devoted to Mediterranean and Oriental goods, and other items sold by weight or measure. Weights were originally the property of the counts, and Troy weight survives to this day, but the *aume,* a cloth measure of about three feet eight inches, varied widely. The settlement of all accounts was done on the final four days when the notaries drew up 'letters of the fair' and seals were placed on the all the important contracts to guarantee their validity.

Other Fairs

The Lucca fair in Northern Italy was at the very heart of the silk industry. It attracted a great deal of attention from the international silk merchants who traded not only local silk, but also silk from the Levant, Syria and Persia. Dyes, including indigo and cochineal were sold at the weights and measures section. In the Midi, there were two large and important fairs, the St Gilles and the Beaucaire. The fairs were a great stimulant to the local economy and many included clothes, haberdashery, tassels, headdresses, purses, gloves, second hand clothes and ribbons, all dear to a lady's heart. Although some fairs had a questionable reputation, many a young girl slipped off to explore with a friend, to see what was new, exciting and in fashion that year.

Some fairs became famous, as much for their roistering and entertainments as for the commercial activity. There was plenty to amuse the crowds of people, jugglers, dancing bears, wandering minstrels, and the fabliaux and plays, like the romance 'Hervis', or '*La Bourse Pleine de Sens*'. It was necessary to be on one's guard because there were montebanks and swindlers, thieves, runaway serfs, pick pockets, thugs, beggars, discharged soldiers, prostitutes and drunkards. Despite the hazards, a fair could be the highlight of the year, and many a young man's thoughts turned to love as he searched out a 'fairing', a silk ribbon or other little gift to give his girl.

The Spanish still had a virtual monopoly of trade to the Americas, and the big fairs at Valladolid and Seville flourished. The sale of goods was enormous at the three great fairs in Castille, the Medina del Campo, the Villalon and the Medina del Rio Seco. They were centres of high finance, that included raising loans for the expansion of the silk industry, private loans for the king and discounting bills of exchange, all totaling millions of ducats.

Woodcut of the market where friends and neighbours would meet. A big fair or market would attract traders from vast distances

There were fairs all over the west, the Levant and Near East, including one at Vervena in the Peloponnese held in mid June where in 1296 a landlord planned to sell his cocoons. Flanders also had six important fairs, two at Ypres, one each at Bruges, Thourout, Lille and Messines. There was a great fair at Geneva on the shores of Lake Leman and from the fifteenth century it became a major commercial and financial centre, along with Basel and Frankfurt. Peter Lutzenkirchen, the husband of Fygen Lutzenkirchen a very successful silkwoman, regularly visited the Frankfurt, Antwerp, and Brabant Fairs at Bergen op Zoom around the 1490s. He was an important Cologne merchant and agent for several trading houses including the Ravensburger Handelsgesellschaft, through which he imported silk from Valencia and gold yarn, destined for Genoa and Venice.

The heavy taxation imposed by the French kings and wars compounded the problems and the Champagne fairs suffered and lost their appeal. The Venetians tried to avoid the trouble spots by increasing their maritime galley routes to Bruges and London, via the Straits of Gibraltar, rather than going overland. Louis XI (1423-83) had become increasingly disturbed by the reduced revenue from the failing fairs and the large amount of gold leaving France for the purchase of silk. He chose to promote and support the fairs of Lyons, rather than those of Champagne, and brought in legislation to prohibit trade with other centres like Geneva. The Lyon spring fair was held on the right bank of the Soane, the French side and the autumn fair on the left bank, the Imperial side. By 1296 the Florentines had changed their alliance to Lyon. Their presence and custom was so important, that it was almost impossible to save the Champagne fairs once the Italians, with their money and expertise had gone. By the beginning of the fifteenth century the international importance of the Champagne fairs had ceased. They had become financial rather than commercial centres, offering currency and bill quotations rather than active trade. By 1550 the Champagne fairs had virtually disappeared from the records.

Money, Credit and Finance

Trade was not the only business conducted at the fairs. Many dealers took the opportunity to reclaim rents or negotiate contracts. The Jewish money-changers and local bankers were available to exchange currency, transfer funds and arrange loans. They had a table covered with a chequerboard, with a pair of scales and leather bags with coins and ingots. For everyday transactions, bezants were used but the coins of Provins were the most readily available. Silk had an acknowledged value, so sometimes it was used instead of cash to round off a debt or achieve a balance. Legally all deals had to be settled at the time of the fair, but arrangements sometimes needed to be carried over.

The Italian merchants used bills of exchange for short-term loans to pay for foreign goods, especially the silks. The bills enabled funds to be moved between different locations, without the risks of physically transferring the heavy bags of coins. They usually gave thirty days credit from the time

the bill was drawn up, and by the end of
the thirteenth century they had transformed
the fairs into the first international capital
markets. Control was in the hands of these
newly rich merchants and bankers. As
banking and credit arrangements became
more sophisticated there was a need for all
year round banking facilities, not just at the
times of the fairs.

The social rank of the fair traders had
declined because the great merchants no
longer travelled to the fairs, but handled
their business by correspondence. They
employed factors, brokers, couriers and
carters to ensure continuous
communication and the safe transference
of both the funds and the valuable silks.
These merchants acted on a national scale,
fuelled by the inflow of new capital and
the development of credit. The largest
international deals were done by the
prestigious Italian bankers, known as the
Lombards. They put together the complex
financial arrangements and received a set percentage that
concealed an interest charge, because usury was still
condemned by the Church. Financial partnerships provided
for a division of the profit and risks in proportion to the
initial investment. Silk was an international commodity. It
often required substantial lines of credit and vast complicated
loans and partnerships to get it from the eastern suppliers to
the western manufacturers and out to the markets.

In 1343 one of the great banking houses, the Peruzzi
collapsed, followed by the Bardi. Both had been fatally
crippled by the failure of Edward III of England (1312-77)
to honour his debts. Then the third largest Florentine bank,
the Acciaiuoli also failed and this triggered an international
banking crisis. Gradually other banks like the Pazzi and
Rucellai, took the place of the failed banking families and
one of the most illustrious was the Medici. They expanded
by combining commercial and political expertise and they

*Italian bankers with chests of gold
and silver coins. Deals and loans were
recorded and a line of people waited
their turn. 15th century.*

became an international holding company with many branches. The Medici were appointed bankers to the Pope and the Papal court and they were richly rewarded. Included in their vast network of financial dealings was the collection of obligations and indulgences, rents from church estates, trade in relics and the acquisition of the finest silks. The Medici and many of the Popes shared a passionate love of the arts with a desire to accumulate the greatest treasure on earth. They combined this with a ruthless pursuit of power and wealth, but this left them open to corruption and bribery, because they were offering guarantees both temporal and spiritual. Up until 1434, the Medici drew half their revenue from the Papal branch in Rome, but their fortunes fluctuated and the pursuit of art and luxurious living became more important than their core business of banking. By 1451 their silk shop was one of the last profitable ventures, an exotic caprice, pandering to a passion for luxury and desire for conspicuous consumption. The bank became a hollow shell, just the outward and visible sign of former wealth and power.

Merchants and trade

Some cities became renowned for their silk industries while others like Montpellier developed into finishing and distribution centres. Direct imports of silk came from the Levant, and in 1221 the consuls of Montpellier ordered a magnificent silk cloth of gold for Jacme I of Aragon on the occasion of his marriage to Eleanor of Castille. Other records note a Lucchesi merchant engaged in 1248 in shipping refined spun silk and gold from Marseilles to Montpellier. This was in turn re-exported as finished silk from Marseilles to Ceuta. Merchants were also involved with the export of 150 *livres* of coloured silk, destined for Toulouse in 1293. Johannes Ferrandes of Burgos and two associates bought *merces de Lucca* in Montpellier in 1341. The Cabanis brothers had a base in Montpellier. They were relatively small investors in the Levant trade, dealing in raw silk, China silk and dyed Lucchesse silks. The brothers had business dealings with Vitalis and Bartholomeus Calvalerii of Cahors, who bought small amounts of *merc de Lucca* ranging in price from 20 to 80 *livres*. One merchant sold a fardel of partially processed silk, *cirici torchie* to a Montpellier silk merchant for *206 livres 9 sous petits tournois*. Many merchants used Montpellier as a financial clearing centre, borrowing funds in their home cities through exchange contracts, and clearing their debts in Montpellier.

Sericulture did continue to expand in Lucca, but the production of raw silk was insufficient for its finishing industry so it still had to import silk from Spain, Genoa and Asia Minor. The notary records sometimes included not just the type of silk but its origin as well; *pro cerico de Romania* was silk from Byzantium. Another silk was the silver brocade of Lucca, *argento de Lucca cerico*, along with raw silk described in 1293 as *cerico crudo refracto,* perhaps because it was damaged or broken. By the 1330s, some Lucchesse merchants are recorded as negotiating for thousands of pounds of China silk.

There were three kinds of silk merchants in Cordoba. The 'desk' merchants the *mercaderes de escritorio* who did not travel but used agents to buy large quantities of raw silk and have it spun. Other merchants redistributed it to the weaver and the third group, the *mercaderes da vara* distributed the woven silk to the retail merchants, who sold it. Granada exported more raw silk than textiles. An Italian, Giovanni Scriba wrote a contract for the shipment of ten pieces of *tela Yspanie*, while other contracts dated 1200, 1224 and 1238 specify *cendates*, another variety of fine silk cloth.

By 1473 silk was big business. The Italian silk merchants had expanded throughout Europe and had agencies in many countries including France, the Netherlands and England. They rarely specialized, but their businesses

Woodcut of a merchant at work in his warehouse, bales and bundles of cloth and sacks of goods. Of prime importance was to keep accurate records and a close eye on profit. With such valuable merchandise, watchmen would be hired, with others to pack, stack and dispatch the stock.

encompassed lots of commodities as well as silk, furs, woolens, pepper, wax, dyes, foodstuffs, metals and gems. They owned shops, selling scarce gold and silver brocades and precious silken cloth. With increasing sophistication in the business of silk, merchants, agents and factors needed to be very astute, and note the minute graduations in quality, lustre, variety and price. They needed to study the markets and be aware of even the slightest political changes, whispers and movements, and not put money into silks that were no longer in fashion. Considerable experience and business acumen was required, a very good memory and a network of trusted colleagues in order to be successful in the post-medieval business world. They were permitted to form 'colonies' in specific areas of the city and conduct their business under their own civil and commercial laws. They were closely watched and only granted a three-month residency permit. Some of the bigger colonies like the *Fondaco dei Tedeschi* in Venice included a warehouse, hostels, public baths, markets and churches. Sometime the Latins claimed whole towns like Chios, Pera, Caffa, Faragusta and the island of Crete.

Antwerp had become a pre-eminent trading centre in Europe and the major Italian silk centres of Naples, Bologna, Milan, Florence, Genoa, Mantua, Lucca, and Venice were all exporting silk to the market in Antwerp. In 1560 a Florentine gentleman, Louis Guicciardini drew up a list of these Italian cities and described the type of silk fabrics exported from each, but only Bologna was exporting silks to England. In 1581 Guicciardini received complaints about the price of silk, especially velvet. The Italians were talented and tenacious businessmen and many like Pandolfo and Vincenzo Galli kept detailed records. In 1595 the Galli's bought vast quantities of silk from both Valdinievole and Pescia in Tuscany, with over 922 pounds from Pescia alone.

Italy had strong ties with Cracow and much is known about the availability of silk from the 1586 inventory of the Italian merchant Jan Cechi. It graphically highlights the many places that manufactured and finished silk in Italy in the sixteenth century. Both old and new styles were imported from Lucca, Florence, Mantua and Pisa, with the coarser silks from Milan. Satin and other delicate silks came from Venice, with smaller quantities from Genoa, Naples, and Bologna. The gradual move of the Polish court to Warsaw between 1596 and 1611 attracted the more expensive silks, brocades and cloth of gold, *drapi d'oro* and cloth of silver, *drappi d'argento* which came from the exclusive Florentine workshops. These, along with the silk vestments were the most highly prized silks although velvet was now less popular. In the seventeenth century, there were two major Italian silk dealers in Cracow, Paolo Antonio Ricciardetti and Marc Antonio Fedderici, and both maintained direct contact with Italian silk manufacturers. The Polish court was in fine form and its demand for gorgeous silks strengthened its strong ties with Italy in the second half of the seventeenth century. Three times a year, goods came overland from warehouses in Verona, via Ausbergen and Leipzig in Germany to Wroclau and Cracow, a journey of six weeks.

Silk was just as liable to loss as profit, through incompetence, bad debts, travel loss or seizure, piracy and war. Two bales, valued at £358 were lost when the ship the 'Devonshire' was pursued by pirates and seized. In 1628 the Dutch imported 1200 bales of silk and like the English, re-exported their surplus to other European countries. This was a small part of the total imports and exports, but what they lost in quantity in comparison with other goods traded, they more than made up for in total financial value and prestige.

Cracow. The tailor's shop, early 16th century. A wealthy person would bring their fabric to the tailor, who would draft the pattern and cut out the fabric, leaving the sewing to the women and apprentices.

Mary Magdalene, Crevelli, 1480. The whole painting glows with gold; the frame, her hair, the jar of ointment, her halo and, above all, her gold brocade bodice, further encrusted with gold embroidery and braid. She is also wearing a rich, red, satin skirt and fine, pleated chemise that shows at the neck and sleeves.

Chapter 4
Gold and Dyes

Gold

Gold has a magical quality, reflecting the mysteries of the sun. It was believed to hold the essence of life, its radiance uniting the spiritual with the earthly. Golden threads woven into a fabric displayed the power of man and magnified the glory of God. The elite of church and state saw it as their duty to possess and wear these extremely valuable items, cloth of gold, priceless velvets, precious brocades, gorgeous furnishings and dazzling embroidery, all encrusted with gold.

The goldsmiths of Augsburg and Nuremberg had experimented with drawing out pure gold and silver rods through a perforated gauge. This fragile metal thread was not flexible enough to use on its own, but had to be wound around a core of orange, red, purple or yellow silk. This gave it added strength and lustre and these threads became a specialty of Cologne. Husbands and wives often worked together but he was the master goldsmith and controlled the capital to purchase the raw silk and precious metals, arrange the contracts and the eventual sale. The actual making of gold thread was women's work and she could have up to three apprentices to assist her. Anything to do with gold, gems or high-class embroidery for the church or court had high status and was considered an occupation of the master craftsman and merchant.

The Italian town of Lucca prohibited the importation of foreign silk products, but made an exception in the case of gold thread from Cologne. Lucca manufactured and exported vast amounts of exquisite gold and silver textiles including *'argento de Lucha cerico'*. Cloth of gold was also woven in Florence, Genoa, Venice, Cologne, France and Flanders, the very places that specialized in silk. Records in Venice clearly indicate how specific some laws could be. In July 1410 a decree forbade the introduction into Venice of silk textiles that had not been made there and it defined the quality of gold to be used. There were severe penalties for using imitation or poor quality silver or gold.

Silk and gold threads were imported into England and used in embroideries and woven into precious braids and narrow ware and were extensively used in the exquisite English embroidery, known as Opus Anglicanum. Vestments for the use of the clergy and robes of state for the king and the court reflected the power and wealth of these institutions. Gold thread was an important element of heraldry. The family coat of arms was emblazoned on many items like the tabard, worn over armour. A replica of the Black Prince's jupon hangs in Canterbury Cathedral above his tomb. It is embroidered in gold thread on red and blue velvet and quilted onto wool and linen.

The amount of gold used was frequently an indication of the status of the wearer but it could cause criticism also as when Henry VII's poet laureat Skelton wrote of the bishops:

> "Ryde with gold all trapped
> In purpall and pall delapped,
> Some hatted and som capp'd
> Richly and warm wrapped.
> God wott to their grete paynes
> In rochetts of fyne reynes, (silk cloth
>   from Rennes)

Chasuble. The cross orphrey is set on red, silk velvet. The fine embroidery features the crucifixion with Mary and the disciples and is worked in gold and dyed silk floss. Bohemia, 1380.

Whyte as Mary's milk
And tabards of fyne sylk,
And stryoppes with gold beglozyd."

Queen Elizabeth of York, Henry VII's wife employed her own embroiderer Robnet, and gave him £2 per annum towards house rent and 1s 4p per week for board and wages. He paid 5 shillings an ounce for flat gold and 4s 4d for round gold. He also paid his embroiderers top wages of four pennies a day and board and was responsible for buying the candles, coal, crewel and thread. On April 29th he purchased for the Queen, 'gold of Venys 8oz, gold of damaske and 10 oz silke Venice.' It cost a further 16 shillings to make these into lace and buttons for the King's Garter Mantle.

Woven or embroidered panels of cloth of gold, with large complex designs, were a very visible display of wealth and status. They were hung prominently in the main rooms and displayed for all to admire and envy. They had the advantage of being transportable from one household to another every time the noble family moved and could either be rolled up or laid out flat in specially made chests for transport or storage.

There is no evidence of an English cloth of gold weaving industry. Even broadloom silks were not widely made until after the arrival of the Huguenot weavers in the sixteenth century. There are however, frequent mentions of the importation of valuable textiles for the English court and church. In 1516 Henry VIII appointed Leonardo Frescobaldo and Antonio Cavallari at a salary of £20 per annum each. They secured silk textiles and gold and silver thread for the court and also arranged contracts with the Florentine merchant bankers. At various times the Bardi, Frescobaldi, Cavalcanti and Corsi bankers were commissioned to secure vast amounts of luxurious silk and cloth of gold fabrics for the king.

One of the most dazzling displays of conspicuous wealth took place at what came to be known as the Field of the Cloth of Gold. It was the meeting in 1520 between King Henry VIII (1491-1547) of England and Francis I (1494-1547) of France. The cousins and their enormous retinues met on a field near Calais for the purpose of establishing a political alliance. They set up numerous tents, gilded and richly

decorated with silks and cloth of gold. A guilded fountain was set up and it gushed forth water, spiced wine and claret, each cascading from a separate spout. The kings and their courtiers paraded each day for nearly three weeks, between June 7th and June 24th in the most exotic and costly garments, each trying to outdo the other. It was an outrageous show of wealth and splendour. The days were filled with jousts and pageants, banquets, masques, processions, balls and even a fireworks display, but to no avail. It nearly bankrupted both courts and King Henry concluded treaties not with France but Spain, the country of his queen, Catherine of Aragon.

Court gossips at the time of Elizabeth the First, maintained that half the gold bullion in the land was for the clothes of the nobility. Bullion was also the name given to a wire thread, coiled like a tight spring and hollow in the centre. It needed to be handled very carefully, and couched or sewn down like a bead. It was usually cut into short lengths and came in three varieties. The first had a dull sheen and was 'rough' or *matte*. The second was 'smooth' or '*glissant*' and the third gave a sparkling effect and was called 'check' or '*frise*'. Gold wire, wrapped around silk was also used to make gold lace and edged the showiest items, ruffs and gloves such as those given as New Year gifts to Queen Elizabeth. Tudor inventories referred to Venice gold. It had been known since the medieval period, and was made using the time honoured method of gilding vellum or long strips of animal intestines, and cutting them into very fine strips. Sometimes these gilded strips were also wrapped around a core of silk or hemp to give them greater strength and flexibility.

Gold thread was always very expensive, whether imported or locally hand drawn. There were tight regulations because poor quality gold tarnished. Unfortunately a garment heavily woven or encrusted with gold could form permanent creases if it was badly packed for storage or transport. It could also get flattened and squashed into ridges when the wearer sat down. Its weight ensured that it was more often used in spectacular outer garments and robes of state where a maid or page could assist by holding up the heavy train. The livery worn by the major guildsmen often included a great deal of gold work. The men were impressive, marching in serried ranks, wearing their livery. Priceless golden garments were mentioned in wills, yet surprisingly few remain. Once the garment was worn out and the gems removed, the garment was burnt to retrieve the gold.

The Guild of Gold Wyre Drawers

The London Guild of Gold and Silver Wyre Drawers were anxious to try and establish just who was the first one to invent or discover the process of extruding gold and silver wire for weaving or embroidery. It was known that Christopher Schutz and Daniel Hochstetter of Cologne had been flattening fine gold wire and spinning it around a core of silk, but Claude Durelle said he was the one who had established a trade in spun gold thread in England '…by spynninge – the first that bought the skyll of spynninge which is nowe knowen.'. The argument continued to rumble on and in May 1611 King James I (1566-1625) granted a patent to Richard Dike and others, because they claimed they alone manufactured gold and silver thread. The Goldsmith's company maintained it definitely was not new, as one of their guildsmen had been drawing gold wire for over fifty years.

Gold and Silver Wyre Drawers and the London Weaver's Company were highly respected and were asked by officers of H M Customs to help when contraband goods were seized. The silk and gold items were so valuable that smuggling was worth the risks. In 1672 the Commissioners asked for help in valuing and selling off great quantities of prohibited foreign silks and gold stuffs on which the import duty had not been properly paid. These items included 'laces, ribands, girdles and corses of tissues or points from beyond the sea'. Eighteen members of the Weavers Company were appointed Searchers and Seizers to assist in this matter. The smugglers had many ingenious ways of hiding the gold and silk items. They concealed them inside ladies turbans or hollowed out loaves of bread. Once they sewed them inside the back of a gentleman's waistcoat, and even hid them in the carcasses of Normandy poultry, destined for the market. The guildsmen took these matters seriously and contributed money when a charge was brought against people illegally bringing in the goods. Sometimes the seizers themselves were rather over zealous and were fined, as when the Company had to pay Elias Turner £75 plus legal fees when his silks were falsely detained.

Natural Dyes

In ancient times, valuable textiles had been dyed with the scarce and precious purple dye obtained from specific shellfish found throughout the Mediterranean. *Murex brandaris* or M. *trunculus* produced various shades of violet-purple and the *Purpura haemastoma* gave an ox-blood colour. The deep violet shade, known as *principalis*, was produced from a mixture of *Murex brandaris* and *Purpura haemastoma*, but the most highly regarded was the purple dye from Tyre, known as Tyrian purple. The colour was obtained by dyeing the fabric first in *Murex brandaris* and then in a bath of *Purpura haemastoma* which added to both the depth of colour and the price. Archaeological evidence suggests that the Minoans of Crete were using murex dyes from around 1900 BC. By 1600 BC there were other centres at Miletus, Sidon, the islands of Cos and Leuka, and Phoenicia, which means 'the land of the purple'.

This purple dye had enormous status and Herodotus (485-425 BC) mentions a wealthy Cretan dyer trading in purple. Aristotle (384-322 BC) maintained that the best season to collect the shellfish was the spring and that it required over 12,000 shellfish to make 1.5 grams of dye. The large ones were removed from their shells, but the little ones were crushed, shell and all. Some midden have been found with shell deposits over 22 metres (75 feet) deep and extending for nearly a mile. The shellfish were kept alive as long as possible because the dye was not released once the fish had died. The dyers were a secretive lot and the actual method, the ingredients, the length of time it had to be soaked, how often it had to be rinsed and renewed were all kept a deep secret. Once there was sufficient concentrated dye, the fibres were prepared and dipped a number of times to achieve the desired shades of reddish-purple. Sometimes the rich colour of ox blood, which the Greeks called *blatta* or *oxyblatta* was the fashion choice, and sometimes a bluish purple.

Medieval dyers. The master dyer watches while the apprentice moves the cloth around in the vats of boiling dye.

Byzantium was prospering, and laws were brought in to prohibit the wearing of purple by anyone other than a person of royal birth. There is something arresting and powerful about brilliant purple, and both Alexander the Great (356-323 BC) and Darius who died in 330 BC, adopted it as conquerors. Alexander found priceless purple robes in Susa that were nearly 200 years old. The flamboyant colour was just to his taste and he attracted a great deal of criticism by flaunting his purple robes, 'just like a Persian'. The hagiographers described Anthony's escape from the battle of Actium on Cleopatra's (69-30 BC) flag ship. They recorded that:

> 'The barge she sat in, like a burnished throne,
> Burned on the waters, the poop was beaten gold,
> Purple the sails…'

Whether the purple colour was murex or vegetable dyes, it still captured the imagination. Pliny (23-79 AD) noted in his writings that only senators could wear a tunic with broad purple stripes, and the stripe broadened as the man's status increased. The Imperial purple of Rome came from another species of mollusc and was so valuable that even Emperor Aurelian (c212-275 AD) refused to buy his wife a silk garment dyed in this purple.

Plictho de l'arte, a book on dying published in 1548.

The price and desirability of the dye led to substitutes and some fraud. The oldest collection of dyeing recipes was found in a grave in Egypt in 1828. It is preserved in a museum in Stockholm and known as the Papyrus Holmiensis, or the Stockholm Papyrus. It has been dated to the third century AD and contains 70 recipes, most concerned with imitating purple. Egyptian Purple was made from woad or indigo and madder. Alkanet, orchil and kermes were also used, either alone or in combination with woad.

With the advent of Christianity, some of the most exquisite Coptic textiles, made between the fourth and the seventh centuries AD include purple-dyed fibres. At least one was dyed with *Murex brandaris*, but most were dyed either from madder with iron or by using a combination of madder and indigo or woad. Purple was also used for staining the pages of some of the most important manuscripts, although Murex purple was now seldom used. The last western centre to have produced purple dye seems to have been Tarentium in southern Italy, and it was from this port that Theodoric (455-526) obtained his supply of purple garments. He sent them to Ravenna, an important city within the Byzantine Empire, and some of the beautiful garments are recorded in the frescos and mosaics there, in the Church of San Vitale.

In Byzantium, purple shellfish dye was produced by women dyers in the *gynaeceum* at Zuexippos under the control of the High Prefect. This dye was now known a *blattae Byzantinae,* and was mostly applied to silk. Under the Norman king of Sicily, Roger I (1031-1101), the purple dyes of Palermo became almost as famous as those from Byzantium. The sacking of Constantinople in 1204 dealt a severe blow to the dye industry, but there was a brief, final revival under the Paleologs in 1261, but soon the Empire came under the power of Islam. After the fall of Constantinople in 1453 the entire shellfish dye industry was lost along with much of the knowledge. By this time the use of kermes insects to produce red dye was more widespread, partly because of the price and also because red was now preferred to purple. In the west in 1464, Pope Paul II introduced 'Cardinal's purple'. In reality, it was not purple from the shellfish but red kermes dye and it was now the luxury dye of the Middle Ages.

Dyes from Plants and Insects

Every community had its dye plants and people gradually found ways to use them and to make the colour stable by applying mordants and other chemicals like the metallic salts of aluminium, iron and copper. This enabled the dyes to be fixed permanently to the fibres and improved the fastness of the colour to sunlight and washing. There is evidence of a silk dyeing industry in Montpellier by the twelfth century when a monopoly was granted by Guilhem VIII, Lord of Montpellier. It had to be relaxed in 1226 and again in 1251. In 1293, a local dyer was known to be dyeing various greens, black and red. Dyeing was a common vocation for Jews in Provence, and over the border, Italy became famous for dyeing scarlet. This was a fine woolen cloth that eventually became the name of the colour itself.

Stained glass in the Barfossecirche church in Germany, showing the three classes of membership of the Dyers Guild: the apprentice, the master dyer and the elderly senior master.

Dyeing was also an important industry in Medieval London and was based in the East End and on the south bank of the Thames River. Shards of stained and broken dye pots, dated between the tenth and the twelfth centuries, have been found in ancient sites around London. In the sixteenth century, villages such as Wandsworth, Putney, Battersea, Lambeth and Southwark became centres of a very successful Flemish and Huguenot dyeing industry and some families specialized in dyeing the valuable silk. It was mostly men's work but if things went wrong, the women were often blamed. Some men maintained that women's quarrelling made the colours 'sad', meaning they were flat and dull. The secret of how to obtain the intense colour was jealously guarded, and only passed on within the family, creating an aura of mystique.

A steady stream of clear water was needed to rinse the fabric and provide the motive power to grind the madder and indigo and for washing the stocks, squeezers and calenders. A local supply of charcoal or wood to heat the baths was also needed. Some London dyers had traditionally used coal for heating the water, but it was considered a poor choice because the fabric picked up the fumes from the coal fires. Nevertheless, coal had been used in Flanders since 1553 by silk piece dyers.

Natural dyes were obtained from plants, lichens and insects, but only a relatively small number of dyes were used on a commercial scale, and many had to be imported into England. Merchants as well as craftsmen specialized in particular dyes. They brought in kermes from the Mediterranean, madder from Holland and France, brazilwood from the East, woad from Picardy and Languedoc, potash from the Baltic and oil and soap from Spain.

Good bright reds were the most highly prized. The main dyestuffs used for the many shades of red were kermes, madder, brazilwood and later, cochineal. Kermes was the most expensive and produced the clearest and strongest colours. It was obtained from the egg sacs of the pregnant kermes shield-louse, *Kermes vermilio*, and was dried and packed in leather bags for export. The insects looked like scarlet berries on the leaves of the evergreen kermes oak, *Quercus coccifera*. It was called 'grain' in Europe and was found in the Middle East and around the Mediterranean. In some places such as Spain and Portugal, Jewish traders and dyers had a monopoly on its collection. It was probably not used on silk in England before the twelfth century, although it was known that Bernard Curuzan in 1248, received a payment of £7.10s to dye cloth 'in the grain' for the king's use. From the fourteenth and fifteenth centuries, kermes dye was found on English wool and silk textiles. In the sixteenth century red from the cochineal insect, *Dactylopius coccus,* found primarily in South America, became more readily available in Europe. Eventually cochineal took precedence over kermes as the favourite dye to get a rich red. From the sixteenth century other important dyes such as logwood, *Haematoxylon campechianum* for purple and black, and fustic *Morus tinctoria* for yellows, were also imported from the Americas.

Lac, stick-lac or gum-lac was another insect dye, imported from India and used on silk to give reds, scarlet and crimson. It made the fabric rather stiff and heavy with a glassy lustre. Lac was a resinous substance emitted by a scale-insect *Kerria lacca* or *Laccifer lacca*, living on the branches of host trees. It was known as stick-lac because it often contained bits of twig surrounded by the sticky resin. It was collected and then exported from India and Indochina but was considered rather precious and rarely used.

Some lichens were used to stretch or enhance other dyes and on selected Italian silks. *Roccella* was traded in the fourteenth century under a Florentine monopoly and called orchil. Some lichens from the north west of England and Scotland give similar colours to those produced from *Roccella* and would have been used locally. Another important source of red dye was brazilwood, or redwood, obtained from trees of the *Caesalpinia* species and brought to the West by the Venetians through their trading contacts with the East. The petals of safflower, *Carthamus tinctorius* produce a red dye but this was inferior to the dye from the brazilwood, although it was suitable for some silks.

In England, red dye usually came from the roots of the madder plant *Rubia tinctorum L* and required a mordant such as alum or iron to fix the dye. The best alum came from a monopoly held by the Papal states. Until alum shale was discovered in Yorkshire in 1604, alum was imported into England from Italy, Spain and Asia Minor. Madder had been cultivated in England since before the Middle Ages but it was also imported to meet the demand. Three madder bags were chosen to form the arms of the London Dyers Company, while in Amiens Cathedral, two men are depicted proclaiming their wealth, by standing on a bulging sack of woad balls.

Woad *Isatis tinctoria L*, was the main source of blue dye and was an excellent base for other shades and colours. It had been cultivated in England since Saxon times, but by the twelfth century considerable imports were coming from Picardy, Amiens, Corbie, Neslé and the Somme region.

Natural dyes

Thuringia and Erfurt in Germany were trading centres for woad, and it was known that Katherina Amlingyn and her daughter traded in woad in Erfurt towards the end of the fifteenth century. Dried balls of pulped woad leaves were imported in casks into London. They had to be moistened and left to ferment at temperatures of up to 50 degrees centigrade before the dye was ready to use. If stored carefully, woad could be kept for years, and was often given as a bequest. Adam de la Pole bequeathed four casks of it to his granddaughter Katherine in 1358. In the twelfth and thirteenth centuries it mostly came from Picardy, and later from Brabant, the Low Countries, Germany, Lombardy and Languedoc. By the fourteenth and fifteenth centuries, many woad-mongers were associated with Baynard's Castle in London and the parish of St Andrews where most of the fragments of ancient dyed textiles have been found.

Indigo, *Indigofera tinctoria,* proved to be a superior source of blue dye and once the sea-routes to India and the East Indies had been opened up in the sixteenth century, indigo gradually began to replace woad in Europe. The plants were harvested and soaked with an alkali such as ash, slaked lime or crushed shells. The liquid was then vigorously stirred to make the indigo precipitate. The resulting paste was collected, dried and pressed into hard blue blocks and spread out on cloths or on the hot sand in the sun to dry. It was sold to the traders and dyers who ground it into a powder. Indigo was later imported from the East and West Indies, Central and South America, Virginia and South Carolina.

Black was usually made from either iron sulphate, iron filings or swarf, a residue from grindstones and blade mills, or a source of tannin such as gall nuts from oak trees. This added actual weight to the silk fabric, and that could be fraudulent. Silk lost some of its weight when the sericum gum was boiled off, and as it was sold by weight some dishonest dyers added antimony or lead calx, known as litharge to the dyes. Black was also obtained by using weld, madder and woad or indigo, in succession.

The main yellow dye was weld *Reseda luteola L.* It was used on its own or over-dyed with woad to give green, and it could be combined with madder to produce shades of orange.

Although there are few written records, enough was probably produced for local use._Saffron also produced yellows but was mostly used in food. It was grown in the Lake District and East Anglia, as was dyer's broom, *Genista tinctoria*.

The colours gained from combinations of dyes and mordants were the most complex and tested the dyers skill. A mulberry-like colour called murrey, was much favoured and often mentioned in treatises on dyeing and painting. This deep purplish colour could be made from kermes, madder or brazilwood. A*lessandrino* was a vivid violet and highly valued. All colours were subject to fashion and changed their use and symbolic meanings frequently, but usually the most expensive and spectacular colours were reserved for the principle religious feasts and court festivals.

Le Teinturer, page from a printed manuscript showing dyers. 1708

By 1630, the silkmen were becoming better organized and they got together to draft a petition to put before Parliament. They complained bitterly about the 'false and deceitful dyeing of silk. These 'deceitful dyes' increased the weight and damaged the yarn, resulting in fibres that were poor in colour, difficult to weave and less durable. The guildsmen made a list of all the unacceptable dye-stuffs including alder-bark and iron filings. They said it was really hard to compete against 'the multitude of broad silks and stuffs imported from France and Holland'. Charles I (1600-49) issued a proclamation setting up an 'Office for the Surveying and Trying of All Silk Dyed and to be Dyed', but it was eight years before he removed some of the restrictions on dyeing in the gum. Eventually he admitted that he was now better informed and understood that it was necessary for the tufted taffetas, figured satins, fine slight ribands, and ferret ribands, both black and coloured, to be dyed in the gum to attain the perfect colour and texture. Colour was always an integral part of the display of wealth and power.

A picnic on the forest, possibly Queen Elizabeth being entertained at a hunting party, with lots of food and wine. The people are shown in a relaxed party setting, wearing their 'ordinary' clothes, silk gowns, doublet and hose.

Chapter 5
The Huguenots and Other Strangers

The Protestant Immigrants

Over the years and during periods of political and
economic strife, the highly skilled silk weavers fled with
their knowledge and expertise to settle in more
sympathetic towns and cities. Some weavers had gone
to Lille, Tours, Lyons and north to Flanders and
Antwerp, offering their skills in exchange for a safe place
to live and work. By the early 1560s harassment and
persecution had reached such a level that they were on
the move yet again to escape from religious intolerance.
In May 1562, around 500 destitute French refugees
began arriving at Rye and other southern English
seaports, including Sandwich, Winchelsea and Dover.
Some continued on to Canterbury, Norwich and
Spitalfields in London. Most were Protestants, some
were French Huguenots, and the rest were Flemings
and Walloons from the Low Countries.

European Protestants had a history of immigrating to England, and many already had family there. The cost of living was lower and there were good opportunities for work. The new arrivals had a variety of trades, but one of the most valuable to the English was their knowledge of silk and silk weaving. The 'strangers' kept a low profile as they set up their looms and sought work. They were fiercely independent, hardworking and self-sufficient and they contributed to the prosperity of their adopted communities. The authorities were supportive, but they set certain conditions. The immigrants were not to take work from the local weavers or proselytize and they were to teach their skills to the English craftsmen. By the end of the sixteenth century, any special privileges granted the newcomers had been withdrawn and they were still paying extra taxes, so many remained pitifully poor.

Some of the first refugees settled in Canterbury. As silk was never successfully grown in England, the weavers had to rely on imported silk, and that made the cloth very expensive. Some used a cheap waste silk like noil or experimented with mixing silk with other fibres like wool or linen. By the late 1560s, bombazine was being woven in a twill weave from 'wooll, silkes and saie'. The warp silk was made of carded and spun noils, or a dull, waste silk called bourette. The weft was a worsted or jersey wool. These mixed fabrics were collectively known as 'silk stuffs'.

Some of the immigrant Walloons from the Netherlands settled in Norwich, and they also wove 'stuffs' and a much more adventurous and demanding tufted silk cloth with an engraved pattern, similar to velvet. These 'mockadoes' came in many weights and were made into doublets, dressing gowns, kirtles and capes and the heavier ones were made into furnishings. Until 1571, mockadoes had been imported from Arras in France and Tournai in Belgium but by 1576 the Norwich Walloons were producing mockadoes of a sufficient quality and quantity to export them back to the Continent. Some English towns like Maidstone had permission to make them, but they produced very little. Compared to Europe, England was technologically backward in silk weaving.

The next wave of refugees

The 1572 riots, known as the Massacre of St Bartholomew, triggered the most serious persecution of Huguenots in France so far, and by 1579 another wave of French refugees started arriving in Canterbury from Tours. A bishop wrote compassionately that they were 'most destitute, labour truthfully, live sparingly'. Once they had settled, they began to make all silk grosgrains with gold and silver tinsel threads, using imported Italian silk. They also wove narrow 'says' using a union yarn with two different fibres twisted together. Other fabrics had a silk warp and jersey wool weft giving a shot effect. The light reflected on these fabric and they shimmered and glowed.

In Norwich, the Flemings made 'stamins' that also had a silk warp and jersey weft. 'Silk rashes' were made from silk and linen, so that the colours changed when it was draped or worn. Also available for the first time was a transparent black silk mourning cloth, produced in Billingsgate Ward from 1572. It had previously been imported from Cyprus and was known as sipers cloth.

The Virgin Queen. Elizabeth as the symbol of monarchy, after the defeat of the Spanish Armada.

When Queen Elizabeth I visited Norwich in 1579 there was enormous excitement and anticipation. A pageant and parade had been planned for her, showing the wealth and pride of Norwich and its craftsmen. The local silk weavers had to wait all day before the Queen saw their carefully prepared float, set up to demonstrate the production of figured silk caffa. This silk was also known as a 'figured russell' because the Russell Company was rather sensitive and possessive about its ownership of patents for the various cloths they wove. In fact caffas were also being made by the Canterbury Walloons and the London Flemings. Around 1580, the Norwich Walloons started making 'saten... part sylke and part cotton woll bumbazin'. It was a rather expensive cloth, used for dresses and soft furnishing, doublets and waistcoats. Within ten years they were making a whole range of fabrics, including brocatelle, a rich satin faced gold and silver fabric with a coloured weft. Its more complicated construction used two rollers so that the pattern was lifted above the ground.

The protestant silk weavers continued to arrive in England in even greater numbers during the later part of Queen Elizabeth's reign. Many of the Flemish velvet weavers went to Stepney and Spitalfields in London and by 1582 they had started to weave silk plush with a silk pile on a linen ground. Large quantities of raw silk were arriving regularly in London and by 1594 the French Huguenots and the Dutch weavers had enough high quality silk to weave the luscious tuftaffeta. It was a velour fabric with tufts of silk and was selling at 3s.4d for 'silk curls' or as 'mixed curls' using a variety of yarns. It was not long before the English weavers in London and Canterbury were also making them, along with a narrow width figurato and a figured double satin, similar to a broken twill satinet. In the warmer summer weather the Canterbury, London and Lichfield weavers responded to changes in fashion, and started producing tiffanies and summery figured silk satins, woven on a light gauze weave.

The problems in France over religion had been increasing and harassment continued until 1599 when Henry of Navarre, in an effort to calm the situation, promulgated the Edict of Nantes. It gave comparative liberty of conscience and freedom of worship to all French subjects, and during this period French silk weaving reached its greatest heights.

In England, London also acquired a fine reputation for its silk weaving. The Walloons were making fustinadoes, described as 'cutt fustyns alias cut uppon taffitie' They also wove a double cloth velour with 400 pile threads. The pile was formed by cutting apart the two separate layers of the double weave fabric. Tobines or tabbies were introduced and flowered damasks woven on a draw loom. These very successful union damasks used mixed yarns to highlight the patterns and they made beautiful, sturdy upholstery and curtain fabrics. One of the silk weavers was John Tyce. He was known to be living near Shoreditch Church around 1615, and weaving top quality wrought velvets, taffeties, tissues and satins.

In Canterbury, silk weaving increased dramatically to around one thousand weavers and looms. A new crewel yarn made of floss silk called filoselle was introduced by the Dutch, along with all-silk buffins and cattaloons. Within ten years, a striped filoselle fabric had become very popular, as were silk camlets and grosgrains, perfect for cloaks, jerkins and upper hose. Although many 'strangers' had settled happily in Canterbury, the big city of London was a powerful attraction and many weavers moved there.

James I

James I (1566-1625) felt he had a problem. He saw that his French cousin Henry IV (1553-1610) had successfully developed a silk industry and he too desired the prestige and financial rewards from producing silk. In 1608 he devised a grand plan to establish sericulture on all the large estates in England. He was obsessive about silk and had mulberry trees planted everywhere, including some at Westminster and Whitehall. James wrote pamphlets and widely circulated the documents to try and persuade his courtiers to organize their workers and as a result, ten thousand black mulberry trees were planted across England. He was guided by his head gardener, who felt that the Morus nigra, the hardy, slow growing black mulberry would stand up better to the English climate. Unfortunately the silkworms much preferred the less leafy but more tender white mulberry, the Morus alba, and did not thrive on the black mulberry.

Despite endless encouragement and support, the enterprise barely limped along. There were many reasons for the failure of this grand scheme. The English weather was too damp and cold, the white mulberry would have been a better choice and offered better food for the silkworms, and there was also the nature of the people. While the men close to the king could see the benefits of cooperation, it was much harder to convince the people on their estates to care for and

Three drapers measuring cloth with a yardstick. The scales and coins are on the table, showing it was a commercial business.

cherish the fragile, temperamental silkworms. The farmers had no experience, did not like getting up every two hours, day and night to clean and feed the silkworms, and really did not like handling them very much at all. During the next 200 to 250 years, most of the mulberry trees were grubbed out, and the land returned to gardens, farm or estate lands, but Charlton House in London is believed to still have one genuine James I mulberry tree. Sericulture did not completely die out and in 1718 John Appleton planted two thousand mulberry trees in Chelsea Park, but this and later attempts were still not commercially successful.

Still enthusiastic about silk, James I in 1619 encouraged Flemish tapestry weavers to come and work on the tapestry looms he had set up at Mortlake. They used a linen warp and a silk weft from Naples, along with gold and silver, jersey and crewel. Gobelin style tapestry weaving was established in other parts of London, in Southwark and Westminster and later in Paddington and Fulham. Traditionally, tapestries were made in Arras, Flanders and Brabant, but some small industries making table covers and cushions, grew up in Norwich and York as well as London. The early tapestries had been woven on a 'high loom' but an easier and faster, 'low' loom was developed in the early seventeenth century and this craft survived until the early 1700s.

The Corporation of Silk Weavers was not established in London until 1629, twenty years after James I's abortive attempt to establish sericulture. England had an open policy towards craftsmen, and the London Weavers' Company welcomed the Protestant silk weavers. By 1635 the Company had expanded. It now controlled all broad loom weaving, including silk manufacture within London, and it encouraged new ideas and techniques. The Huguenot weavers developed a heated roller known as a calender, to press silk plush and to give a watered effect on grosgrains, taffetas and chamblets. By 1640, silk druggets had been given a spot effect by putting it through engraved calender rollers. Hair or mohair from Turkey was often mixed with silk in ferradines, paduasoys and tamarins, producing a corded texture. There was fierce competition to be the first to introduce new weaves and capture the fickle, fashion market.

Lots of new names were invented to smarten up older patterns and weaves, along with new combinations like Norwich Lace and silk odaratoes. In 1653 there were silk chequarettes, 1657 silk piccadillies and after the 1660s silk tammies, silk say and flowered silk calamancos, all containing various proportions of silk and other fibres. In Stepney in 1664 a shag-finished silk became very popular. It used expensive prime silk but then in 1672 a London weaver called Edmund Blood patented a shagged fabric made by passing teasels over a much cheaper waste silk. By 1682, plain and striped gauzes and silk crapes were added and a heavily crimped black crape for deep mourning. It was woven from worsted and silk and shrank irregularly in the finishing, producing an interesting texture. It was made in towns around Norwich, Canterbury and in Stepney for over 200 hundred years. Silk weaving in Canterbury went into a decline after the arrival of cheap novelty silks from China. The fashion for the new Indian calicos and dimities left the Canterbury silks unsold and abandoned. Norwich was more successful with its development of the Norwich shawl. It had a silk warp and worsted weft and was embroidered with crewel work. It was light-weight and it draped very nicely, exactly the right fashion accessory for the time.

A group of singers and dancers taken from the poet Edmund Spenser's work 'The Shepherds' Calendar', 1579. This is April, with Taurus the bull and Queen Elizabeth with her sceptre, in the centre, surrounded by her women wearing silk gowns with richly embroidered petticoats.

The Edict of Nantes in France

In France the difficulties were increasing, especially after 1683. The throwsters, dyers and weavers of Nimes and Tours were mostly Protestant although Lyon with around 1000 Huguenot Protestants, was still a predominately Catholic city. Some Huguenots came from Paris and Normandy, especially from the Pays de Caux. Many were skilled silk workers who had acquired the secrets of making the expensive damasks, taffetas and velvets, for which these cities were famous.

Louis XIV (1638-1715) was in a bind, because although he did not want French Protestants to dominate in any guild, he wanted to at least appear honourable. The Protestants were increasingly persecuted and legislation was used to make it extremely difficult for them to find work or enter guilds as apprentices or as master workmen. Some guilds like the seamstresses in Paris, tried to completely exclude them. Unfortunately, the Protestant Huguenots tended to be the entrepreneurs, and comparatively wealthy. They provided employment for large numbers of people, but their position became increasingly untenable when they were made to swear oaths against their Calvinist beliefs and forced to attend Mass. Louis XIV, influenced by his courtesans and the Jesuit fathers, instigated the enforced conversion of Protestants back to Catholicism, and in 1685 revoked the Edict of Nantes that had given them some freedom of worship. Politics and religion were inextricably mixed and the persecutions continued until 1775.

Thousands of Huguenots escaped to England, Switzerland, Germany, Holland and even America. Louis XIV was apparently unconcerned about losing so many of the finest craftsmen, believing it would not affect his wealth or the industry. But the results were soon evident in France when tariffs were erected against the French silk industry. War and depression shrank it still further and unemployed silkworkers clamoured for relief. They begged the king to relax the persecutions and cease the war of propaganda and to reinstate their religious freedom.

Many of the migrants had mixed motives and only a quarter of them actually claimed that they were fleeing religious persecution. Some were seeking lost family or adventure, others wanted to learn English, or were hoping to trade. Some Huguenots were skilled in international banking and supported the establishment of the Bank of England, set up to finance the war against France. Seven of the twenty-four foundation directors were Walloons or Huguenots and they raised £104,000 of the initial £1.2 million capital required.

England recognized that contented, stable, skilled people were a great asset to their communities, and through their taxes, to the general economy and the public purse. At this time the population of England was around five million people, compared to France's twenty million so England could easily accommodate the immigrants. Around 200,000 people left France, many with nothing but the clothes they were wearing, but bringing with them the silk industry's most cherished secrets.

Spinners, by Diderot

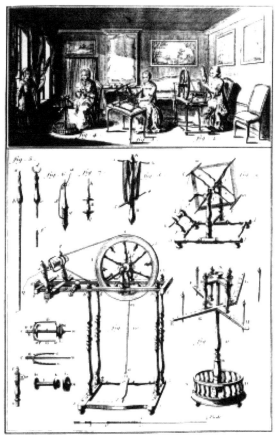

The largest group of French Huguenots arrived in England after 1678, and the local Protestant community raised £200,000 by public subscription. They were welcomed and given assistance, although they were not granted naturalization until 1708, and then only partially. Charles II (reigned 1660-85) issued a special proclamation according them 'all privileges and immunity for the liberty of exercising their free trade and craft'. In England they could work free of guild regulations and restrictions and were absorbed into the existing workforce. Many of the French immigrants from Tours and Lyon were technically in advance of the local English weavers and some claimed they were master silk weavers and their skill could be a great benefit to the nation.

The Great Lustring Claim

In truth, not all were master weavers and some had difficulty substantiating their claim to the court. Two weavers became notorious rather than celebrated. In 1684 Jean Quet and Jean Larguier from Nimes claimed that they knew the secret of making high gloss lustrings and alamodes. The court had never seen such lovely silks before and were amazed by their beauty. The men claimed special privileges but the court rejected their claim to be master weavers. It was not convinced that they had actually woven the samples they produced.

High gloss fabrics were now in fashion. A method had been devised in Lyon to improve the lustre of the warp chain and weft threads, even before the finishing. Lustring was a process applied to many silk fabrics including alamodes and taffetas, grosgrain and velvets, paduasoys and satins. It was believed that this process had been secretly brought to London by a Huguenot workman called Montgeorge. Other weavers like Peter La Dore were granted a patent to gloss plain or figured satins, striped and flowered lustrings. Many other people made claims and counterclaims and amid much controversy, the English Lustring Company was set up. Many weavers began to produce these fabrics. In 1679, John Agace's unsold stock was recorded in London. It included two black and one other piece of silk lustring. The black was valued at 6s 4d yard and the other 6s 3d. An expensive gauze cost 4 shillings, the Jaradine 5s 10d and the Venetian sprig, 7 shillings a yard. By 1698, 768 looms were involved, most in London and some in Ipswich. The lustrings, brocades, velvets and damasks now woven in Spitalfields were rivaling those produced in Lyon, and attracting a good deal of the trade that had formerly gone to France.

Along with their trade secrets, the Huguenots brought new skills, ideas and designs. The silks they wove were made of the best thrown silk from China and Piedmont in Italy, while some other fabrics were made of the cheaper spun waste silk. The new fashion silks, especially the fragile, floral fabrics had a delicacy and brilliance not seen before. These Spitalfield silks came to be known as 'flowered silks' and

Spitalfields silk. Design for a brocaded lustring by Anna Maria Garthwaite. 1747.

became all the rage, although the designs were varied and complex. They included black mourning silks, alamodes and lustrings, coloured and sprigged taffetas used for dresses, linings, ladies hoods and mantels. Rather unusually, two women became widely recognized as superb English silk designers, Anna Maria Garthwaite and Phoebe Wright. Phoebe also became known for her beautiful embroidery designs.

The Huguenots contributed greatly to the English silk industry and every branch prospered. The Weavers' Company noted the dramatic increase in the number of looms between 1664 and 1713. During this period, over three thousand pounds worth of black silk was produced in England rather than imported from France. The range expanded to include paduasoys, ducapes, watered tabbies, plain and figured velvets, damasks, brocades and cloth of gold.

The Spitalfields Community

John Stow, an early recorder and geographer of London mentions the ancient priory and hospital of St Mary Spittle in the East End of London. It was founded by Walter Brune, a citizen of London and his wife Rosia, and in 1197 the priory was dedicated to the Virgin. In 1534 the church and hospital, with 180 charity beds was dissolved by Henry VIII (1491-1547). The area around Petticoat Lane, which leads from Spitalfields to Whitechapel including New Broad Street, became known as Spitalfields, or Petty Fraunce. The Hall of the Weavers' Company was in Basinghall Street and this was the area to which the French immigrants gravitated.

Spitalfields had been an attractive and desirable part of London, with open fields and gardens. Lord Powis, Lord Bolingbroke, Lord Morly and the Countess of Dudley all lived nearby. Sir Walter Raleigh lived at Mile End and Thomas Gresham at Bethnal Green, near where the Bishop of London had a rural seat. With the coming of the Huguenots, the streets were given French names or were named after flowers, like Fleur de Lys Street, Blossom and Floral Street. The more

Girl's dress made from English silk at Spitalfields, London, c. 1736-7.

prosperous merchants, retailer and dyers built elegant houses on Spital and Devonshire Squares, St Helens and White Lion Street. They had imposing facades with window boxes filled with flowers. The ground floor became the shop, with the desk, scales and measuring sticks, and all the paraphernalia of sales. At the back was the warehouse where the bolts of silk cloth were stored.

The Huguenots were welcomed and French was freely spoken in the workplace, schools and factories. Within a few years the area was teaming with new immigrants and two or three families were crammed into every available house. The weavers' desperately needed space to weave and houses sprang up at speed, spreading out over the fields and gardens. They were built in long rows with attics running the entire length of the terrace and large windows giving the best light for weaving. Unfortunately the window tax of 1696 had a detrimental effect as people blocked up their windows to reduce the amount of tax they had to pay. When they could afford it, the weavers installed mirrors and looking glasses to try and compensate and maximize the light.

The day began at 5.45 am, when the Christ Church bell rang. There were half hour breaks for lunch and tea, and the curfew was rung again to signal the end of the working day at 7.45 in the evening. The church was central to their life and work. There were sixteen rather plain, undecorated Huguenot churches in Spitalfields, and seventeen in Wapping. More were built, yet at times there was such a crush at the services that people had to stand outside in all weathers. Jean Durel translated the liturgy into French while he was minister of the fashionable Savoy church. By 1640, French churches were established at Southampton, Norwich, Canterbury and Dover. Dutch churches were at Norwich, Yarmouth, Colchester and Sandwich Bay.

The Huguenots wore austere, plain clothes, sang traditional hymns, and some never learnt speak English. They had a strong sense of community and helped their less fortunate brethren by providing soup kitchens and charity schools. They kept their own customs and so it was some time before French workers like Louis Goujon described himself as a silk weaver rather than an 'ouvrier de soie'. Some family names like Courtauld became famous. Other people anglicized their names but it took three or four generations for many to become completely absorbed into the nation. Gradually some of the strangers began to move away and to attend the local parish church. They intermarried and were admitted to the guilds, were able to buy property and became full citizens.

The late seventeenth century could be described as a golden age for the Huguenots in England. They had work, a new home and security. Their church united them and they continued to form a compact community despite spreading to Stepney, Bethnell Green, Mile End, Aldgate, Bishopsgate, Shoreditch, Thames Street, Broad Street, Long Acre, Seven Dials and around Soho and St Giles. Some silk-weavers moved north, east and west from Spitalfields and formed new colonies.

As with any group there were people who brought problems as well as skills, and when jobs became short, the English weavers started to complain of competition and tempers flared. Then the immigrants had to deal with resentment, anger and antagonism because their neighbours felt that any charity or assistance should be given to them before supporting any incomers. With discriminating legislation and too many people chasing too little work, there were riots in 1766 and 1767 and attacks on looms and weavers' premises. Sometimes the expensive silk was forcibly cut off the looms and thrown into the Thames River and in desperation, the weavers appealed to George II 1683-1760) for protection.

Changes

Christ Church, Spitalfields

Change was in the air and after 1675 the silk factors and agents at Leadenhall market began selling materials on their own account, including silks and dyes. They offered 'day' or two weeks credit to the merchants and the debt could be partly cancelled by goods supplied. The increased use of factors meant wholesale drapers and merchants from other cities no longer had to keep a partner resident in London to transact their business. These agents were tradesmen, general merchants, suppliers and retailers of clothing and provisions. They were neither the industrialists nor the workers, but were people in the middle and many became relatively wealthy because they manufactured or supplied parts for the looms and other machines or services to the industry. This group included the designers, draughtsmen, dyers and later, the highly esteemed jacquard machinists.

By the 1820-30s, the population of Spitalfields and Mile End was around 100,000 with over half entirely dependent on silk manufacture, or closely involved in the supportive industries, throwing, winding, reeling, and finishing. The silk throwsters and winders were some of the first to suffer whenever there was an upheaval. The industry was controlled by male masters and throwsters who employed large numbers of semi-illiterate women and girls, especially the wives and daughters of sailors living in the East End. All too often they had the least resources and women like the silk winder and widow Anne Ramsbottom of Petycote Lane appear in the courts on minor charges. Isabel Dodd was a 31 year old widow who rented a room from another widow. She told the court she had three jobs to try and maintain herself; she wound silk, knitted, washed and scoured it. Another throwster committed suicide by hanging herself in her lodgings because she could continue no longer. As the families became poorer, the children began spinning waste silk for a mere pittance, because 'they had no other means of getting a living'.

Row of weavers' cottages in Fournier Street, Spitalfields, London.

The situation deteriorated further. The weavers saw themselves as master silk weavers and were most reluctant to move from handloom weaving to using steam power and so the average wage for a Spitalfields weaver dropped to 5 shillings per week, if periods of waiting were taken into account. Legislation had raised the wages of the weavers and should have protected their work, but it just made things worse because their wages were now uncompetitive with the rest of the country. The industrialists refused to pay and moved out of the City to Essex, Suffolk, Norfolk, East Anglia, the West Country, the Midlands, Chester and Manchester. They set up silk mills and supporting industries and paid wages that were only two thirds that of London.

London was losing its craftsmen and its silk industries. The port set high duties on goods destined for export and so London was avoided. To minimize the fees, some merchants favoured a particular port like Southampton to export their broadloom silks to the Low Countries, Germany, Portugal the Americas or the West Indies. London was still the largest and most important city in England, but the silk industry was moving away.

Ambrogio Lorenzetti, 1345. The Virgin Mary is sitting on the floor in
an attitude of humility with Joseph and Jesus. This wooden panel shows her
knitting, her hands held over her four needles as she knits a small item.
In the centre is the round bobbin rack, the tiny spools of silk prominently
displayed. Such a range of colours suggests that the item is a little relic bag,
similar to those found in ancient church treasuries.

Chapter 6
Knitting

Early knitted silk and the Madonna

The introduction of silk to Europe changed knitting, because silk unlike wool, does not felt easily. Felting added to the weatherproofing and wearing qualities of everyday items, whereas silk was always comparatively fragile, delicate and precious. It was more difficult to spin than wool, much more expensive and less readily available. Silk has many moods. It could be lustrous and flexible, a fabric that molded to the body. It could be woven into heavy rough furnishings or knitted into a fine lacy fabric or even imitate a brocaded fabric, richly embossed with gold and silver threads.

The earliest knitted silk items still extant date from the twelfth and thirteenth century. These fine Spanish and Italian liturgical gloves, relic bags and cushions are therefore five to six hundred years later than the eighth and ninth century woollen sandal socks and caps that have been found preserved in the dry conditions of Pre-Islamic Egyptian tombs. Careful examination suggests that these early fourth to sixth century woollen items have been made by knotless netting, nalbinding or sprang. These techniques use separate lengths of yarn and a large sewing needle to make the loops. In comparison, true knitting could be described as an elastic fabric, composed of rows of stitches, using a thread of unlimited length, and two or more needles.

The earliest needles were bone, wood and occasionally metal. Some first century needles have been found at Taxila in Pakistan, where Alexander the Great attended university. Ivory needles, each around 28cm long were found near Nimes and dated to the beginning of the 2nd century AD, suggesting that knitting was known to the ancient Gauls. The largest collection of medieval knitting needles was found in a Latvian excavation, along with a cap and five pairs of gloves. In the early paintings, it is always stocking stitch on four or five needles, never two needles. It is not known when the purl stitch was developed, allowing knitting to go forward and back using two needles only. Perhaps that was first explored when turning of the heel of a sock. Certainly the oldest silk liturgical gloves would have been knitted on four or five needles.

Virgin Mary by Tommaso da Modena (1325-75), one of the three sections of a polyptich. She has the Child tucked in the chair beside her as she knits in the round a garment big enough for a little shirt for him. On her knees is a large round board with four small bobbins and from their shape, also probably silk.

The Knitting Madonnas

The irrefutable evidence of complex, sophisticated knitting with silk, is clear in some of the paintings of the Madonna knitting, dated between 1300 and 1400. In every one she is knitting in the round with four or five needles. One of the earliest paintings is by Tommaso da Modena. He probably painted it in Bologna sometime between 1325-1375 and it is now in the Pinacoteca Nationale at Bologna. Here the Virgin sits on a throne in an arcade, knitting with four needles, and using a fifth. The knitted item could be a little shirt for baby Jesus who sits beside her. She has a large round board on her lap with small spools

of yarn, almost certainly indicating that it is silk. Wool is usually wound into a ball while silk is fine and slippery and needs to be wound onto a spool or bobbin or it will unravel.

Another painting from around 1345 comes from the studio of Ambrogio Lorenzetti. It is of the Holy Family, and the Virgin is knitting purple silk. She has a range of coloured silks on spools collected on a small circular tray in front of her. This painting is one of the *Madonna dell'umilta*, or the Madonna of Humility. She sits humbly on the floor in a domestic interior, with Joseph on the right and Jesus close by while she knits on four needles. This item appears too small to be a shirt and too large for a sock, so it is possibly a relic purse. They were made to contain a precious fragment, believed to have come from a saint. Relics were highly revered and so it was quite usual for the little purse to be made of the most precious yarn, dyed silk. This painting is now in the Abegg Collection at Berne

A third Knitting Madonna, is by Vitale degli Equi (1308-59) and is in the Poldi-Pezzoli Museum in Milan. Again the Virgin sits on the floor and behind her stands a martyred saint on the right, and St Catherine with a fragment of her wheel on the left. Baby Jesus reaches out for one of his mother's knitting needles with one hand and grabs a spool of silk from the round, two-tiered spool stand with the other. The knitting is on four needles and has an allover brocaded pattern, similar to her beautiful dress and the band on her veil. The small knitted item is in two colours, so possibly she is also knitting a little relic bag.

Probably the best known of the knitting Virgins is called 'The Visit of the Angels', *'Der Besuch des Engels'*, by Meister Bertram of Minden. It is part of a triptych altarpiece, painted around 1395 for the Benedictine nuns of Buxtehude. Here the

Virgin Mary Knitting, by Vitale degli Equi called da Bologna (1309-1359/61). The Virgin of Humility with St. Catherine of Alexandra and a martyr saint, wood, 41 x 21 cm (inv.1574) Milano Museo Poldi Pezzoli.

The Madonna of humility with St. Catherine and St. Christopher, by Niccolo di Buonaccorso, died 1388. In the centre panel of the golden triptych, the Virgin Mary sits on the floor with the Child on her lap. Behind her, on a bench, is what appears to be knitting but, from its position on the needles, could not be so and is more likely to be a frame for making a beaded purse or relic bag. Certainly the little tiered bobbin stand holds the silks.

Virgin sits in splendor, in a delightful folly in a garden, wearing a luxurious and highly fashionable silk gown. She is using four needles to pick up the stitches to knit the neck of the little red tunic, possibly for the Child. This time it is wool not silk, as three balls of yarn lie in a basket beside her as she knits. All is not quite as it seems, because this is really a subtle reminder of Christ's Passion.

There are two other pictures that might have been thought of as Knitting Madonna, but are not. One is dated 1356-88 and is by Niccolo di Buonaccorso. It is in the Timken Museum in San Diego. Behind the Virgin, on a bench is a little bobbin stand, with four bobbins of silk red, blue, white and yellow and three more at the rear. Also on the bench is some work on four needles, but from the angle of the needles it is clear that they are being used to frame a little relic bag, probably being beaded, rather than knitted. Another, the 'Holy Family' by Veit Stoss 1480-85, is a Polish engraving. In it Joseph has a large aul and the Madonna holds a coat on a T-shaped hanger. She is holding thread but not knitting needles.

Medieval silk gloves, bags and cushions

Knitting was a man's trade in the Middle Ages, so it was probably the traders, sailors and Coptic missionaries who travelled across the Mediterranean and Central Europe to Spain, Germany and Italy, who introduced the skill of knitting. In Moorish Spain, with its history of sericulture, the long glossy filaments of silk were perfect for experimenting with knitting. Knitted items belonging to the Infante Fernando de la Cerda who died in 1275 have been found in his tomb at Las Hueglas, a Spanish Monastery near Burgos in Old Castile. One cushion is 36cm square, knitted in stockinet stitch in two colours, probably originally crimson and gold, with a diagonal pattern containing the heraldic elements of fleur-de-lys and eagles. The other side has octagons containing golden castles and rosettes, with the Arabic word for 'Blessing' on each edge.

Tombs, like the graves at Seville and church treasuries are the richest source for the delicate knitted silk gloves, cushions and relic bags. The Cathedral of Sion in Switzerland has a number of fourteenth century silk relic bags, knitted in the round in multi-coloured stockinet stitch and tied with a drawstring at the top and with tassels along the bottom. All have horizontal patterned bands in various combinations of green, red, blue, violet, beige and white silk. They feature stars and shields, birds and crosses. It is known that nuns did some of the exquisite silk embroidery, so possibly they also made the knitted items. To make such delicate articles, the knitter needed soft hands, not roughened by housework, and the leisure to knit these fine, often complex designs.

Silk was considered ritually pure so it was appropriate, after the seventh century, for knitted silk gloves to be part of a Bishop's regalia, like the 'two gloves made for the high clergy with needles', '*deux gants de prelat faits a l'ésguille*'. Gloves were usually in natural cream, *écru*, or liturgical colours of red, green, blue or violet but never black. A twelfth century bishop's glove preserved at Speyer, was not knitted but used an early technique known as knotless netting. In Italy, there are knitted silk gloves from the same period in Trinity Church Florence, and in the cathedrals of Narni and Agagni. Papal bulls sanctioned the wearing of gloves, and the gloves can be clearly seen on the monument erected to Pope Innocent IV who died in 1254. Another Bishop, Siegfried von Westerburg, who died in Bonn in 1297 had knitted coloured silk gloves with blue and gold eagles and rosettes with eight petals. Usually gloves were close fitting with a long cuff, often with a sacred symbol in a medallion, like the ones at New College Cambridge. These gloves came from the tomb of William of Wykeham (1367-1404) and were of crimson silk decorated with gold octofoils and the IHS emblem. Cluny Abbey in 1385 listed twenty-two pairs of gloves. They are nalbinding, not knitting and made in *écru* silk for Abbot Peter de Courpalay who had died in 1334. Other gloves have two-inch cuffs and are lined with red silk for protection. Some have a split on the back of the finger to allow the bishop's ring to come through while others have simulated gold rings and gems embroidered on each finger and thumb, and

Spanish knitted glove, 16th century, knitted in the round in red silk with silver-gilt, the floats twisted in the back so they don't catch. The cross is incorporated into the design and the glove is trimmed with gold bobbin lace and plaited braid outlining the fingers.

Silk stockings. 17th century embroidered clocks in silver gilt and gold thread, probably knitted in London.

elaborate tassels on the back of the hand. When the Bishop raised his hands in blessing, the gloves would have glowed like jewels and been clearly seen, even by the villagers right at the back of the church. Silk gloves were part of lay attire also, although it took a highly developed technical skill to knit five fingered fashioning. They were expensive and a symbol of authority, dignity and grace. The presenting of a glove could express a contract, flinging down a glove an open challenge, while a knight could carry a lady's glove high on his standard as a token. Silk gloves, rather than cloth or wool, were precious and added to the importance and significance of the occasion.

Silk Stockings and the Guilds

Traditionally, stockings and leggings had been made by a tailor out of cloth, cut on the bias with a seam up the back. From 1320, knitted woollen stockings, leggings and Bishops' gaiters were occasionally mentioned in inventories. They were appreciated for their greater elasticity and gradually replaced the cloth ones. Silk is not mention for stockings until 1537 when the future King Henry II of France had hand-knitted spun silk hose, and in 1547 Henry VIII of England ordered ' six pairs of black silk hose knyt'. Spain is usually given credit as the first exporter of silk stockings and it is known that Sir Thomas Gresham imported them for both Edward VI and Queen Elizabeth. They were certainly a valuable gift because the silk took the dyes beautifully, and they felt wonderful and fitted more smoothly than wool. They were only available to the elite due to their cost, sumptuary laws and the technical skill needed to deal with the fine, slippery silk.

One of the earliest knitting guilds was set up in Paris in 1268, confirmed again in 1366, 1380, and 1467. Etienne Boileau in his book of medieval crafts, the *Métier de Livre* of 1292 did not think very highly of the craft of knitting. The craftsmen knitters in Paris were called *bonnetiers* from the word bonnet, and they made four types of head covering: hoods, berets, knitted caps and nightcaps. The guilds often honoured a patron saint and the Barcelona Knitting Guild chose St Lucy and St Ursula for their guild in 1496.

Many of the English towns and counties like Bristol, Norwich and Cheshire formed knitting guilds and made a wide range of knitted items, including garters and braces, aprons, narrow belts, girdles, pockets, cushions and little bags, and the finest were silk. Although there is no record of a London guild before the fifteenth century, the silk knitters could be members of other guilds like the cappers and haberdashers. The guilds set rules and required each apprentice to complete a set piece of work to show that he was now a master knitter. The 'master piece' could be a small furnishing item, patterned waistcoat, breeches or a large, finely detailed knitted carpet or table cover in wool, silk or a mixture. One of the largest recorded was 3 x 2 metres. That would have been extremely heavy and bulky to handle so possibly it was made on an early knitting frame. These extraordinary carpets were made mostly in Southern Germany, Austria, Silesia, Slovakia and Alsace. The Guild in Vienna had a statute dated 1609 that required the apprentice knitter to make a table carpet in six colours, a beret and pair each of silk gloves and silk stockings. The real test was the ability to handle the expensive, slippery silk. All masterpieces had to be an original design, using birds and flowers, biblical scenes, coats of arms etc, and incorporate up to twenty different colours. After he had completed his apprenticeship, the journeyman spent the next three years travelling around Europe, footloose and fancy free, gaining experience and all too often becoming a hazard as he banded together with other young journeymen on some adventure. Other journeymen knitters migrated more permanently to Champagne, Languedoc, Normandy, Tournai, Toledo, Naples, Milan, Genoa, Switzerland, Austria and Poland.

Knitting had become an established and skilled craft all over Europe by the sixteenth century. In England, an Act of Parliament in 1552, notes 'Knyt hose, knyt petycote, knyte gloves and knyt sleves'. Yellow knitted silk breeches, with

Man's trunk hose, knitted for the Elector of Saxony and listed in his dress inventory of 1552-55. It is yellow silk, knitted in separate panes in a pattern of arrowheads and lined with yellow silk taffeta.

Crimson knitted silk stockings, found with the body of Eleanor of Toledo when her tomb was opened up in 1857. She was the wife of Cosimo I de'Medici, the Grand Duke of Tuscany and only 40 years old when she died of malaria in 1562. The fine stockings were knee high and held up with garters. The top welt had lacy lozenges and the main part was in stripes of alternating double moss stitch and garter stitch.

yellow silk taffeta lining, are in the collection of the Dresden Museum. They belonged to August, the Elector of Saxony, (1553-86), and are listed in his 1555-6 clothes inventory. These unusual breeches were very dashing. They were paned, each strip knitted separately in faggot stitch, forming arrowheads. The panes were then joined together with the body of the garment to give the fashionable, slashed effect. Men's short padded breeches drew attention to the legs and made fine, decorative silk stockings almost essential. When the Lord Chancellor, Sir Christopher Hatton (1540-1591) was painted by Cornelius Ketel in 1587, he was wearing white silk stockings with an elaborate all over diamond pattern. Eleanor of Toledo, the wife of Cosimo I de Medici, Grand Duke of Tuscany died of malaria in 1562. When she was exhumed in 1857, it was found she had been buried in her priceless wedding dress, made of richly patterned silk velvet in brown and gold. With it she wore exquisite scarlet silk stockings patterned in garter and moss stitch, with a diamond zig-zag design around the turnover tops. In England, sumptuary laws in the sixteenth century prohibited commoners from wearing silk stockings. Even royalty could only wear them on Sunday, because they were imported from Spain, and silk imports were deemed to be a threat to the English wool economy.

The Queen and Mr Lee

There are lovely stories about Queen Elizabeth I and the way she used to knit in her spare time, while considering weighty matters of state. She used her knitting needle to jab a hole in lists of names, to ensure that there would be no mistakes or misunderstandings and her chosen men were selected.

Queen Elizabeth was given a gift of Spanish silk hose, and declared '...I like silk stockings so well because they are so pleasant, fine and delicate, that henceforth I will wear no more cloth stockings'. In 1560, her silkwoman Mrs Montague, made her a gift of a pair of black, silk stockings. It became fashionable for women's skirts to get slightly shorter, which gave added importance to decorative shoes and delicate silk stockings.

The Queen was concerned about poor relief and in 1578 she visited a knitting school and saw a tableau illustrating the work. There were eight little girls spinning and another eight knitting stockings. More knitting schools were set up in many towns to teach the 'arte and misterie' of knitting; at Ipswich in 1587, then York 1590, Lincoln 1591, and Norwich in 1592 and more followed. Poor children knitted woollen stockings and hose, petticoats and caps, gloves, scarves and waistcoats for a ready market.

A knitting school came into another tale of love and industry. William Lee (c1556-1610) was believed to have fallen in love with a lady in Nottingham who ran a knitting school, and in a fit of pique, he decided to make a machine that would knit and give her more time for him. More probably, growing up in the country he understood machinery, and with his good education at Cambridge saw designing a knitting machine as an interesting challenge. William is credited around 1589 with being the 'first inventer of an ingyn to make silke stockings'.

William Lee is shown watching a woman nurse her baby while hand knitting. She is thought to have been the inspiration behind his invention of the knitting machine in 1589 because knitting stockings was a constant occupation for a busy housewife.

William Lee continued to refine and improve the design of his machine, and three years later went to London to solicit the patronage of Queen Elizabeth. She was not impressed with the rough, machine knitted wool stockings, and didn't care for the noisy machine, either. She thought it would take away useful employment and so she denied her patronage. She said, 'I have too much love for my poor people, who obtain their bread by the employment of knitting, to give my money to forward an invention which will tend to their ruin by depriving them of employment.' Elizabeth rarely supported the arts or new inventions, and only left a vague promise that if Lee could make silk stockings that would not effect the income of her poorest subjects, she might reconsider. But a lack of success in achieving a patent from the Queen, left Lee profoundly depressed and discouraged and he decided to accept an offer from Sully the French Ambassador, on behalf of Henry IV (1553-1610) of France. William and his brother James travelled to Rouen with nine skilled men and set up their knitting frames. Lee must have seen his future back in London, because the London Weavers' Guild has an application from 'William Lee a weaver of silk stockings by Ingyn admitted as a forren brother on the Seventh day of March 1608.' A contract dated 1611, was found in Rouen. It appears to be between William or his brother James, and Salomen and Pierre de Caux, de Format and le Tartrier. It provided for the manufacture of both silk and wool stockings, 'by ingyn'. In Rouen he got caught up in the civil disorder and persecution of the Protestants, in the aftermath of the Revocation of the Edict of Nantes, and in grief and despair he went to Paris. His patron, King Henry IV was assassinated in 1610 and Marie de Medici, Regent for her son withdrew all patronage.

James Lee went to Paris to visit William, but by then William was dead, so James brought the machines back to Old Street Square in London. He was preoccupied with designing a round stocking frame, to function like knitting on four or five needles. This was eventually abandoned in favour of a machine with the needles in a straight line making stockings with a seam up the back. At the time, the knitting frame was the most sophisticated textile machine in common use. It was composed of over 2000 moving parts, but it still needed the loops to be smaller, finer and closer together to knit silk well. Probably, in the early days any increase in the speed was discounted by the uneven quality of the finished stockings. James returned to Nottingham. There was interest in the machines from Europe, and some were sent to Venice and France and installed there, but the enterprise limped along until James returned to London in 1621. London prospered and many silk articles were knitted on the frames, including stockings and purses in the silk parishes around Spitalfields.

Hand and Framework Knitting in Europe

In Europe, St Brigid, who died in 1335 was believed to have introduced knitting to Sweden. She was only 12 years old when legend says that she was taught to knit by a guardian angel, making knitting a blessed occupation. In 1533, for the stunning state occasion in Venice when Henry II of France married Catherine de Medici, he wore hand knitted silk stockings. By then handknitting was an important industry, but handknitted silk was much rarer.

Knitted silk stockings were one of the most prized items and Erik XIV of Sweden (1533-77) in his 1566 'handknit inventory' included a wonderful range of silk stockings; red, violet, pink, yellow, brown, black and gray. Johann III was buried in 1594, and when his tomb was opened up in 1945, there were crumbling yellowed silk stockings with a well defined seam of purl stitches down the back. Around the same time, the King of Denmark was presented with a pair of fine, fully-fashioned knitted silk hose. They were made in Holland and he was so impressed that he encouraged Dutch knitters to come to Denmark and teach his people how to knit silk. Framework knitting spread in the seventeenth century throughout the British Isles, France and Italy. Soon Spain, Southern Netherlands, Saxony and Copenhagen had frames and by the eighteenth century knitting machines were in Germany, Austria, Hungary, Poland and Russia, some for knitting silk.

Diderot's 18th century engraving of stocking frame knitters, with the male knitter and his female assistant who did the spinning and throwing.

Machine knitting in France initially had state patronage and it spread to the silk districts of Nimes, Lyon and Paris, where both silk and jersey gloves and stockings were knitted. The machines were costly and complicated, and the men operating them needed support and supervision. Quality control was essential. This was more difficult when the frames were worked in the home, rather than in a factory or mill. Around 1656, there was some reverse migration when some English Catholics took their frames and knowledge of silk knitting back to Avignon during the Cromwell years of religious intolerance. There was a thirst for knowledge and the immigrants were welcomed.

Knitting machines were constantly being refined. Diderot published in his Encyclopaedia, an old set of twenty-four technical drawings of knitting frames, copied by an industrial spy, Jean Hindret around 1656, and these drawings were widely used and adapted. In Lyon by 1667, a machine could make ten pairs of stockings per week, three pairs of unicoloured ones and two pairs of patterned silk. Designs were becoming ever more complex and one exquisite pair of toeless silk stockings had an all over ribbon design, with tiny portrait medallions of a French financier, Jacques Nécker (1732-1804). They were knitted in bands of yellow, green, pink and blue, and are now in the Metropolitan Museum of Art in New York. Handknitted stockings were superior and more expensive than machine made, and both the handknitters and the Guild and continued to be profoundly resistant to any change.

Spain had traditionally supplied France with a great deal of silk. In 1586, buyers from the French court ordered stockings in various colours; 3 *paires de vert marin, 3 argentees, 3 rouge, 3 bleu céleste, 3 gris foncé, 3 chatain, 3 coleur de pigeon, 1 jaune, 1 blanche, 1 violette, 12 noires.* Expensive coloured silk stockings were still high fashion and four years later in 1590, Diego de Camp put in an order for stockings: *4 paires fauves, 3 gris cendré, 3 blue-ciel, 2 jaune, 2 vert et cramoisies…*' This quantity was probably organized by a Guild, like the Catalonian Knitting Guild. It had been established in 1426, and continued to be active until the end of the seventeenth century. At first most knitters had linked up with the haberdashers, but from 1745 the imported machines gave a great boost to the craft and more items were machine knit.

The Spaniards were very dexterous and full of innovations. They added decorative 'clocks' up the sides of the heel of the stockings by inlaying gold, silver and coloured silks. In 1700, Cordova was exporting silk embroidered, openwork mittens, gloves and hose to England. They had been made on the knitting frame by transferring stitches by hand and this simple but slow method resulted in some exquisite and intricate lacy patterns. The Spaniards invented a method of frame knitting waistcoats, that produced 'shading, brocading and flowering in gold and silver and all shades of colour.' In 1767 they produced a knitted silk velvet pile fabric that had '… a very smooth and brilliant appearance, whilst the web was also elastic.' These fabrics were used for a multitude of garments and 'all agreed that the productions were the handsomest articles that had yet been made either from

Exquisite coral pink and silver-gilt thread knitted brocaded silk jacket, probably Italian and 17th century.

the stocking frames or the loom.' They were however, very expensive and so had limited long term appeal.

The Italians gained both raw silk and information from Spain, and began producing knitted silk stockings and other garments in rich colours. Venice, Genoa and Turin at various times, all had Englishmen of mixed competence, ability and honesty promoting the knitting frame to make silk stockings, and applying for a warrant and monopoly. One Englishman Italianized his name to Tommaso Harnaggi to enhance his proposal. In 1658 he wanted to manufacture silk stockings on the knitting frame in exchange for a grant from the city for 15 years. His grand plans failed because he was unable to attract workers with the right skills and raise sufficient finance for his scheme. Another Englishman John Hanford moved to Turin in 1663. He also wanted a monopoly there for fifteen years, tax exemptions for himself and ten companions and permission to open shops. The Milan merchants turned him down, fearing that it would reduce the price of stockings and destroy a traditional craft. At the time 8,000 people handknitted stockings and the merchants baulked at supplying every family with a knitting frame. In the event it was not until 1722 that the frame was officially permitted in Milan

By 1575, the Italians had developed the technology to use reverse stockinet stitch to emphasize the pattern sections and were making jackets from the cheaper filoselle and floret 'refuse' or spun waste silk. Some of the exquisite knitted brocade waistcoats and shirts were called 'Florentines' though they may not have even been made in Italy. They were made of rectangular panels and shaped by the addition of side gores. Silver and gold threads added sparkle to the floral design, and they were fastened with many tiny buttons. Many were lined with thin dyed

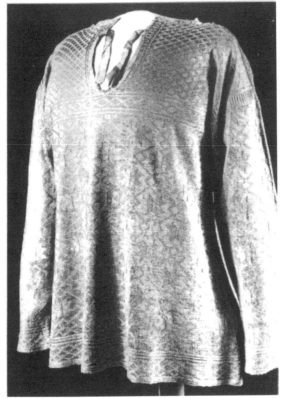

Pale blue knitted silk 'vest' similar to the one Charles I wore when he was executed in 1649. The damask effect is made by alternating plain and purl stitches in a complex pattern.

silk fabric because they tended to be rather untidy on the reverse, with long floats, unavoidable in the early days of the knitting frame. In the seventeenth century, the fashionable elite wore silk garments and matching silk stockings and the city fathers saw an opportunity to promote and extend the range of silk fashion accessories. In 1724, Turin had 153 frames and these increased rapidly to 237. Two years later a guild was formed and over 10,000 pairs of silk stockings were exported. Milan recognized an opportunity, and in 1762 set up a factory in Parma to make even more stocking frames.

English Knitted Silk

The English and the French had long been trade rivals. In London, the advent of the knitting frame saw a marked upturn in the production and trade in silk items. There were also many more incidences of the French smuggling and then copying the English frames. Paris was like London in that it dealt mainly in fancy goods, while Nimes was more like Derby, and specialized in knitted silk.

London became a much more sober place with Oliver Cromwell in charge. In 1649, he sanctioned the imprisonment of Charles I and Charles went to the block wearing a fine, sky blue knitted silk shirt, with a row of little buttons down the front placket opening. It was knitted in the round in a damask pattern that gave it a soft, yet tailored feel. It was probably made by an Italian Master knitter and is now in the London Museum.

Around the time of James Lee's death in 1657, the London Hosiers asked Cromwell for the right to form a Guild. They needed to protect their technology and to prohibit the export of 'any frames and machines for knit workers of silk stockings', and this was granted on 14 June 1659. Within ten years there were 400-500 frames in use in London and of those, three-fifths were for knitting silk stockings. Then in 1695, Charles II gave a charter to the parishes within ten miles of Spitalfields in the City of London, and 1,500 stocking frames were recorded, mostly in private homes. By the early

1700s there were around 5,000 knitting frames throughout England, though exactly how many were exclusively for silk is not known. It took some time for the knitters in the Midlands to change to knitting frames but the idea caught on and many towns became knitting centres, mostly of jersey wool but some like Nottingham and Derby were silk cities. Handknitters everywhere were particularly hostile to the frames, fearing for their livelihood. Knitted items now formed a significant part of the export trade, as did the frames and expertise.

Silk stockings were hand knitted in Norwich and later Diss, but although few could afford them some people did have as many as 'two or three pairs of these silk netherstocks.' The popularity of silk stockings 'in the English style', meant that by 1750 Nottingham was the largest framework knitting town south of the Trent River. Derby was already a silk town and the use of knitting frames spread to Sherwood Forest and many other provincial towns including Leek and the Peak District, Chester, Gloucester, York, Oxford, Berkhamstead, Maidstone, Godalming, Christchurch, Reading, Guildford, Lewes and Leicester. The cost of a frame had dropped significantly and was now between £10 and £15. A second-hand one could be bought for as little as £3.00, and to rent one cost only 1s 6d a week. There was a new group of businessmen called bag-hosiers who rented out the frames. Timothy Harris owned between 70 and 80 silk stocking frames in Nottingham in 1794, and became a very rich man on the proceeds. The fashion was for heavy silk stockings, around 4oz the pair but the only way the Nottingham silk knitters could compete with London was to use embezzled or stolen silk and produce finer and finer stockings, barely one and a half ounces a pair. The most beautiful examples of hose date from

Knitting frame, 1770, that produced stockings that were shaped but still had to have a seam up the back.

this time, when traditionally a lady's fine silk stocking could be pulled through her wedding ring.

The machines were continually being adapted for specialized use, new styles of silk yarn, complex designs, fashions and garments. There are isolated references to hand-knitted petticoats, which in the early days were described as 'petycotes' or small undercoats, rather than underskirts. There was a good export market to Europe for expensive silk goods produced in London, mainly waistcoats, hose and gloves, but many workers were reluctant to be innovative and to adapt to changing fashions so there was instability and decline. The knitters lost status because they had become less inventive and entrepreneurial and were no longer considered skilled freemen and master craftsmen. The next step was to adapt the knitting frame to produce lace.

Queen Anne of Denmark, an anonymous engraving, published in 1613 after her death. She insisted that the now deeply unfashionable Elizabethan gowns be worn at court, with the drum farthingale, low neckline and fanned out fine lace.

Chapter 7
Lace

In the early days, a lace was a tie or braid. The concept of making an open-work border to decorate the edge of the neck or sleeve, came much later. Soon it was found that threads of a loosely woven fabric could be distorted and gathered together, or whipped and braided into an attractive lacy pattern. Some threads were pulled to make a little hole, and those holes were grouped into a fine, filigree design. The ideas were expanded and soon groups of individual threads were knotted into long strips of lace in complex patterns and were used to join garment sections together. Some threads were combined into fragile floral motifs and made into collars and larger items, and fine gauze and silk tulle were over-embroidered to make delicate nets. Bobbins, pins, needles, patterns, weights, lace pillows and other aids were developed to make it easier to make the lace. Soon making lace became a fine art.

Traditionally, the finest lace was made of linen, but silk was lustrous and precious and the long filaments were found to be suitable for making delicate lace. The earliest piece of bobbin lace, dated 1480 was a piece of insertion in a sudarium or napkin, now in Uppsala Cathedral. Lacemaking was highly skilled and also very time consuming, so any articles made of silk were considered very desirable. To add a further richness, gold or silver wire was wrapped around a silk core and this metallic lace was used to decorate and embellish the flashiest and richest garments.

Some of the earliest examples of true lace were recorded in a Venetian pattern book of bobbin laces dated 1536. The designs, known as 'R.M' *Nuw Modelbuch* were further developed in Switzerland and published by Froschauer in Zurich in 1561. These laces were obviously very special because the book recommends that they be made in expensive gold and silver threads or coloured silks. Early laces were also made in France, Belgium and Northern Italy, cities already famous for their silk.

Lace came into stunning effect with the appearance of the lace ruff in France. It was first just a little frill at the edge of the collar of the doublet or bodice or at the wrists. Catherine de Medici was fourteen when she left Florence to marry Henry II of France in 1533. She was credited with introducing the ruff to soften the neckline of the black or white gowns she usually wore. In Italy and Spain the ruff was decorated with lace from Flanders, and was higher at the back than the front. Elizabeth the First of England used large, extremely delicate and expensive ruffs to frame her face and emphasize her regal power and might. In the Netherlands, the cartwheel ruffs became a major sartorial statement. Lace was now all the rage within the royal courts and among the rising courtiers and wealthy nobles of Europe.

Elizabeth I employed Alice Smyth and her husband Roger Montagu to sew and do needlework on silk and linen for her. Another silkwoman Dorothy Speccart, along with her husband Abraham were paid:

> "First to Dorothy Speccart, seamstresse...2 dosen of ruffs of fine cambricke, one dosen of them edged with bone lace... 6 dosen fine handerchers stitched and edged with bone lace...:
> "To John Sheirston for 148 yards of broad bone lace for Bandes, Ruffes, and Shirtes, all Xs the yarde, £74.00.00
> "For 408 yardes of Bone lace at 2s per yard £40.16.00

Nüw Modelbüch/
Allerley gattungen Dæntelschnür/so diser
zyt in hoch Tütschlanden gæng vnd bräuchig sind/zů
vnderricht jren Leertöchteren vnnd allen anderen
schnürwürckeren zů Zürych vnd wo die sind/
getz mwlich zůbereit/vnd erstmals in
truck verfergket durch X. W.

Pattern book of lace designs known as 'R. M.' New Modelbuch, published in Zurich in 1561.

Abraham Speccart's bill included £14.08.00 for two combing cloths to protect the clothes when powdering the hair, and two cushion cloths of fine Cambricke 'verie rich with gold and silver and coloured silkes'. Other lace edgings were 18 pennies to 4 shillings a yard along with silk thread for making up.

A specialist seamstress called Mary Kent, supplied the Earl of Bedford with regular cravats and cuffs. Without a qualm in one year alone, he spent another £87.18s.6d on glorious gold and silver thread lace. In England, this 'orris work' was a lucrative section of the London weaving guilds. During the reign of James I, the Guild of Gold and Silver Wyre Drawers was on the rise, gaining its charter in 1623. These valuable laces became known as 'statute lace' because their quality and availability were highly controlled. Some men gambled or spent vast sums to acquire the finest lace. At this time of over-decorated, excessive display, even they were criticized for squandering their fortunes and becoming effeminate.

Galerie du Palaise, an engraving by Abraham Bosse of a draper's shop in Paris in the 1640s. It shows lace, collars, cuffs, fans and falling bands. Behind the counter, a lady serves the fashionable customers.

John Eaton was laceman to Charles II in 1674. He supplied 'Poynt de Venize for cravats and cuffs, narrow poynt, poynt de Spaine, bone lace for 18 night shirts, 12 yards of Bone lace for 6 cappes and six long pillowbeeres in total Seaven Hundred Threescore and seaventeene pounds two shillings and a penny'. Lace was used to embellish an ever-increasing range of items, including hats and spangled garters, shoe roses, wraps, handkerchiefs and collars.

Some of the finest lace came from the Low Countries. Buyers and agents had to be very astute in order to source the most exquisite lace in the newest patterns, as their fastidious customers were always on the lookout for something new. About 30 per cent of Antwerp's population in the 1650s were involved in the textile trades. The wages were poor, and it was mostly the women who were employed in working linen, silk or lace. Little girls began to make lace from the time they were six years old, and they earned the derisory sum of less than one *stiver*, the equivalent of a few pennies per day. With the expansion of the lace industry, there was increasing competition from other towns. The manufacturers took the opportunity to build mills and factories in the country districts around Antwerp where they could employ the local people and pay even lower wages.

A lace shop in Paris, 1678, engraved by J Berain, showing the range of gloves, stockings, tippets, shawls, ribbons and bows. The lady wears a lace hood, covering her hair and her dress, with the long, pointed bodice, has the sides gathered up and drawn to the back. Her companion wears a highly decorated baldric to support his sword. Note the full bottomed curly wig, the lace cravat and the number of buttons used for decoration.

Silk Blonde Lace

Silk lace was usually described as 'blonde' from its natural creamy colour, and by the mid-seventeen hundreds, its delicacy and sheen had made it very popular. Blonde lace was made in many places including Milan, Genoa and Lucca, although comparatively few examples of these lovely silk laces have survived. The intricate patterns mirrored the designs popular in the fashionable woven silks. The patterns were becoming increasingly complex and technically demanding, requiring a high degree of skill to handle the glossy silk. Some blonde lace included rococo scrollwork designs, chinoiserie birds and flowers, fountains and figures.

The elite of Paris society demanded more and more of the beautiful silk lace and the Parisian lace makers responded by producing a new range of geometric patterns, including some cheaper ones on a rather coarse mesh ground. Paris became famous for its delicate blonde silk 'fancies' and other accessories like a 'head'. This was a cap, consisting of a frill and lappets that hung down the back or sides. The shape and style of the lappets changed during the century, and by the 1760s they were very fine, with delicate trailing flowers on a mesh ground. In general, the lace grew lighter, becoming more suitable for trimming the neo-classical gowns that were now high fashion.

Some designs were constructed on a base of net or tulle and over embroidered, needle-run or tamboured. This was a kind of lace running or darning, made with a needle threaded with thicker silk. Tambour work had been introduced from the East around 1760. It was done by professional embroiderers in France, China and India, mainly in white but sometimes gold or silver thread. The fine muslin or silk net was tightly stretched in a circular frame, and a hook was inserted from below so the silk thread formed little loops on the surface. This work was popular for aprons, collars, cuffs, caps and other accessories. Later in Scotland, it was available with the designs already printed on the fabric. Pattern books, dating from 1797 have been preserved and show many different lace designs worked in white cotton, white silk and black matte silk. By the 1820s, lovely blonde laces were used for the little capes called pelerines, flounces, stoles, veils, or even whole gowns for the wealthy.

Chantilly

In the late eighteenth century, Chantilly was still a small town north of Paris. It produced some of the finest blonde bobbin lace, markedly different from modern cotton Chantilly lace. Early blonde Chantilly lace was almost always black and featured dense, shiny patterned areas in thick floss silk. A corded silk was used to outline the pattern, on a 'fond simple' ground. Sometimes 'kat stitch' or 'Paris ground' were used on the hexagonal mesh, giving the effect of a six-pointed star. Black Chantilly lace was used in fashionable lacy ruffles and collars, and was suitable for older ladies and for mourning wear. The blonde silk was dyed with a black dye that was acid and contained iron, which unfortunately tended to oxidize and lose its colour and rot the silk.

French lady in the latest fashion for 1693. Her lace headdress has got higher, the lace sleeve flounces fuller and her trained mantua gown is neatly waisted. Her scarf has been looped like a Steinkirk cravat and on her face are the tiny, black velvet patches or beauty spots. In her hand, she carries a fan.

Production of Chantilly lace flourished between 1740 and 1785 under the patronage of Louis XV (1715-74) and Louis XVI (1774-93) but declined during the tumultuous period of the French Revolution and its aftermath (1789-95) when it became foolhardy and dangerous to display any aspects of wealth. With the restoration came a period of relative calm. Emperor Napoleon I gave silk lace a boost in 1804 by decreeing that only Chantilly lace and fine lace from Alencon should be worn at court. By the 1840s, dull black silk known as grenadine, stiffened with gum arabic was highly fashionable, as well as the cream bobbin lace. These silks were worked in fragile, naturalistic floral designs, creating a delicate fabric that looked wonderful when worn over a contrasting underdress. A thick silk gimp was formed by bundles of shiny threads and used to outline the pattern. To make the larger patterns, the motifs had to be divided up and split into smaller sections and these were later joined with minute, invisible stitches. Beautiful flounces and Chantilly shawls were fashionable at the French court until the fall of the Second Empire in the 1870s but lost favour with a change of political climate and new ideas. The drastic reduction in the market meant that lace was now hard to sell at any price.

Le Puy

The districts around the Auvergne have a lacemaking tradition, going back to the seventeenth century. Many of the country areas produced some of the simpler and cheaper laces as well as blonde, both creamy white and dyed black. Its popularity suffered a decline during the early 1800s, but revived again during the 1820s and 1830s, with the latest patterns coming from Paris.

In the Haute-Loire, the two main lace making *arrondissements* were Le Puy and Yssingeaux. They had a total population at the beginning of the 1800s of around 30,000 people, rising to 100,000 by 1870. In Le Puy there were two streets in particular where the women sat in their doorways making lace. These streets, the rue Chenebouterie and the rue Raphael were just narrow passages in the centre of the town but became well-known and something of a tourist attraction. Passers-by and visitors to the town would stop to chat and watch the women working. The patterns were pinned to a lace cushion and the women quickly and smoothly twisted the bobbins of thread over each other, building up the delicate lace.

Many of the lace makers lived in the remote villages around Le Puy, in the general area where silk was grown. Sometimes the women sang as they worked, and in the evening they gathered together in a specific house to continue working and share the cost of candles. Although they were independent artisans, they did not have a contract, but dealt with an intermediary called a *leveuse,* who travelled around the villages. He took a percentage of the price and paid the lace maker on the length, quality and accuracy of the design. The lace was measured with a *demi-aune*, a length of around 60cm. The higher the quality, the newer and more fashionable

Black blonde silk lace collar from Le Puy.

the design, the more the women were paid. The lace was then passed to other women who specialized in joining the lace strips together, or adding them to specific items. The lace was collated and sold back to the Le Puy lace merchant who had initially supplied the thread and patterns. Unfortunately there were frequent disputes. The women had no control over the designs or the amount of payment and there were many unscrupulous merchants.

There was a long standing belief that women's lace work was only a hobby, was morally desirable and even healthy, an entirely suitable way to keep her busy and in the home. Although wages were poor, some married lace women still preferred to work from home rather than working in the new ribbon-making factories in the region, but many young girls were not attracted to lacemaking. They thought it was old fashioned and indicated that the family was poor. Some country girls wanted to be modern and wear smart clothes and earn a wage and preferred to work in the factories in the towns.

Despite the 'mere pittance' the married lacemaker received, she sometimes earned more than her husband did growing grapes, although his work was considered 'skilled' and hers 'supplementary.' In truth, much of the land was very poor yet the income she brought in was often essential to keep the family fed and together. The coming of the railroad to the Haute-Loire in the 1860s signalled a change for many women. They could now travel into the town and strike their own deals with the Le Puy merchants. This cut out the services of the *leveuse*, but lace was always subject to the vagaries of fashion and it could be very difficult to sell.

Especially between the 1820s and 1840s, Caen and Bayeaux in Northern France also produced beautiful blonde bobbin lace. The fine lustrous silk lace with the simple floral patterns incorporating daisies or wheatears was made in Caen as early as 1745. In the summer it was a common sight to see the women making the lace, known as 'white blonde'. Great care had to be taken to keep the hands clean and so when the

Blonde silk bobbin lace fichu collar, 1835-40, probably made in Northern France.

weather got colder, rather than sitting by a smoky fire, the women were reputed to have worked in the lofts above where their animals were kept, and so they benefited from the animal's warmth. Caen became renowned for the large double fichu collars, shaped to fit the shoulders and they became extremely popular. Some exquisite collars have been preserved in museums and lace collections. One typical example had a scalloped edge, each scallop filled with a flower, with leafy sprigs flowing into the net ground. The Normandy silk laces had a naivety and freshness that was most attractive. Sometimes it was little more than a Valencienne ground with rows of small dots and a picot edge, perfect to edge a baby's bonnet.

After the 1851 Exhibition, the Report of the Jury noted that by this time hand worked silk blonde in Caen had almost disappeared. It had been replaced by Chantilly piece goods, luxury items, scarves, berthas, ladies robes and shawls. L Radon of Caen and Paris, produced silk and gold and white silk lace lappets, while A Duval exhibited both yellow and white silk yarn for making blonde lace. More worryingly, the jury noted that a Chantilly style silk lace was being machine made very successfully in Buckinghamshire in England and Grammont in Belgium. There was a revival of patronage in 1854 when Empress Eugenie began placing orders for Chantilly lace, a shawl from Lefebure and a flounce from Pigache and Mallet. While the manufacture of Chantilly lace had almost disappeared in the Chantilly region, the designs were flourishing in many other parts of France. Heavy silk blonde became all the rage once black silk parasols and shawls became fashionable. Unfortunately, the end of the Second Empire in 1870 meant the end of royal patronage and a decline in silk lace.

By 1900, the black silk lace industry of Normandy had fallen into a serious decline, with less than 1,000 workers in Calvados compared to over 50,000, fifty years before. Aristocratic patronage had been falling and the manufactures blamed the decline on a fall in apprenticeships, a direct result of the Education Acts of 1881 and 1882 that made full-time schooling compulsory for all children up to the age of thirteen. Even more important was that vast quantities of lace could now be produced quickly and cheaply by machines.

Auguste Lefébure was a leading French lace manufacturer. He modernized the local lacemaking school and established a trade supplying lustrous lace for the Spanish market in cream, white or black silk. It was known as blonde matte or Spanish blonde and was more heavily patterned than French blonde and that suited the Spanish taste. Spain was still a producer of silk, but Spanish bobbin lace was not widely available and never very fashionable. The lace was made using two weights of silk; the finer lower denier for constructing the ground and the heavier, higher denier for outlining the motifs. Catalonia in the nineteenth century had its own blonde industry and continued to make shawls, black mantillas and other items, both for the home market and export to the colonies. In this strongly Catholic country it was traditional for women to wear these delicate black silk mantillas to church each Sunday. Some Spanish blonde lace used a coarse thread of a rather uneven colour that tended to brown with age. It was not valued as highly as the French articles because of the poorer workmanship and coarser designs.

Maltese Lace

In the 1830s, Maltese lace was revived, partly due to the arrival of some Italian silk lace workers from Genoa. There had been a terrible famine in Northern Italy and it was said that Lady Hamilton Chichester was profoundly moved by the plight of the lacemakers. She was influential in bringing them to Malta, to try and establish lacemaking there. Fashion now tended towards fuller, richer designs and the Maltese cross was quickly established as a distinguishing feature in the lace. When the rest of Europe was moving towards machine-made lace, Malta survived because of the popularity and cheapness of its handmade lace. Unfortunately that was partly due to the rather low standard of workmanship and the coarser threads. Maltese blonde lace came into its own and looked wonderful when it was made into parasols and the huge enveloping square and triangular shawls. They were graceful and decorative and balanced the wide crinolines, worn in the early 1860s.

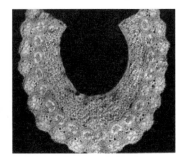

Maltese blonde silk lace collar. The Maltese cross in the border is clearly part of the scalloped design. (Private collection).

Lacy silk 'fascinators' were highly fashionable between 1850 and 1875. These lacy head coverings featured a cap with lappets at the side, long enough to tie under the chin if required. They had an almost three-dimensional appearance when worked in thick, lustrous cream floss silk. They featured the central cross of Malta, set in a scalloped border on varied grounds of twisted and plaited 'brides' or decorative joining threads. These were combined with 'wheatears', a group of individual leaves in a star formation. Most fortuitously, there was a revival of interest in Maltese lace between 1890 and 1900 and a subsequent improvement in the quality. The local lace makers began making dressing table sets, place mats and silk edged handkerchiefs, as *souvenirs* for the British soldiers stationed there.

Maltese silk 'fascinator', a delightful, shaped head and shoulder scarf, dated around 1850.

Machine made lace

Knitting frames had been used for nearly 200 years before they were adapted to make machine-made lace. Up until the early eighteenth century, the frames only produced a plain knit. If an elastic, textured rib was required, it was made by letting the stitches run down like a ladder, and then latching them back up again by hand. This was both tedious and time consuming and therefore expensive.

There was a flurry of inventions and new adaptations to the knitting machines and one of the first was a tuck presser, manufactured in Nottingham between 1725 and 1742. It was an iron attachment that hung in front of an ordinary knitting frame. These 'tuck ribs' were an imitation rib and did not have the elasticity of a real rib. They were extremely popular and were a first step to machine lace. Then, in 1758 Jedediah Strutt patented his Derby rib attachment. It produced a genuine rib, quickly and more economically than by hand. Strutt and many Quaker industrialists were concerned about setting a high moral tone and were particularly conscious of the health, social, educational and moral welfare of their workers. They were paternalistic and set high standards, so that many Victorians saw these men as the new leaders of society.

By 1783, most of the wide shawl frames had a form of 'oilet hole' attachment that transferred stitches quickly and made the fabric loose and open. The slippery silk laddered easily and the fabric was rather weak and unstable, making these nets less popular. The next adaptation was a 'square net' made on a version of the Derby rib frame. Although this silk net proved to be far too expensive, it was described as 'lustrous and durable' and was used for mitts, gloves, purses, shawls and wig foundations.

By the late eighteenth century, the latest fashions were rather soft and dreamy so the manufacturers and inventors tried to make a fine six-sided tulle that was sound and durable. An attachment was patented that made 'point net'. This net was quite regular but also rather unreliable and the fabric had to be stretched and stiffened with gum arabic to make it transparent and shiny, otherwise it was described as '…a miserable article, shrinking to a fabric resembling a rag of crape.' The pin, or point machine was never very popular in England but in 1786 under orders from Louis XVI, the Duc de Laiancourt pirated the machine and copies were set up in Lyon and later Paris. It produced a single and a double silk net and by 1800 there were 2000 pin machines working in Lyon. These nets were decorated and embellished with tambouring, and lace running stitches using a thicker silk. Hundreds of women were employed over-embroidering plain silk net and it became an important industry in its own right.

Another variation produced a good copy of blonde Brussels lace. It was made by using a heavy glossy silk gimp to outline the pattern on the silk net. Some of these laces were so good that only the cut ends of the threads indicated that it was not a handmade lace. William Gardiner, visiting Paris in 1802, found that these new machine-made laces were greatly admired for their beauty and cheapness. Another type of Chantilly lace, featuring sprigs of flowers was worked on black machine-made silk net and produced in Exeter in England. It was made by needle-running using floss silk, and the veils, flounces and neckerchiefs sold very well. There is some evidence

Parasol of heavy, cream blonde silk lace from the area of Lyons known as La Croisse-Rousse, where the canutes, the silk weavers, were concentrated.

that silk laces were being made in Honiton. Mention is made of beautiful motifs, worked in coloured silks and appliqued on to black machine made silk net. They were exotic and unusual and of excellent design. The merchants saw an opportunity and hired people to try out new designs to test their accuracy and suitability. Some women specialized in joining the strips of lace together to make a saleable length of 33 metres, while others were *crocheteuses* who joined different parts of the pattern to make a large overall design. Unfortunately few pieces of lace have survived as the enterprise was not commercially successful.

Mittens were also fashionable. Until 1804-5, they were made two at a time on the lace knitting machine. For variety, some were made lengthways and were known as 'opposition mittens'. The *Framework Knitters Advocate* reported that silk gloves had become an important and valuable part of the trade. By that time the cotton trade was expanding at the expense of silk and Nottingham was becoming far more important for lace than hosiery.

The race was now on to produce a viable, economical machine made silk lace. In 1809, John Heathcoat (1783-1861) invented a bobbin-net machine. It produced a superior net almost identical to those hand-made in Lille and Buckinghamshire. The big change was that it no longer used a stocking frame, but had each thread on a separate bobbin and this eventually led to a real lace being made on a machine. In Nottingham, in the high days of silk net production, an experienced lace knitter could earn up to £2.10s per week.

There was a downside. With the increase in machine production, the independent master weavers and lace knitters were becoming desperately anxious about their future. The troubles were escalating and disaster struck John Heathcoat on the 26th June 1816 when the Luddites, supported by other discontented young men, rioted and wrecked his factory at Longborough. They smashed fifty-five of his frames and destroyed his valuable stock of silks and other materials. John Heathcote was completely crushed by the unfairness and wanton damage. He was eventually awarded £10,000 in compensation, and was urged to set up again in the town, but he had lost heart and refused to do so. He accepted the money and moved to Tiverton in Devon.

Machine Lace in the 1800s

There was enormous excitement in the silk trade when Princess Charlotte married Prince Leopold of Saxe-Coburg in 1816. Her wedding dress was a weft knitted, ivory silk net with silver threads, bordered with silver lamé. It was a wonderful example of the perfection that had been attained by machine lace, but joy turned to despair when she died in childbirth the next year. The silk makers who had raised loans to increase production in anticipation of a happy and prosperous new era with bright silks and baby ribbons, were crushed. This just compounded the serious problems of a lack of parity over import duties. More than 24,000 yards of silk weft nets had been flooding the English market annually. The French only paid light import duties and this made the English silk lace and nets in comparison, ruinously expensive.

Three new inventions had a profound effect on the market. Between 1813 and 1814 both the Levers and Pusher lace machines were developed. By 1841 both had incorporated the new jacquard technology which enabled them to insert a liner automatically, saving hours and hours of handwork. Then in 1846, John Liversay developed a curtain net machine that became the basis of the Nottingham lace industry. It produced a good imitation of the black Caen and Chantilly silk lace. The judges at the 1851 Great Exhibition were most impressed. They compared it to handmade lace, saying '...the patterns of which are most correctly copied, while the difference in price is seventy-five percent...'

Silk laces were on a fashion and economic see-saw. Many lace machines had been extended in width to 100 or even 150 inches and were worked by steam power and could produce vast quantities of lace. The English designers combed the French and Italian archives for new ideas and complicated patterns. Many tried to sustain and reinvigorate the lace trade, but there were many cyclic slumps between the 1830s and 1850s. Merchants tried to keep in close touch with fashion trends, but by the time an order had been fulfilled, the fashion had often moved on. Then disaster struck. The European silk industry was almost entirely wiped out in the

Chantilly, blonde silk lace fan, 1880, with blonde tortoiseshell ribs.

Black silk lace fan.

1860s when a disease known as Pebrine, struck the silkworm population. The silkworms failed to thrive and they died in their millions before they could spin their cocoons. Louis Pasteur worked tirelessly to discover the cause and save the French silk industry. Scientifically improved methods of detection, care and production were established and hygiene was stressed to control the disease, and slowly the industry recovered.

With dramatically reduced domestic production, glossy, high quality silk threads had to be imported in large amounts from China to help support the damaged silk industry. They were mixed with locally produced dyed silk and metallic threads. Black and white stoles, scarves, head coverings and flounces were made, mostly in Lyon, while in Spain, the lace industry was revived using locally produced silk, known as *blonde Espagnole*. The Pushers machines were ideal for making the stylish silk shawls, but by the 1870s, they were no longer high fashion. By then the Franco-Prussian war had effected all the European textile trades, by disrupting trade routes and supplies.

Another major change came with the Swiss invention in 1883 of the revolutionary chemical or burnout technique. The background silk net was chemically dissolved, leaving just the fine cotton tracery of the design. It was frequently used for lace collars and flouncing and was considerably cheaper to produce than handmade lace. It was widely available and the slightly fuzzy edges were often the only clue that the lace was not handmade. Silk nets continued to be produced, though almost none in England after the late nineteenth century.

Edwardian silk lace dress from Nottingham, 1907.

Engraving of Charles II and Catherine of Braganza.

Chapter 8
Buttons and Bows

The Spitalfields Act of 1744 changed the lives of the London silk weavers forever. It set minimum wages and that was what the weavers wanted, but they had not understood the predictable outcome. The silk manufacturers refused to cover the wages and left London and set up in other parts of England where land and labour were cheaper. They avoided the rigid controls imposed by the London weavers but in general paid the country people well below the Guild rate. The London weavers suffered because with the exit of the big silk manufacturers there was almost no work at all.

Silk was a luxury trade. Producing silk items was labour intensive and the new industries required many people to do the supporting tasks of winding, reeling, throwing, warping and finishing, as well as broadloom weaving. The minor silk industries, collectively known as *passementerie*, included making silk trimmings, braids and tassels, weaving ribbons, making purses, caps, lace, and stockings, embroidering buttons, and sewing all types of clothing. These trades contributed significantly to the continued prosperity of many smaller communities. Mills were built, and attics and lofts were quickly and cheaply converted so that work could start immediately. In the eighteenth century in the English counties, there were lots of new opportunities for everyone.

Lombe's Mill

Around 1704 Mr Crocket started a small silk throwing mill in Derby. This town was the centre for silk hosiery and he saw a need for an efficient and effective throwing mill to produce organzine silk for knitting and weaving. When Crocket went bankrupt, his former apprentice John Lombe leased the mill, with his half-brother Thomas putting up the money. Thomas was born in 1685 and was already a successful mercer and framework knitter, trading in silk in London. The Lombe brothers installed imported Dutch machinery and hired local labour.

Water powered mills had been used in Lucca for three hundred years but had not been developed in England. The Italians were experts at throwing silk mechanically, but the English could not match them for quality using their less sophisticated machines. When John took over the mill he was a bold young man of twenty. He was reputedly a good draughtsman and an excellent mechanic, but by 1717 the Lombe brothers were tired of paying exorbitant prices for top quality thrown Italian silk from the Piedmont mills, so they devised a secret scheme, little short of industrial espionage.

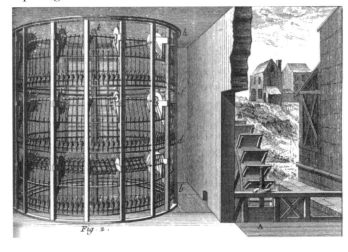

Diderot's version of V Zonca's water powered throwing mill, first published in Novo Teatro di Machines, *1607. This diagram clearly shows the S shaped flyers on top of the bobbins and the reels.*

116

John probably understood the design and working of the water powered throwing mill, because plans had already been published in Padua in 1607 by V Zonca in his *Novo Teatro di Machines*. A complete description of Italian methods had been published again in 1620 and 1686, and John had probably read it, because it was widely available. But, there is no substitute for careful observation of working machinery and hence his trip to Piedmont. He disguised himself as an outworker and became friendly with the locals and through subterfuge and bribery, gained private access to the machines at night. He carefully sketched out the details and hid the plans in a bale of silk. The silk was loaded at Livorno by Thomas Lombe's agent as part of a regular consignment and the plans were safely retrieved in England. John stayed on in Piedmont, hoping to learn more. He certainly knew the risks he was taking because the punishment was 'hanging by one foot from a gibbet until dead'.

Eventually his actions must have aroused suspicion because he escaped just in time, his boat pursued by a Sardinian man-of-war. William Hutton in his *History of Derby*, claimed that the Italians were furious when they realized that the Lombe brothers had stolen their invention. They planned revenge and sent an Italian woman to work at the new Derby factory that Thomas had built in John's absence. When John returned in 1722, he was a fit young man of twenty-nine, but quite suddenly he was taken ill, doubled up with intense stomach pains. The circumstances were highly suspicious and within days he was dead.

Thomas had applied for and been granted a British patent in 1718 for the pirated "new invention of three sorts of engines never before made or used in Great Britain, one to wind the finest raw silk, another to spin, and the other to twist". In 1720 he had taken a lease on a swampy island in the middle of the Derwent river for £8 pa, where he built a modern mill at a cost of £30,000. It was a masterpiece of the Industrial Revolution, an eighth of a mile long, with eight throwsters' rooms and 468 windows. The giant water wheel revolved three times each minute and for each revolution it moved 67,415 m (73,726 yd) of organzine silk thread, an amazing 291,240,006 m (318,504,960 yd) per day. During the fourteen years of the life of the patent, between 1718 and 1732, the mill was reputed to have made £80,000 profit. Thomas worked tirelessly to reduce costs and undercut the Italians and the money rolled in. He imported raw silk from Persia, Piedmont and 'perfect white China sorts' from Canton. The mill employed 300 hands, many of them women. By the standards of the day, the factory was very modern, with good light and air but the workers were strictly controlled with draconian rules, long hours and harsh treatment of the children who worked there.

At the end of the patent in 1732, Thomas tried to get an extension but it was denied. His critics were still murmuring that his invention was not new, but based on a machine that had been used in Italy for a hundred years. Eventually Thomas was paid £14,000 to put a prototype on display in the Tower of London for all to see and copy. Thomas Lombe was now a man of stature and influence and an alderman in the city of London and was made the city's sheriff in 1727. He died in 1739 on the 3rd of January leaving a very substantial fortune of £120,000 to his widow and his two daughters, Hannah and Mary.

William Taylor took over Lombe's Mill, making sarcenets, *gros de Naples*, and other rich silks and many were as fine as those made in Spitalfields. He had 220 looms and employed 300 local people. There was a big push towards expansion and specialization and many other manufacturers tried to imitate Thomas Lombe's success. Throwing mills were built by entrepreneurs wherever there was a constant flow of water to drive the complicated mechanical machinery. Silk mills were built at Stockport in 1732, Macclesfield in 1743, Sherborne 1740 and Congleton 1754. Silk throwing and weaving mills were also set up in Tring, Sudbury, Taunton, St Albans, Glemsford, Lancaster and Pebmarsh.

Expansion in Industry

It was a time of enormous industrial growth and energy. Communications improved with new roads and canals. Scientific and technical knowledge was avidly sought

and the textile industry attracted enlightened men and the brightest minds. **The real need now was for a more mechanized system of spinning silk that would expand production and produce a more consistent product.**

There had been handspinning devices and spindles for over four thousand years. The spinning wheel was thought to have originated in ancient India, and was originally designed to spin cotton. The spindle wheel was used for silk and offered considerable improvements. Around 1555 there was another big advance when the

Woodcut of a spinner outside her house. !6th century

Saxony wheel had a flyer and bobbin added, and a pedal for foot power so both hands could be used to handle the fibre. There were some experiments with double wheels and ingenious designs for multi-spinners in a bid to increase the output. Even Leonardo da Vinci once drew a design for a primitive spinning machine. All these devices had the limitation of being hand or foot powered, so the drive was for a more mechanized arrangement that would enable many threads to be spun at once.

Fine reeled silk was very expensive, but various waste silks had arrived in London from China or accumulated from the throwing mills. The silk was tacky, dirty and almost unrecognizable as silk and virtually unusable until Israel Reynolds and Henry Geange in 1568 developed a primitive machine for cleaning and milling it. Although they turned the silk into a useful form so it could be spun, it was probably not a proper carding machine. It was 1748 before Lewis Paul, a prolific designer of textile machinery, patented a carding system using two sets of hooked cards mounted on cylinders that rotated one against the other. Another engine supplied the power. It was claimed that 'when 20 to 30 women and children drew out the threads, assisted by one child of 9 or 10 years turning the handle, it would spin re-constituted waste silk into a useful yarn'. It was also understood that the machine had a social value, as it would give these children 'good employment'.

Now carded silk was available, the next problem was to find a mechanized way of producing silk thread that was sufficiently strong and even enough to be woven or knitted. Around 1735 Lewis Paul and his partner John Wyatt designed their first roller spinning machine. It was not commercially successful but in 1758 they patented another spinning machine that was further developed by Richard Arkwright as the spinning frame. Almost concurrently, around 1764, James Hargreaves tried to patent his spinning jenny but it was judged invalid because he has disclosed his invention. These machines were initially designed to spin cotton for stockings, but soon they were adapted for spinning the silk used by the machine knitters in the hosiery trade.

Both pedal looms and drawlooms, using a system of individual cords, had been in common use for centuries. In 1733 John Kay had designed a flying shuttle. It was initially only used in baize making, but John's son Robert developed it further by introducing a drop shuttle box, so two or more shuttles could be used in the same weft. The looms were not completely mechanized until they were connected up to a source of waterpower to drive the engines. Once mills had been established, production increased dramatically. Some firms wove plain silks, velvets and chenilles while others began producing heavy silks and stuffs, taffetas and damasks. Wealthy, fashionable people craved the new and exotic and in these prosperous times, even the less affluent people in the towns bought the cheaper light silks and half-silks and had them made up into men's waist coats, women's petty-coats, linings and soft furnishings.

Industrialists, Merchants and Other Workers

Another group of important merchants did not have a factory, just an office and warehouse. They controlled up to two hundred looms and the weavers worked in their own homes, but exclusively for him. The merchant's job was to get the orders and manage the workers and distribute the finished silk. He calculated the weight of organzine and tram silk thread and gave

the skeins to the dyer. Only occasionally did he have
the facility to throw or dye the silk, preferring to
subcontract that out to the specialists. The skeins of
silk then went to the winder, who wound them onto reels
for the warper to lay the threads. The silk had to be
calculated exactly, for length and the number of threads
per inch. It was wound onto a 'hand stick' and weighed
and given to the weaver, along with the bobbins of tram
for the weft. It was the weaver's job to take the hand
stick of yarn and the back roller from his loom to the
warp spreader who would wind on the warp. The weaver
also arranged to have the silk tram wound from the
bobbin onto the quills, and he paid for both. When the
fabric was woven, the weaver took the completed cloth
from the loom to the warehouse where the merchant
carefully checked, measured and weighed it. Any debts
or cash advances were settled and the weaver was paid
the balance. This system produced vast amounts of silk
fabrics, but rarely the exquisite and complex ones. They
were still made by the master handweavers.

Many arrangements worked very well but there were
endless opportunities for dissention and mistrust. Some

*Winding a silk warp, Diderot
engraving, showing the warping mill
and the bobbin rack.*

Cottage industry, spinning and reeling, an engraving by William Hincke. The family, all contribute to get the work done for their shared welfare. 1791. The fire is interesting because it could be for cooking, washing the yarn or boiling cocoons before they are reeled.

merchant weavers and masters too, allowed their weavers to draw some of their wages before the weaving was completed. This way the weaver lived from hand to mouth and was rarely out of debt. It was a downward spiral and the fluctuations in the market, politics and changes in fashion resulted in extremely low wages. In the latter part of the eighteenth and early nineteenth century the average contract weaver had in his hand, between four and eight shillings per week. This meant that all the members of the family had to contribute their earnings for the family to survive. Even then, their combined income was rarely more than 20 to 25 shillings per week.

Some of the smaller, but successful master weavers owned a variety of looms including lace looms, great looms and drawlooms. To keep their costs down, some went against the Guild laws and used semi-skilled boys rather than apprentice or journeymen weavers. An independent weaver with only one or two looms required his wife to take a turn at the loom and the rest of the family to help. Some impoverished weavers owned neither looms nor materials, but were dependent on the more successful masters for continuing work.

Silk winding seems to have been part of the normal work of the weavers' shop. The eighteenth century Norwich Freeman's Register occasionally mentions throwsters and silk winders. There are references to the hexagonal reels on which the filaments were wound, called 'silke swiftes', and 'silk blocks' and 'horns' on which the bobbins were set. The throwsters situation varied. Some major throwsters with access to capital set up water powered mills and had the silk thrown by skilled women. Even with all the petty controls, long hours and generally awful conditions, some women liked handling a little money and the limited freedom from household drudgery that working in the mill allowed. The mills were seen as a social asset because many people still believed that women had to be controlled at all times, to protect them from themselves and their baser nature. Silk was very expensive, so a mill enabled quality to be more easily controlled and theft reduced. It was hoped that the expense of building a mill would be offset by an increase in production and quality. Unfortunately the machines were still rather rudimentary and there was a lot of waste and many throwing mills failed.

Throwing did not have the status of weaving and many small scale throwsters were women on their own, working from home for a master. All silk was subject to fluctuations in demand and unpredictable fashion. The throwster was the most vunerable of the silk workers, and her family was dependent on her income. The children had little or no schooling as their mother worked the silk and managed the family. Many children understood very early in life that this was their lot; to spin, wind quills and bobbins, knit, weave or make buttons. It is one of the ironies of life that in this luxury trade, were some of the poorest workers.

Fancy Buttons

Button making, covering the moulds and hand embroidering the buttons.

Buttons started to appear on clothes in Europe in the first half of the thirteenth century, more for decoration than practicality. They gradually replaced the brooch as a fastening for wrist and neck openings. The fashionably laced and fitted garments also used buttons and a matching strip of eyelets. Surviving examples of early cloth buttons show they were made over a wad of material and attached with a shank of silk thread, with the matching buttonholes worked in 2-ply silk.

Button making was a cottage industry, to be fitted in by the women

Suit of silk clothes with matching fine silk embroidery 1785-90. A real feature is made of the matching handworked buttons and buttonholes, both functional and decorative, right down the front and on the wide cuffs. The Hermitage Museum.

and children around the agricultural seasons and other household demands. The buttons were hand sewn with a needle in a variety of designs. Some small buttons could be covered all over with little knots and other fancy stitches, or worked over a ring of horn or a wooden mould, using coloured silk, mohair and silk twist. The mohair probably came from the Levant in Turkey and the silk from the local mills or by packhorse from the London merchants.

Making handmade buttons was always outwork. Forty-five pennies per week was pitifully little for such fine handwork, but during difficult times, even that could be an important addition to the family income. Button making was also taught to the poor in the hope that they could support themselves. The majority were women and they lacked the bargaining power of a guild, so the low wages continued until they became organized. The 1709 Act regulating Button-Covering and Buttonhole bindings states that, '..no taylor and other person whatsoever...shall make or sell or use or bind...on any clothes or wearing garment any butons or butonholes...' This Act and others added restrictions and did nothing for the women's wages or conditions.

Button making became a growth industry in many English towns and villages. The Flemings introduced button making into Canterbury using combinations of silk, goats' hair and jersey wool and by 1630 silk buttons were also being made in Sherborne. Buttons, ribbons and a binding called ferret were made in Leek by French Huguenots who had moved on from Coventry in 1685. Buttons and buttonholes were also made in Shrewsbury, using a splendid white horsehair that took the dye beautifully. Some buttons were cheap and coarse, with fabric scraps pulled over a wooden mould, but the better ones were of silk, worked in intricate patterns. Congleton was famous for its gloves and buttons, and they remained its staple until around 1730. Edward I had granted

Congleton a charter to hold a fair three times a year and buttons and other *passementerie* items were sold there.

Making *passementerie* or 'narrow ware' was ideal when other job opportunities were limited. Most could be done within the home and required little in the way of expensive equipment. It did not need a long period of formal training or an apprenticeship and women were used to doing handwork and fitting it in around their family and household tasks. P*assementerie* industries developed around Maidstone and Colchester, while in Sandwich loom laces of linen, silk, wool and hair became a specialty. These crafts were already established in London, but they spread into towns around Norwich, Chester, York, Kings Lynn, Sudbury, Reading and Bristol. Narrow ware and buttons became important industries in Warwick and Coventry and into the Flash and Peak Districts around Leek, Buxton, Stockport, and Macclesfield.

Making passementerie and braids.

Buttons and Macclesfield Silk

In the middle of the eighteenth century many Huguenots left London and moved to Manchester, Salford and the Macclesfield areas. At least eleven Manchester and Salford testators between 1648 and 1791 describe themselves as silkweavers, but with names like Bayley, Smith, Goring, Budworth and Thorpe they were unlikely to be of foreign origin unless they had all anglicized their names. The first silk throwing mill was built in Macclesfield in 1756, but scores of mills were later built in the town. Macclesfield became famous for its quality silk thread, complex, heavy woven fabrics and button making. The Macclesfield town accounts of 1574 note 'a debt for making buttonz of ye value 15s 2d'.

Macclesfield silk was controlled by just a few families, the Brocklehursts, Pearsons, Smales and Turners. The company of J J Brocklehurst was founded in 1745 and they

The medieval chapman, Godric of Finchale, who began as a peddlar, taking his pack of wares to the towns and outlying properties. He became very successful and embarked on international ventures, eventually becoming a saint.
This wooden sculpture is in Swaffham Parish Church.

wove all kinds of broad silk, and were one of the earliest to spin waste silk. They had an excellent reputation for their foulards, dress goods, mufflers, fancies, crepes, linings, waterproofed silks and buttons. In 1789 they exported buttons to the value of £300 to Kruger and Reisenkaroff. Brocklehurst was a successful and tenacious businessman and obtained government orders to supply silk handkerchiefs to the Navy. He continued to sell handkerchiefs and scarves even during economic downturns and when they were no longer fashionable. Some people believed that the first tie was originally a simple Macclesfield square, folded in seven.

The main centres for button making were the districts around Macclesfield. These haberdashery items, including buttonholes and silk twist were sold by peddlers, and one group called themselves the Flashmen. This was partly because they congregated and built their cottages on a piece of common land called 'the Flash' on the banks of the river between Leek, Buxton and Macclesfield. They formed a gang who had a reputation for cunning and speaking a kind of slang, and their wild and outrageous behaviour earned them a name for being unreliable. As well as Macclesfield buttons, the Flashmen hawked the ribbons made in Leek and handkerchiefs from Manchester. There were other gangs of peddlers and chapmen, including one known as the Broken Cross Gang.

In the eighteenth century, peddlers and chapmen sold their wares at the fairs and markets. Some peddlers took the silk twist and buttons as far as London. They had waggonettes with sliding drawers, with all their haberdashery items classified into different qualities. Completed buttons were mounted on cards, with a blue top for the best and yellow for the poorest, with pink and blue for export.

Handmade buttons continued to dominate the market until around 1725 when metal and horn buttons from Sheffield and Birmingham became cheaper and more fashionable. It was estimated that by 1765 there were between 12,000 and 15,000 silkworkers and button makers in the area, including the villages of Knutsford, Mobberley and Wilmslow. With button making in decline, throwing silk was a more lucrative way to make money.

Coventry Ribbons

Many English towns became well known for their exquisite ribbons, as well as their broadloom and mixed silks. Around 1627 some Huguenot weavers had moved to Coventry from London. They began weaving broadloom and mixed silks as well as making silk ribbons, galloons, buttons, lace and gloves. Ribbons were very important, especially in the millinery trade and fashion trends fluctuated. Work was sometimes scarce, and the silk workers experimented by forming a body for their own protection. Later they joined an older established group, and finally in 1703 they once again formed a separate guild.

Up to the end of the seventeenth century, ribbons were handwoven in exquisite detail by master craftsmen or by women using the little portable box looms used for *passementerie* and braids. Making ribbons one by one was very slow. Fashion demanded lashings of ribbons to decorate every part of the garment and the person, so the drive was on to find some way to make a machine that would weave a number of narrow ribbons, all at the same time.

The earliest multi-ribbon loom was called a Dutch engine and it was developed in Leiden in 1604. It had up to two dozen shuttles and as many warp beams, one for each ribbon being woven. By 1610, multi-ribbon looms had been installed in London and by 1636 there were probably over 100 looms. This encroached on the local ribbon weavers who were still trying to make a living using their single looms. King Charles was petitioned and asked to prohibit the installation of these looms. He did, but the major ribbon weavers ignored the directive because they saw the value of the multi-loom as it allowed many ribbons to be woven at once, still by one man. The new loom put hundreds of men, women and children out of work, and the situation gradually got worse and in 1675 there were riots. Many of the old pedal looms were standing idle because fashion had turned away from the expensive, delicate handwoven fancy ribbons. Now people wanted the new plain ribbons in a multitude of colours that could be made quickly and cheaply on the new Dutch engines.

Coventry ribbons, showing a small sample range.

Joseph-Marie Jacquard (1752-1834) a weaver of Lyons, who adapted his loom so that it could reproduce patterns using a string of cards, the basis for all modern complex weaving. This statue was erected in 1970 in the Place de la Croix-Rousse in Lyon.
Below: sample pattern cards.

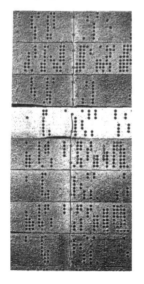

The new Dutch multi-ribbon looms required relatively unskilled men to work them. The standard dropped significantly as ribbons were now produced quickly and to a price. By 1801, Joseph-Marie Jacquard (1752-1834) had introduced his improved loom. His jacquard loom worked on a system of punched cards that allowed the pattern to be reproduced automatically. These looms were ideal for the fine silks, but were very expensive and their popularity increased slowly as people learnt to use them

From Feb 1813 to autumn 1815 everyone wanted the latest fashion, a purl ribbon with little knobs along the two selvedges. The loops were woven by passing the weft thread over stiff horsehair outside the natural edge. This period came to be known as the 'big purl' and everyone had work. Wages rose and fortunes were made, but just as suddenly the fashion changed and the market collapsed.

To add to the confusion, in England an Act had been in force since 1765 that prohibited the importation of silk goods. With the lifting of the Act in 1826, French silk goods had flooded the English market. These ribbons had finesse and offered variety at a cheaper price. The fashionable women, starved for novelty for so many years, turned as one to the delicious French silks, and ignored the locally produced ribbons. The weavers panicked and in the volatile situation, a List of Weaving Prices was introduced to try and stabilize the wages. Unfortunately the variations in wages for different jobs were so numerous that there were endless disputes and strikes in 1819, 1822, 1831, 1834 and 1835. The List had not really addressed the problem. People were just not buying English silks and so the weavers had little work. The miseries were not confined to Coventry, and there was great distress in all the silk towns and cities.

The weavers became desperate and in 1831 steam power was introduced. Many saw this as a further threat and the innovation was violently opposed and mills were burnt. The weavers knew that eventually they had to accept the steam-driven jacquard and multiple looms. In a bid to finance and utilize steam, long terraces of three-storey cottages were built, each group with a steam engine set up in the lane behind their houses, and connected to all the looms in the attics.

The Quakers John and Joseph Cash, renowned for their name ribbons built several weavers' cottages adjacent to the local canal. A new town was built at Hillfields, near Coventry with over two thousand houses entirely for silk-weavers. The upper storey of the weavers' cottages contained the looms. They had large oblong windows with between sixty and eighty panes of glass for maximum light and by 1838 the Coventry silk ribbon trade had once again settled down.

The years between 1854-6 of the Russian war saw a period of prosperity, and the weavers supplied a hundred thousand pounds worth of plain ribbons to a London wholesale house. But it was not long before the reality of the 1860 Commercial Treaty with France had created panic. Once again, remembering the last time the French had had open access to the English market, no-one placed big orders because they feared the market would be flooded with novel silk items of better design at a cheaper price. One million pounds worth of silk goods prepared for the spring trade, languished unsold in the warehouses. There was panic and despair, strikes and a rush on the savings banks and money was withdrawn.

It was not all gloom and in 1872-75 here was a brief respite and plain ribbon was once again fashionable. It was called Coventry Souple Oriental, and these ribbons with a moire finish were in demand. There was also a call for utility and war ribbons with silk combined with other fibres. Silk ribbons, tapes and hats manufactured in Coventry contributed to a period of prosperity in the town.

French engraving from Cahiers de Costumes français 1779. The lady's full court dress with ruffles and festoons was made of 'Pekin' a type of Chinese silk. Her hair is upswept and carefully coiffured and decorated. She is accompanied by an ecuyer or equerry, whose silk suit is comparatively lightly decorated with gold and silver braid and embroidery. The silk stockings were de rigueur for court life.

Shops in the Exeter Change, 1777. This building on the Strand housed lots of little shops, milliners, drapers, bookshops, hosiers and became a fashionable place to meet.

Chapter 9
Home and Fashion

In 1477 the Swiss forces overcame the Burgundians leaving Charles the Bold dead on the battlefield. It was the custom to go on campaign surrounded by every luxury so the tents were resplendent with tapestries and sumptuous silks, and the knights had dazzling clothes and accessories. Apparently the jubilant Swiss soldiers fell on the silks, stripping the tents bare, and claiming everything as the spoils of war. They decorated their battle worn garments with the torn shreds of silks. The effect of the slashed garments stuffed with bright silks looked so comical that legend says, at their triumphant homecoming the people copied them and a new fashion was born. Slashing and puffing was in.

Fashion ideas travelled across borders, but slashing was never so extreme as in Germany where the new style was adopted with joy and alacrity. The doublets and breeches were literally cut to ribbons, the cut edges sealed with wax and the coloured lining pulled through. In some instances the fabrics were not slashed but a contrasting fabric was appliquéd on to resemble the silk lining or undergarments poking through.

German tailors, 1568. On a hanger is a gown with a skirt stiffened with rows of inserted canes. The two men sit crosslegged on a low stand near the window, with the best light, while the tailor is cutting out fabric.

Underneath the table is the box of off-cuts and fabric scraps that he will probably sell off – as the saying goes, 'turn your silkes into golde'

In the sixteenth century, Spain already had a well establish silk industry. The influence of Ferdinand (1452-1516) and Isabella (1451-1504) was still very strong and the Catholic Church took a high moral stand to control what people wore. The fashionable Spaniard chose a dark brocaded silk doublet with paned breeches, fine hose and a cape, all with rows of stiff gold and silver braid. Spanish women wore the cone shaped vertugarde or farthingale. The shape was achieved by threading canes horizontally on the outside, in cascading circles. It was matched with a stiffened embroidered and laced bodice. The neck was low, exposing the breasts until the strict etiquette of the court of Charles I (1500-58) required the women to wear a fine pleated or embroidered chemise that ended with a frill, high at the neck, the forerunner of the ruff.

The Italian women were influenced by Spanish fashions but chose a softer less structured look that showed off the gorgeous damasks and other silks for which their country was famous. The girls decorated their hair with fresh flowers, braids and circlets, and the older women covered their hair with a fine silk veil. The Italian authorities, under the influence of the Catholic Church banned daringly low necklines in Genoa, Milan and Rome and in 1514 Venice issued sumptuary laws limiting spending on rich silks.

There had been a history of using sumptuary laws to limit the colours and cost of the clothes people wore, because different fabrics, especially silks were seen as appropriate for different social classes. English Sumptuary laws go back to 1379, but they were constantly being tinkered with, repealed and re-enacted. Despite some harsh penalties they were often ignored because there was no real way of enforcing them. The 1455 laws specified the quality of silk and furs that a knight could wear and it was extended eight years later in 1463 and again in 1482 when wearing foreign wrought silk textiles was prohibited. Birth was more important than wealth so the nobility required an income of £200 per year while merchants needed goods worth over £1000 before they could wear silk. The colour, texture and sheen of fine silk was associated with power and importance, in contrast to the drab colours and rougher textures often worn by the poor. Tradesmen's wives were criticized for trying to wear the latest fashion, and maids who gave themselves airs when wearing their mistresses cast off clothes. Sir John Harrington wrote ...

> '...Apparells great excess;
> For though the laws against yt are express,
> For each Lady like a Queen herself doth dress,
> A merchaunts wife like to be a baroness.'

Henri IV 1599. The canopy, the plumed and caparisoned horse, the attendants, the king's clothes, all contributed to reinforce the message of wealth and ultimate power.

The Tudor Period

In England, Henry VII (1457-1509) had made a politically expedient marriage when he had married Elizabeth in 1486 to unite the rival houses of Lancaster and York. Elizabeth was tall and fair and eight years younger than her husband but they grew together and she gave him the love and companionship of a real home and family and he was faithful to his marriage. In comparison to Queen Elizabeth Woodville, her wayward and ambitious mother, Elizabeth of York was gentle and pious and her modesty influenced English style. She and her ladies wore flowing silk gowns that fell in heavy folds to the ground. The gabled bonnet framed the face and only partly covered the softer hairstyle with its central parting.

Elizabeth of York patronized many mercers and spent vast sums on silk fabrics. On May the 5th 1502, she spent £40 13s 5d for 'certain velveteens and other stuffs, and on their occupation by them, delivered to the use of the Queene'. In November she ordered more velvet at 10s 6d. Payment could be slow and one London mercer was repaid in quarterly installments for his bill of '£107 10s for certain silks and other stuff of his occupation'. Her embroiderer Robnet was responsible for fitting out the 'Queene's riche Bedde' He employed three men and three women for 52 days and the expenses for the seven weeks amounted to £5 13s 1d which was refunded on Christmas Day. Sadly Queen Elizabeth died in childbirth on the 11th of February 1503 on her 38th birthday and so enjoyed her beautiful 'bedde' for only a few weeks. The king was grief stricken and retired from court where he 'privily deserted to a solitary place and would no man should resort unto him'.

Elizabeth of York's second son Henry (1491-1547) dominated the sixteenth century in England. He was a big man 6'2" tall, of great charm and wit. He was loud, fickle, impetuous and his multiple marriages changed the course of history. Henry VIII and the men of his court wore the broad, heavily padded doublet, slashed to reveal the white puffs of the undershirt and lavishly trimmed with precious stones. The doublet was waisted and fell nearly to the knees with the cod-piece prominently displayed. Over the doublet was worn a massive, heavy shouldered and puffed gown that fell in ample folds. On his legs he wore close-fitting white nether hose that showed off his splendid legs.

His gentle, pious wife Catherine of Aragon was his dead brother's widow, and she brought with her to England her strong Catholic faith and her Spanish style of dressing. Catherine is reputed to have introduced the Spanish farthingale into England. She favoured a modest neckline, with a little ruffle. Her dresses often had a matching petticoat and inner and outer sleeves, and she wore her hair pulled back under a cap, similar to the gabled headdress worn by her late mother-in-law, Elizabeth of York. Catherine went to her coronation carried in a litter,

The two women sitting working at their tapestry looms illustrate the story of Arachne's downfall at the hands of the powerful goddess, Athene.

> '...borne on the backs of two white palfreys trapped in white cloth of gold, her person appareled in white satin embroidered, her hair hanging down her back, of a very great length, beautiful and goodly to behold, and on her head a coronal, set with many rich stones.'

Bessie Blount also came to court around the same time as Catherine. She was enormous fun, danced and sang beautifully and had energy and high spirits to match the king. In 1519 she gave birth to Henry's son, Henry Fitzroy, later Duke of Richmond but in 1514 she was just one of the four 'Ladies of Savoy' who wore blue silk velvet with a gold bonnet at the Christmas festivities.

Richard Smith, Elizabeth of York's Yeoman continued to serve Catherine of Aragon and became responsible for the preparations for all the royal births. He arranged for the nursery to have new hangings, bedding and carpets. Included were two silk velvet counterpoints of estate, one purple and the other crimson, trimmed and powdered with ermine for 'what tymne she laye in childebedde'. The inventory compiled after the annulment of her marriage in 1533 showed her wealth had been greatly reduced to 24 pieces of tapestry, 19 cushions, 17 carpets and one cloth of estate. Despite many marital changes, Ralph Worsley managed to remain Yeoman of the Robes to Jane Seymour, Anne of Cleves and Catherine Parr. Officers of the Robes and Beds had a grant of black silk livery annually, consisting of a doublet, coat and gown with fur trim. When the French Admiral visited England in 1546, the liverymen wore coats of crimson damask 'guarded' with yellow velvet and lined with black buckram.

Henry's queens brought their own subtle differences in dress, depending on their personalities. Anne Boleyn wore a large gold letter 'B' on a chain around her neck and favoured a flattering, closely fitted French style bonnet edged with pleated silk and pearls. She was vain, demanding and immensely strong-willed. She spent heavily on her wardrobe and after her execution there were many debts. Pictures of Jane Seymour who died soon after giving birth to her son Edward in the year following her marriage show her wearing a gable bonnet. The gowns worn by Catherine Parr and her step-daughter Elizabeth had close-fitting bodices that became longer and more pointed, emphasizing the split skirts and rich petticoats.

The Queens had their own households and Wardrobes of the Robes and Beds, based in London at Baynard's Castle. It was the traditional residence of the Queen consort and was similar to the King's Great Wardrobe but more modest. In 1538 at the age of six months Prince Edward was provided with his own household. Henry Fitzroy, Henry's illegitimate son and also his two daughters Mary and Elizabeth, were dependent on the King's generosity and that could at times be rather thoughtless and intermittent.

The Great Wardrobe

The Great Wardrobe had a keeper, clerks, tailors, skinners and embroiderers, with yeomen employed on a daily basis to assist them. As clothes and furnishings became worn they were recycled or sent to the Standing Wardrobe or various houses including the Tower of London, to be cleaned or stored.

Henry's clothes required special care, especially his purple and velvet coronation robes valued at £200, a doublet of purple cloth of gold worth £49 and a frock of 'white tincel' £26.13.4d. The Black Book records the duties of perfuming and cleaning the royal textiles. Perfumes scented everything, including the gloves to mask the fishy smell of the glue. Violet and musk were popular and lavender was burnt as a fumigator. Rose petals and distilling herbs were grown in the royal gardens and used to perfume Henry's beds and protect the textiles from moths, while rue was used to discourage fleas. The Wardrobe supplied soap, ashes and lye to make a bleaching solution but records suggest that stains could be difficult to remove. Every self-respecting lady had her 'book of secrets' with cleaning and dyeing formulas. The real problem was the dirty air, the soot from open fires and candles, and getting things properly dried and aired. Whenever possible, the maids laid the washed linens out over the hedges to bleach and dry in the sun. A little flat pan

Woman cutting out a pattern. Boccaccio. Late 15th Century France.

full of hot coals called a smoothing iron, was used to iron the fabrics. Some harsh cleaning methods shrunk the clothes, so most silks were just brushed and spotted using fresh bread.

The court was constantly on the move and the king's newest clothes and fashionable furnishings travelled with him. The decorated silk lined boxes and coffers were protected inside stronger crates for the actual travel. Some small boxes were embroidered and trimmed with gold, silver and 'passamayne lace of Venice,' and some had drawers. Cases were especially designed for specific items, like the boxes lined with white quilted sarcenet for his doublets. Less precious items were packed in bags and cloth sacks, wicker baskets, iron trunks or *cuir bouilli*, a stiff boiled leather. There were wall hangings, beds, cloth of estate and cushions. The whole household was designed to appear luxurious despite being constantly dismantled, transported and reassembled.

The Later Tudors

Henry died in 1547 and was succeeded by his young son Edward VI, who reigned for 6 years until 1553. He was followed by Mary, the Catholic daughter of Catherine of Aragon, who reigned for five years until 1558. Her marriage in 1554 to Philip II of Spain had a profound effect on the nation and like her mother, she was strongly influenced in dress and etiquette by her Spanish connections. Stays made of stiffened canvas and reinforced with whalebones flattened the breasts and emphasized the narrow waist. Dark colours, padded hips, cone shaped skirts and high collars that discretely filled the neckline, all gave a feeling of rigid inflexibility.

France was influenced by Spanish stiffness but softened the line, and retained the lower neckline. A thick cord of silk or gold with a pomander of musk or sweet smelling herbs was worn around the waist to ward off nasty smells and diseases. Sometime after 1540 men's hose separated into upper breeches and lower stocks or nether stockings. When the doublet and jerkin were shortened, the hose became one piece, called the trunkhose. Around 1570 the codpiece was discarded

Ceollo. The Infanta Isabella Clara Eugenia, still a child in 1579, wearing the rather stiff, formal gown and high ruff favoured by those at the Spanish court.

and the form-fitting canions in contrasting brocade or satin, became fashionable. They lengthened to the knee and were matched with smart silk stockings held up with a garter.

Catherine de' Medici (1519-89), the daughter of the Duke of Urbino, did not have much success as a wife, as her husband King Henry II of France, who reigned from 1547 to 1559, openly preferred his enchanting mistress, Diane de Poitiers. Catherine's sons, three of whom became inadequate monarchs, were a disappointment too. The third son, Henry III who became King of France in 1574 was much more interested in being a leader of fashion rather than of men and his country. His highly effeminate behaviour and his penchant for cross-dressing meant that he spent a great deal of time primping and fussing and consequently was late for both his wedding and his coronation. He favoured the peascod belly doublet, an idea brought back from Poland and reputed to be a shape that would deflect an attack. By the 1570s, hair was shorter, collars had risen and he took exquisite pleasure in his delicate cartwheel ruffs. Henry's weak interest in government was fortunately compensated by his support of France's silk textile industry. During his reign, sericulture was given serious attention and both Tours and Lyon became famous for silk manufacture. Silk factories were established at Montpellier, Nimes and Orleans and later, silk stockings were knitted at Dourdan.

Mary Stuart, Queen of the Scots (1542-67) was Catherine de Medici's daughter-in-law and grew up in France. A document dated the 25th November 1561 mentions a silk parasol, possibly given to her by Catherine.

'Item: ane litle cannabie of crammosie satine
of thre quarter lang furnisit with freingeis and
tassis maid of gold and cammosie silk mony

litle oaintit buttonis all serving to mak schaddow afoir the Quene.' (Item: one little canopy of crammosy satin of three quarters long furnished with fringes and tassels made of gold and crammosy silk many little painted buttons all serving to make shadow over the Queen.)

Fans were also becoming fashionable and she had a fan with a mount of brocaded silk and silver tissue, in softly graded rainbow colours. On New Years Day she received a gift of 'two fannes of straw wrought with silke of sundry colours'. Her Catholic faith, dress and manners were entirely French and she was treated with suspicion when she returned as a widow of eighteen to her birthplace in Scotland.

Elizabeth I

Elizabeth, I was a dedicated setter of fashion during the 45 years of her reign from 1558 to 1603. She loved clothes and once she had some control of her money and her destiny, acquired beautiful textiles and jewels. When she was a child, her father mostly ignored her and at times her wardrobe was in a parlous state. Her devoted lady in waiting, Catherine Champernowne, later Ashley, whom she called Kat, had to beg for suitable clothes for the growing girl.

Elizabeth never forgot these times of penury and she was always tight with money becoming skilled at eliciting the perfect gift from her courtiers and swains. She was fragile and small of build and often suffered illness but her indomitable spirit always shone through and gave her the strength she needed. She was demanding and vain, proud of her small delicate hands and feet. The late portraits were almost always political statements, with her hand on the globe, or the Armada in the background, her clothes embroidered with snakes and eyes. Her embroiderer John Parr and other professional and domestic embroiderers often depicted little birds and insects, interlacing coiling stems, roses and oak leaves on jackets and doublets. Embroidery was not only used to decorate a garment but also to strengthen the seams, and on occasion to disguise soiled areas or stains.

Elizabeth was reputed to have 3000 gowns, many of the later ones featuring the long pointed stomacher and bombasted leg of mutton sleeves, festooned with pearls, encrusted with jewels, bows and minute gold sequins. The silk skirt became marginally shorter and the drum farthingale came out at an angle from the hips to balance the lacy ruff that she wore, in one form or another all her life. She often wore the delicate fanshaped Medici ruff that framed her face and showed off her white neck. Ruffs were starched and goffered, and the folds were set using poking sticks of wood and later metal. Coloured ruffs were known but in contemporary paintings they are all white. Between 1560 and 1640, the ruff was characteristic of both male and female dress. Some of the cartwheel ruffs reached enormous proportions, especially in the Netherlands. They must have been uncomfortable and restricting to wear, making meal times somewhat hazardous.

The Seventeenth Century

When James VI of Scotland arrived in England to be crowned James I in 1603, he was impoverished. His wife Anne of Denmark was most offended at the suggestion she wear the late queen's hand-me-down gowns, even if remodelled, but even James had to borrow silk stockings. Boots had become funnel shaped revealing lacework frills with satin or taffeta garters knotted under the knee. The short cape slung over one shoulder got longer, with a satin sash tied over the doublet. Some women wore the sash along with a less rigid farthingale.

As collars grew higher, wigs got shorter, with tight little curls fixed with a powder made of finely pulverized starch, scented with cyprus oil, or violets for brunettes and iris for blondes. Most women used the much cheaper rotten-oak powder that gave their hair a rusty tinge.

From around 1620 the farthingale hoops and bum rolls were discarded and the beautiful fabrics were allowed to fall naturally. Silk was still chosen for the most splendid gowns. They were open down the front but tightly fitting into the waist, like a redingote and hitched up to show the underskirt. They drew attention to the exquisite quilted and embroidered petticoats of silks and satins in contrasting colours, trimmed with gold lace and pearls. Lace was still a very obvious sign of luxury and wealth and a variety of ruffs, kerchiefs, whisks and handkerchiefs were worn. Falling collars were universal by 1635, some as big as shawls.

During the seventeenth century there were advances in printing, literacy and scientific discovery, trade expanded and the silk manufacturers were working overtime. At Tours in France there were around 8000 looms producing silk velvets, satins and taffetas, and Lyon had over 12,000 workers making brocaded silks. Fashion artists, including Hollar in England and the Bonnarts in France recorded the change into Baroque style. Dress became flamboyant with buttons, bows and lace decorating everything. Sleeves were set low on the shoulders and now became shorter with the forearm daringly exposed with cascades of lace. Spain retained the farthingale but flattened and turned it into the *garde-infante*, as depicted in Velasquez paintings. At his court at Versailles, Louis XIV (1638-1715) dominated manners and fashion. It was an extremely decorative period with ribbons, furbelow, lace and feathers. Men's clothing changed radically during the reign of the *Roi Soleil*. The vast petticoat breeches were worn with a sleeveless doublet called a *Moliere brassiere* that showed the chemise. The *justaucorp* or long coat was embellished with gold braid, buttons and ribbons called goslings, a fashion that lasted for 25 years. Around 1670 the doublet or pourpoint became more like a long undercoat or vest and the lace collar was replaced by a cravat, a style that had been worn by German soldiers for thirty years. Louis XIII had worn a wig but it had gone out of fashion until Louis XIV lost his fine head of hair and started to go bald. Then the wig was revived and the whole court followed suit.

In England, Charles I (1600-1646) was increasingly at odds with the Puritans. Part of the problem was that his Queen, Henrietta Maria was a practicing Catholic and this was seen by some as a threat to national security. Charles had

'The Habit of an English Gentleman' is a satire, dated 1640s, mocking the extreme fashion, the ribbons, lace, wigs and patches that were popular at the time. A warning is included to be prepared for death because time is running out and noting his "long wasted dubblet unbuttoned half way... his sleeves unbuttoned... his breeches out... his codpiece unhooked, open at the top with a great bunch of ribbands."

A woodcut from the frontispiece of a little tract attacking the excesses of fashion. It shows a peddler displaying her wares, patches on her face and holding a mask, fan and ribbons.

many admirable qualities, was temperate, a good father and husband and a sincere Christian, but he was weak and avoided any difficult decisions. She was a gentle but determined Queen, seeking especially where her Roman Catholic faith was concerned, to be influential over her husband. The paintings by van Dyck from around 1630, show her dressed in the luscious plain silk satins she favoured. The short waisted bodice, with a peplum over the moderately full skirt was very flattering to her small build. At the neck she wore a falling collar or a folded square of lace, and her hair had a low fringe of short bangs, with side curls over her ears.

After the execution of Charles I, the period of Cromwell's leadership was defined by severe social constraints and political priorities, wars and taxes, but in 1660, the experiment in republicanism was over and Charles II (1630-1685) was invited to return to England and was crowned. In 1662 he made a politically expedient marriage to Catherine of Braganza, daughter of the King of Portugal. It was said that she loved her husband and he cared for her in a general way but she was unable to have children and he consoled himself with a series of beautiful women, including the actress Nell Gwynn. The people loved him and called him the "Merry Monarch' but it was a period of rather effeminate fashions, flounces, laces, bows, an excess in everything. Catherine's clothes were thought rather odd when she arrived in England. She wore simple full-skirted dresses, with a waisted bodice, full elbow length sleeves with a deep band of lace around the neck and dropped shoulders. The parasols in her trousseau, made from specially woven silk were considered most unusual and the children laughed and called them walking sticks with petticoats. Possibly they came from Goa where Portugal had trade links.

Everyday clothes were made to last as long as possible, and were turned, dyed, scoured, cut down or let out. Even the humblest household tried to get help with the monthly wash. Samuel Pepys recorded in his Diary that the laundry was started before dawn at 4am, and was still not finished by night fall. Pepys spent three or four times as much on his clothes as he allowed for his wife Elizabeth. He was the son of a tailor and he felt he just had to have the latest wigs, velvet cloaks and suits trimmed with gold buttons. In 1665 he noted that his new silk 'camelott suite' cost £24. That was the annual wage for a middling class family, but even he was criticized for trying to dress like a gentleman and rise above his station when he wore gold lace sleeves.

In 1686, Mrs Groves was seamstress to Elizabeth, the Duchess of Somerset. Silk velvet varied in price but a fashionable lady could expect to pay 26 shillings a yard, and even a mixture like silk and wool or silk and mohair was 5 shillings a yard. Mrs Grove's charges to make up the fabric included 11 shillings for silk to line a petticoat, 8 shillings for some black 'sassnet' to line another petticoat, more silk to lengthen it and add pockets and 8 shillings for making a 'lustring manto', a loose gown of glossy silk. Other costs included the interlining, buttons, embroidery floss, metallic threads and any alterations.

Some fortunate little girls had dolls, called babies or poppets. One preserved at the Museum of Childhood in London had been bought at the Bartholomew Fair. It was fashionably dressed in striped silk with an apron and mop

Lady Isabella Stuart with her doll, carefully dressed in fashionable garments. 1577, Hardwick Hall.

cap. It had leading reins attached to the shoulders, just like the dress worn by its little owner. The Victoria and Albert Museum has two fashion dolls from the 1690s. Lord Clapham is wearing fully fashioned white silk knitted stockings with red clocks and blue ribbons and Lady Clapham wears a white Chinese silk damask mantua trimmed with lace. Her mask is made of black silk on a molded foundation. The mantua, from the French 'manteau' meaning a cloak or tunic had started out in the 1670s as 'undress', a loose kind of negligée, open at the front to reveal an embroidered corset or stomacher. It was rather déshabillé, and worn by the 'beauties' of the Restoration period, but it gradually evolved into daywear. Lady Clapham's shoes were white silk, brocaded with silver and trimmed with pale pink ribbons.

Panniered gown of extreme width, designed to show off the vastly expensive silk fabric. Eschelles were still very popular and the bows, from the neckline, emphasise the small waist.

François Boucher (1703-70) and Antoine Watteau (1684-1721) both did paintings of men and women dancing and relaxing in delicious idealized situations. The pretty girls had shorter more informal skirts, tiny waists, fitted bodices and sleeves with cascades of lace, ribbons and flowers. Rich fabrics were still popular along with plain or delicately patterned silks woven with amusing bizarre grotesques. Watteau painted his '*L'Enseigne de Gersaint*' in 1720, showing a style of gown with two large box pleats that fell from the back of the shoulders. Variations of this style both loose and fitting became known as Watteau gowns and were popular for some decades.

When hoops were reintroduced in England in the 1720s, they became flatter and were supported on the hips by a wicker frame or pannier. They were at their most extreme by 1750, and then lost favour. It was rumoured that the main doors of St Paul's in London had to be widened to allow the ladies to enter. The flat expanse of the skirt was the perfect shape to display to the fullest the extremely expensive woven and embroidered silk cloth. Accessories became very important with watches, belts and fans that either matched the gown or were in contrasting brocaded silk, damask, braid or lace, embroidered with gold or silver.

The *robe a l'anglaise* was a redingote style, with a tight bodice and without panniers but with stiff petticoats and a little *cul de Paris* cushion tied at the back waist to support the skirt and train. A quilted silk petticoat with two or three thickness of fabric stitched together for warmth was worn under the split skirt with running or back stitch used to outline the large stylized floral or feather motifs.

When Louis XV (1710-74) gave a fancy dress ball at Versailles on the occasion of the marriage of the Dauphin to the Infanta of Spain, he decided to invite some of the most beautiful women in Paris, even if they were not titled. The woman who caught his eye was Jeanne Antoinette

Poisson (1721-64). She was intelligent, gifted, fond of intrigue and came to have enormous power over the king. Despite her meddling in state affairs, the king showered her with gifts and entitled her the Marquise de Pompadour. She gathered a salon about her and encouraged the arts and artists, and made the *robe a la française* her own. It had a huge over skirt of crisp silk taffeta, in bright soft colours or floral patterns, divided to reveal a petticoat festooned with braid, rouched ribbons, flowers and jewels. The bodice was inset with bows in graduating sizes like a ladder, called *eschelles,* and she wore a matching little bow on a ribbon around her neck.

In England, George II's wife Queen Caroline was large, blonde, lively, intelligent, and loved expensive silk and lace. In 1733 when she was fifty years old she paid John Denay 100 guineas for an exquisite Brussels point headdresses. One length of 27 yards of 'white and gold brocade armoz' was acquired by John Thompson for the enormous sum of £68.9s 6d. Most of Queen Caroline's silks were somber greens, blues and purples but she also wore striped lustrings, a brown flowered silk, scarlet flowered velvet, and a 'printed satteen'. John Green made her a pair of silk slippers with red heels that she wore with silk stockings, decorated with embroidery. Alas, in 1737 she died of peritonitis and George despite his philandering, was bereft without her.

Mantua gown, an anonymous French engraving of around 1700. There was a great deal of criticism of the excesses of fashion and her petticoat was deplored as having 'enough fringe to sweep the Mall.'

Interior Decoration

The interior designers were using rich silk textiles for wallhangings and upholstery. Chairs now needed high straight backs to support the lady in her tightly laced bodice and towering headdress. In the late seventeenth century the sofa had appeared, in imitation of the exotic, oriental Turkish bed and the simple day-bed or couch in the dressing room evolved into the single bed. The master bed had hangings for privacy and to keep out the draughts with a feather mattress over another horsehair mattresses, wool blankets and a silk quilt or coverlet to match the hangings. A baby born into a noble

The 'incroyables' and 'macaronis' were ultra fashionable men who favoured an excessively flamboyant style of dressing, to the point that they were often accused of being effeminate.

family had a 'cradle silk quilt and a little Holland sheet with a suit of bedlinen'. People were well aware of the damage sun and damp could cause to valuable silk textiles, so furniture was covered much of the time with dust covers. It was the practice to change the drapes in autumn to heavier lined and padded ones to keep out the cold and damp. There was a good second hand market for silk drapes and there are reports of thieves creeping up to an open window and dragging them off their poles with a grappling hook.

Clothes were kept in a garde-robe, closet or dressing room off the bedchamber. On the dressing table were brushes, a looking glass, candles, potions and powders, puffs, salves and rouge. Muslin cloths were used to protect the carpet and clothes while the hair was dressed and powdered and perfumes were worn to hide the smells of unwashed clothes and bodies. Patches made from gummed black silk velvet, satin or taffeta, were cut in circles, rings stars, half moons, or even a coach and four. They could be positioned as a lover's secret signals or more usually, to hide the scars left from smallpox. Elderly women continued to wear masks to protect their face outdoors, but younger women wore them more to flirt or conceal their identity. In the 1760s, coiffures were stiff and heavy, although fragile and difficult to sleep in. Vermin could be a problem and slits were made through the hardened paste to try and get rid of them.

France

Marie Antoinette (1755-93) was the fickle, demanding and rather undisciplined wife of Louis XVI of France. She loved amateur theatricals, and played at being a country dairy maid, wearing her skirts swept back into a three part puff called a polonaise. The hoop petticoat had been worn since 1710 but by 1780 had gone out of fashion except for court wear. In 1786, Elizabeth Vigée-Lebrun painted Marie Antoinette wearing a long sleeved white *robe en chemise*, made of transparent silk mousseline. It was tied at the back, and worn over an underskirt and corset of rose taffeta, with a fichu of linen gauze. The public was scandalized and the painting had to be withdrawn.

Rose Bertin was Marie Antoinette's main dressmaker. She was one of the first great couturiers and she introduced gauzy fabrics with tiny floral designs, narrow stripes and dainty braids and trims. Rose had customers in nearly every European country, called upon them in person, and sent them her fashion dolls, called *filles des boutiques*. The terrible time of the Terror and the Revolution resulted in Louis XVI being beheaded in January 1793 followed in October by Marie Antoinette.

It became dangerous to appear on the streets in rich silks, and so simple transparent cylinders of white muslin with a sash at the waist, and the neck gathered with a drawstring were favoured. By 1796 the 'incroyables', 'macaronis' and dandies flaunted an unkempt look with huge buttons, vast cravats, gypsy earings and tight pants tied or buttoned at the knee. They wore a little sleeveless spencer jacket, short waistcoats and over jackets with extreme lapels. By the end of decade, pantaloons and sans-cullots, taken from the peasants working breeches had been replaced by long trousers.

In 1796 Rose was 49 years old and her aristocratic patrons were destitute, dead or in exile in Coblenz, Turin, even England. The market was flooded with second hand clothes, luxury goods and jewels. Rose had a lucrative sideline in buying up superb lace and other confiscated goods and delivering packets between émigrés and their families in France. Life was much harder and she was no longer sought after and on the 22 September 1813 she died, aged 66.

Three ladies, a 1796 fashion engraving by von Heideloff. The ladies are wearing soft, high waisted silk robes with plumed headdresses.

Shops and Shopping

Small shops with men and women's clothes were often located within large important buildings like Westminster Hall and the Royal Exchange in

Cornhill. Some contained over 200 shops and many sold beautiful silks and luxury accessories like gloves, ribbons, stockings and fans. Even well established shops could have some second hand goods for sale. Shopping became the new fashionable leisure activity and the shops catered for their wealthy clientele with fine counters and looking glasses, and even pretty girls to tempt the men to spend. By the end of the eighteenth century some manufacturers were producing for the wider market with millinery warehouses in Jermyn Street and workshops where skilled sewers and embroiderers made up waistcoat shapes and petticoats.

Appropriate clothes were needed for funerals and sometimes existing clothes were quickly dyed to make them do. The Huguenot weavers saw an opportunity and started to produce a dull kind of black silk, known as mourning crape and in Denmark, the king chose this silk for mourning hat-bands and it became the universal choice for dresses and accessories.

Women received gifts of clothes in wills but many sold them on for cash. Clothes were also pawned for example when Jean Edmonston, a lawyer's wife gave a silk gown, petticoat and piece of silk as a pledge to Lady Dalmahoy.

When Jean failed to pay the money back, Lady Dalmahoy kept the silks. Second hand clothes dealers often settled in a particular district and sometimes their stock included stolen items, even stolen on demand by the unscrupulous. Court records note an alamode mourning hood valued at 2 shillings. Theft was big business and washerwomen and servants were sometimes accused of stealing clothes and linen. Janet Brown was accused of steeling a Brussels lace stole from her employer Lady Dunlop and Jane Blair was indited in the Old Bailey Sessions Papers for stealing three silk gowns and three silk petticoats along with money and other valuable items of silver from her employer.

Fashions were changing rapidly and the newspapers responded. The first issue of the Ladies Magazine contained coloured engravings of a Lady in Full Dress, and every edition showed some fashion plates of exquisite men and women in dramatic poses showing the styles being worn in London. By 1824 the Ladies Monthly Museum was announcing the newest parasols, made of Lyonese silk in a lilac colour. The market was becoming unified and common standards were imposed. Fashions were now advertised and the ideas were becoming accessible to a wider variety of people, although standards and expectations were rigid and social lines could not be crossed.

Left and below: The Tailors and the dressmakers, by Diderot

World Trip jacket, London, Paris, Vienna, Rome, Hong Kong, Auckland, New York, Home, handknitted from handspun tussah silk.

Chapter 10
Practical

Knitting with Silk

There are a number of Priceless Secrets when knitting with silk. The first is that it is silk, not wool, cotton, rayon or any other fibre, it is silk, and it will handle differently. Silk has less bounce than wool, but more than cotton, and by its very nature it is slippery and silky. Unless you really enjoy knitting on very fine needles, or need a thin yarn for a delicate lacy pattern, the silk should be spun into a light and lofty yarn, similar in thickness to a commercial knitting yarn.

Secret Number Two is that while silk does not stretch it will drop up to four inches in length and must be knitted on needles at least two sizes smaller than for wool. The first challenge is to find a pattern, because there are few patterns specially designed for handspun silk, although some yarn companies do produce designs for knitting their own mixed silk yarns. These may not be suitable for your silk, so it is better to know how to deal with all handspun yarns.

Secret Number Three is to approach the problem from another angle. Pattern companies design garments and specify a particular yarn, double knitting, Arran, three ply, sports, etc. With handspun, once you have knitted a tension square and decided on the best needles size, you simply choose a pattern by the needle size, not yarn.

Tension squares are fun. First choose a pair of needles and a ball of your silk yarn. The sample should be around 12cm square, so cast on approximately 40 stitches, and knit six rows in the stitch you plan to use for the garment. This is important because rib will pull in and garter or lacy stitches can be wider or looser than stocking stitch.

Hold your sample up to the light to check the feel and 'handle', and see if it is too loose. Chose another pair of larger or smaller needles and do another six rows. Keep experimenting, testing different stitches and needles until you are really happy with the look and feel of your knitting. Continue until you have a big enough sample, cast off, and pin it to a piece of paper and carefully draw around it. This gives you a record of its size and shape before it is washed.

Secret Number Four is to wash your sample because major changes take place. Use warm water and a few drops of liquid soap or detergent, rinse and roll it in a towel. Give it a good shake every so often as it dries. The silk looks dreadful when it is wet so the more you shake it, the better it will look and feel as it settles into its final size and shape.

When it is dry, place your knitted sample on your traced pattern and see whether it is narrower than when you started, or even more likely, that it has been knitted far too loosely and has dropped. Choose the section that looks and feels just right and use those needles to knit this silk. With practice you will be able to almost guess the best size to use. Don't forget that ribbing needs to be even firmer and on even finer needles.

Designing for Knitting with Silk

Start with the easy way first. If your new garment will be similar in size and style to one you already have, then spread it out on a large piece of paper. Carefully

draw around it, noting exactly the shape and position of the underarm, neck, cuffs and bands, increases and decreases, every detail of size and shaping. Take some time to make it right. Trace out the sleeves as well. You now have a template that you can use to test your knitting against.

Next, check your measurements. It is often easier and more fun with the help of a friend. There are three essential measurements, and some others as well.

- First, the centre back length, from the knob at the base of your neck, down to the bottom of the band or welt.

- Second, the bust measurement, straight across the back, and right around across the point of the bust. To this you need to add 'ease'. This is the amount required to make the garment fit and feel comfortable. In principle, the finer the yarn the closer the fit, but not always, as a fitted skinny rib might be an inch or so less than the bust measurement. Most fine garments require between 3 and 5 inches (7-12 cm) ease added to the bust measurement, while a big heavy jersey or jacket may need 10 inches (25cm) or more. It's a design decision.

- The Third measurement is the underarm sleeve length, from the knob on your wrist to the underarm. Sleeves of different shapes require some adjustment here too. For example, a square set sleeve needs another 1 ½ inches (4cm) added, to fit into the armhole, while a dropped shoulder on a wide garment may make the underarm sleeve length seem very short. The width of the sleeve effects this length too.

Other measurements that could be useful include:

- The width across the back from shoulder point to shoulder point.

- The width of each shoulder.

- Across the front of the bust for a heavily breasted women, who may have a narrow back.

- The circumference of the upper arm, and don't forget to add ease here too.

- The wrist.

Taking your measurements

153

- The depth of the armhole.
- Occasionally for a fitted sleeve, an outside measurement over the bent elbow from shoulder point to wrist can be useful.
- The underarm to hem length at the side.
- The waist measurement.
- The hip measurement.

Every body shape is different. Please note these are just numbers, and have no social or emotional value whatsoever. We can get very worked up about our numbers. They are not a scale to measure our worth, just numbers.

Check these measurements on your traced out pattern, including an allowance for ease. Lengthen or shorten the garment, adjust the neck or sleeves. Cut out and colour extra strips of paper to represent cables, zig-zags or chevrons. Experiment with pockets, bands, Fair Isle or other patterns or motifs. Place them at random until you find the perfect arrangement and balance. The advantage of working from a paper pattern is that you can experiment before you knit and during the knitting you can check your progress. It is so easy and it allows you to be the DESIGNER.

Working out the tension

Take your washed and dried sample and pin it on to a board, without stretching, wrong side up. It is easier to count the rows and stitches on the wrong side. Place a pin about ½ an inch (1 cm) from the right hand bottom corner and measure exactly 4 inches (10cm) across the

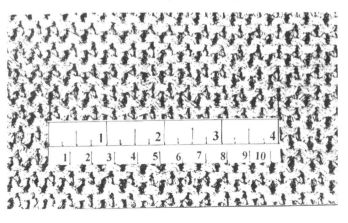

Working out the tension. Work from the wrong side of your tension square and count the number of stitches. This sample has 12½ stitches to every 4 inches, or 12 stitches to every 10cm. Do the same vertically, counting the number of rows.

154

knitting and place another pin. Now measure up the knitting for 4 inches (10 cm), and place a pin there and on the other side to make a square.

Carefully count the number of stitches across and rows up. The larger the sample, the more accurate, so don't be tempted to make it less than 4 inches square (10 x 10 cm). Include half stitches as well because they can effect the final count.

Let us take a really simple example to try out the method. If your finished bust size including ease is 40 inches (102cm), then the front will be 20 inches (51 cm) across, and the back will be 20 inches (51 cm) also. On your tension square you have counted, say 23 stitches across the four inches (10cm), therefore 4 inches multiplied by 5 = 20 inches, so cast on 23 x 5 = 115 stitches for the front or back of the garment. If it was 23 ½ stitches to every 4 inches, round it up to make the total 115 + 2 ½ stitches (5 half stitches) = 118 stitches.

The length is calculated the same way, but there are usually fewer rows because the stitches tend to be longer than wider. In this sample there were 20 rows to every 4 inches (10cm) and a back length of 30 inches. Divide 30 inches by 4 inches (20 rows) = 7 ½ which is 140 rows plus 2 inches (10 rows) = 150 rows.

In real life it is rare for it to work out so neatly, so just add the extra stitches or rows as required. Many people like to work on proper knitting graph paper and carefully transfer these measurements and calculations and all the shaping onto the paper. Other people are happy to work on plain paper and keep checking the knitting against it. There are as many ways of designing and calculating as there are knitters, and if your method works for you, then it is the right way to do it. With silk, the most important aspect is to work out the calculations on the washed sample. Silk does not shrink but it will drop for sure.

It is usual to start by casting on for the back or front, but priceless Secret Number Five, is to start with the sleeves first. They have relatively few stitches, so it is easy to experiment with the tension and pattern, and there is very little to undo if you don't like it.

Knitting jacket in hand spun, hand dyed, hand knitted silk, adapted from a painting by Robert Rooney

Spin your silk to the thickness you require for your garment

There are other very good reasons for starting with the sleeves. The final tension cannot be worked out until you know exactly how much it will drop after it is washed. By completing the sleeve, and then drawing around it on a sheet of paper to record its original unwashed size, before washing and drying it, you can really see the changes. Allowance can be made when deciding on the exact tension and needle size.

The washed sleeve can be adjusted as required. If it has a shaped head, and needs to be longer or shorter, undo it back to the armhole, unravel the rows, or add more before shaping the head again. If it is not wide enough, undo it back to the part where it begins to be too narrow, then increase at the side edges more frequently. It will probably need to be washed again, but once this sleeve is just right, then knit the other sleeve, using the washed and corrected first sleeve as a pattern. You now have two sleeves that are exactly right and they are perfect for using to calculate exactly the number of stitches and rows for the body of the garment

Once you know your yarn and knitting tension there is an argument for knitting both sleeves at the same time, especially if you are using a complicated pattern or a variety of colours. Cast on using one ball for the first sleeve, and then take another ball and cast on for the second sleeve on the same needles. With this method the sleeves are sure to match.

Now for the body of the garment and Secret Number Six. When using handspun silk, wool or any yarn where the colour is uneven, it is always better to knit the front(s) and back as one, so that the colour is consistent, especially across the two fronts. It may seem daunting to have so many stitches, but the result is always worth it and if you are doing competition work, it is essential. Add extra stitches for the front bands.

Silk is not very elastic, so if the bottom welt or band is ribbed, then reduce the number of stitches you cast on by 1 in 8. Our sample had 115 stitches for each front and back, so doubling that would make it 230 stitches all around. Divide that by 8, which is approximately 29. The number therefore to cast on is 230 minus 29 = 201 stitches. After the welt is completed these 29 stitches will be evenly increased across the last row making it 230 again. Even a garter stitch band benefits from being a little firmer, and so use the 1 in 8 calculation for that too. Sleeve cuffs are adjusted by 1 in 4 stitches.

Single and Double Cast On

Single cast on

There are lots of different methods of casting on but silk is slippery and the most foolproof method is to knit the cast on. To get a nice ropy edge that is elastic and wears well, use the double knitted cast on method, putting the needle between the stitches. This is quick and stable and does not require any calculations, you just knit up the number of stitches you want. If you want a more fragile edge for a lacy finish, with little loops that are easy to pick up for a crochet, picot or folded hem, then use a single knitted cast on, inserting the needle only through the front of the stitch.

Double cast on

Increasing can be done by wrapping the yarn around the needle, by knitting twice into the stitch or by picking up the loop between the stitches, depending on how open an effect is required. To give a fully-fashioned look and make sewing up easier, knit 2 or 3 stitches from the outer edge before you K2tog to decrease, or increase into the next stitch.

When picking up for the neck, leave one clear stitch along each side before the K2tog, Leave the centre stitches of both front and back on a spare needle, rather than casting off, to help keep a smooth finish. If there are too many stitches, they can be decreased evenly during the first rib row.

Short row shaping for shoulders and sleeves

For a professional finish without the steps and stairs of casting off in groups of stitches, use the short row method to shape the shoulders. Count the number of stitches for the shoulder before you start shaping, and divide by three. For example, if you have 30 stitches, there will be three groups of ten stitches. For the left

Short row shaping

shoulder, and starting at the armhole edge and right side facing, knit across all 30 stitches. Next row, purl to the last 10 stitches, turn and slip the next stitch and knit to the neck edge. Next row, purl 10 stitches, turn, slip next stitch and knit to neck edge. All the stitches remain on the needle, but the shoulder has been shaped. Slipping the stitch when turning still leaves a little hole and that can be disguised in a final complete row by knitting into the back of the loop between the stitches where you have turned, and knitting it together with the next stitch. Continue to the end, eliminating the other hole also. To increase the angle of the shoulder, divide the stitches into four or even five groups rather than three. The right shoulder has the shaping reversed so begin at the neck edge and knit to the last 10 stitches, turn, slip the first stitch and purl back to the neck edge. Knit 10 stitches, turn, slip the next stitch and purl to the neck. Knit across, eliminating the holes by knitting the loop between the stitches with the next stitch.

The shoulders on the back of the garment and the head of a classic sleeve are done exactly the same way, with equal shaping on both sides. Knit the back to the same length as the fronts before shaping the shoulders. Turn on 10 stitches like the fronts. Knit to the last 10 stitches, turn, slip the next stitch and purl to the last 10 stitches. Turn, slip the next stitch and knit to the last 20 stitches. Turn, slip the next stitch and purl to the last 20 stitches. Turn, slip the next stitch and knit to the last 30 stitches. Turn, slip the next stitch and purl to the end. Do a final knit row, eliminating the little holes and leaving all the stitches on the needle, ready to graft on to the fronts.

The classic sleeve is done the same way. You might like to first try out the shaping on a sample, and then lay it on your paper pattern to gauge the shape. Complete your sleeve to the required length at the underarm, and cast off the 3-5 stitches as usual. Decide how steep you want the curve. Turning on 3 stitches will give a steep curve, 6, 9, 12 etc an increasingly shallow curve. Knit across to the last 3 stitches. Turn, slip the next stitch and purl back to the last 3 stitches to match. Turn, slip the next stitch and knit to the last 6 stitches. Turn, slip the next stitch and purl to the last 6 stitches. Turn and continue in this way making the curve even on both sides until it is the shape you require. All the stitches remain on the needles, so when you come to graft it into the armhole, it is just as easy as a straight edge. It sounds far more complicated than it really is, and it does give a beautifully smooth finish to the sleeve and you have control over its shape at all times.

Grafting

This is a technique that gives a perfect finish, strong, even, smooth and essential for competition work. Many people like to use a needle and thread to do the grafting, but that will not be strong enough to take the strain on the shoulders and set-in sleeves, although it may be perfect for joining side and other seams.

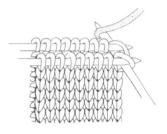

Grafting: Place the two needles together and, using a third needle, knit as one stitch. Repeat for the next two stitches and cast the first stitch off over the second stitch.

Three needle knitted graft. Graft the shoulders by placing the fronts and back together, right side facing, and starting at the outside shoulder. Place the right hand needle into the first stitch of both needles, ie of the front and back and knit both as one stitch, repeat with the next stitch on each needle, and draw the second stitch over the first one to cast off. Continue until all the stitches have been cast off.

To reinforce the shoulder, use either smaller needles or knit more tightly when casting off. They can also be reinforced at a later stage by crocheting along the cast off edge, missing a stitch every so often to tighten it as required. It can look almost gathered, but when it is pressed, the seam will lie flat and will not stretch further.

Grafting in the sleeves. First graft the shoulders. Leave all the stitches on the needle after completing the sleeve. Divide the total number of stitches on the needle in half. With the two right sides together, and the garment in the front and the sleeve on the needle behind, pin the centre stitch of the sleeve onto the outside edge of the shoulder seam. Now place a pin at each underarm and then divide each section again by pinning the sleeve and armhole together halfway between the underarm and the shoulder. The sleeve and the armhole are now pinned together evenly in five places.

The edge of the garment will look as if it has 'loops and knobs' and the usual proportion for picking up the edge is 'loop, knob, loop, miss a knob' ie pick up the end stitch on 3 out of 4 rows. You may have to adjust this, which is why it is very important to pin the garment and sleeve evenly together. It is a bit experimental, but start casting off at the underarm edge and pick up a loop first and knit it together with the first stitch on the needle. The next stitch is a knob, so pick it up and the next one on the needle and knit it, and pass the first stitch over the second to cast off. Repeat with the next stitch, which is a loop but skip the next knob. Continue across the whole edge.

This method looks as good on the inside as the outside, with all the stitches evenly incorporated. The joining up is done as part of the knitting, not something to be tackled later. This method works equally well whether it is a square set sleeve, dropped shoulder or round headed sleeve.

Raglan sleeves can be knitted into the garment from the top neck down or the underarm up. This is a very good shape for comfort, and for incorporating Fair Isle, fancy textures or pattern. Use a circular or set of needles and incorporate small balls of yarn, so the colour is spread evenly right round the yoke. For comfort and fit, short rows must be incorporated across the back neck to make it higher than the front. Also expect the shape to increase (going down from the neck) or decrease, (near the neck) rather quickly, to allow enough breadth around the shoulders. Keep checking your knitting against the template of your jersey.

Folded hems. To make them lie flat, use needles two sizes smaller than for the body of the garment. Cast on loosely with a single cast on and continue for the depth of hem as required, for example 7 rows, ending wrong side facing. Knit this row to form a neat base line, or repeat (K2tog, Yarn Over to make 1) for a picot edge. Stocking stitch another 7 rows, ending with the wrong side facing. Take another fine needle and working from the far end towards the yarn at the right hand edge, pick up all the cast on loops and count them to check there are exactly the same number of stitches on both needles. Fold the knitting in half wrong sides together, and with the two needles together, and using a third needle pick up the first stitch from each needle, purl together but do not cast off. Repeat for the next two stitches, and continue until all the cast on stitches have been incorporated into the main body of the work. Change needles to two sizes larger for the body of the garment. Tucks can be made at regular intervals using the same technique.

Backwards knitting is Secret Number Seven. To save constantly turning your work, use backward knitting for all narrow bands and complicated Fair Isle designs because this method allows the pattern to be worked entirely from the front. Knit across the row as usual. Keep the yarn in the right hand, and without changing the needles or turning around the work, place the point of the left hand needle into the back of the end stitch. Using the point of the first finger on the right hand, draw the yarn behind, over and towards the front of the needle, then draw it through to make a stitch. Continue to the end of the row. Carry any coloured yarns loosely at the back and twist them every 3-4 stitches. It is better to be rather loose because nothing can stop the puckering if it is too tight. If you tend to be a tight knitter, consider using a larger size needle when doing Fair Isle. To do rib or moss stitch, knit as above, but when doing a purl stitch, bring the yarn forward between the stitches and place the point of the left hand needle behind and into the back of the stitch on the right hand needle. Draw the yarn under the front right hand needle and pull it through to form the new stitch, finally re-placing it on the left hand needle. Return the yarn to the back.

When Front Bands have been knitted separately, wash them also before sewing them onto the garment, as the length alters rather unpredictably, and they are much easier to adjust before sewing in place. With a knitted-on band, pick up 3 out of every 4 'knobs' and 'loops' along the edge and at the required depth, cast off or fold it and graft it off. Another hem finish that is successful with silk uses fine stocking stitch,

Veronica Jersey, Handspun and knitted tussah silk with three pearl shell buttons on the shoulder.

Bombyx mori jacket with crochet edges and cables of dark tussah silk from Botswana.

Five colours with black. This jersey uses ever changing combinations of the five colours for stripes, slashes and crosses.

without any rib to keep it flat. The edge forms a smart rolled edge when it is loosely cast off.

Buttonholes can be done from the right side, without turning the work. Cast off the 2 stitches for the buttonhole and continue to the end of the row. On the return, purl twice into the last stitch before the gap, and then twice into the next stitch across the gap, and continue to the end of the row.

Trouble shooting

Colour change is the bane of any knitter's life, especially with handspun. Always try to have sufficient silk to complete the garment. Top quality new silk should be even in colour and quality. Priceless Secret Number Eight is that if you are using both old and new silk, then keep the two lots absolutely separate. Mark one bobbin 'old' and spin all the old silk on that one, and all the new silk on another, then ply them together. It is essential to be consistent or it will show up when it is knitted.

Try to complete the spinning before you start to knit. Wash the skeins and check them very carefully for the slightest differences in colour. Group the skeins into shades, then ball them up into large balls to limit the feelings of confusion later when you are no longer sure which ball goes into which pile. You could tie matching pieces of coloured thread onto the balls, or stick a little sticker on the ends of the yarn, anything that will help to differentiate them. Once they have been balled, it is very hard to see the differences. Then weigh the silk and check you have sufficient for the garment. If you have another completed handspun silk jersey then weigh it, and that will give you an idea of how much spun silk you will need, then allow another 50-100 grams so you have plenty on hand to choose from. In general a small jersey takes about 350-400 grams and a large one 500-650 grams.

Insufficient Matching Silks

If you think you might be short of silk yarn, lessen the impact and turn it to your advantage by:

- Working the front and back as one so the colour goes right around especially if the garment has a front opening where a colour change will be noticeable.
- Knit to the underarm on the body and sleeves and transfer them all onto a circular needle, knitting the yoke as a contrast.
- Knit from the neck down as a yoke or raglan, working the sleeves and body evenly, so any colour change will be balanced and the same over all.
- Divide the remaining silk in half and knit the sleeves from the top down, so that the tops match the garment and despite the change in yarn, the bottoms will match each other.
- A change of texture will help to disguise a colour change so consider bands of basket, moss, garter, rib or other flat patterns.
- If you run out before doing the bands, consider crocheting them in a different or contrasting shade.
- Keep the finer yarn for all the bands and cuffs, collars, pockets etc, and use the main yarn for the body and sleeves.
- Use three balls of different yarns. Knit one row in A, the next in B and the third in C. If they are fairly close in colour, the overall look is surprisingly even. If you have only two shades, then it will look rather striped, so still use three balls, even if two are the same.
- Create a shaded or ombré effect, by starting with the darkest or lightest colour yarn and graduating the change.
- Even a simple Fair Isle pattern can give a great lift to a garment and disguise a colour change problem. Include bands of contrast on the body or sleeves or around the yoke.
- You could treat the different shades as an asset and do the whole or part of the garment striped, in moss stitch, or salt and pepper, or alternating light and dark stitches

Rose Jacket.
Hand spun and hand knitted rose jacket, both natural and bleached tussah silk.

· If you discover after the garment is knitted that there is a colour change, even after the garment has been washed, you could consider dyeing it, but the change may still show. Unfortunately there is really no alternative but to undo the offending part, remove the yarn and knit it up again. It will be fine for cuffs and bands, as nothing is ever wasted.

Reduce the effect of dropping and stretching:

· Use needles two sizes smaller than recommended in the commercial pattern.
· Knit the garment side to side. It will not drop as much, but could get rather baggy.
· Spin or ply shiny silk with noil or other novelty silks that are textured and not so slippery.
· Experiment with cables and other patterns that tend to pull the knitting in.
· Knit into the backs of the stitches.
· Take care with lacy patterns, by using smaller needles because the lacy part is likely to stretch more than the plain areas.
· Knit lycra into all cuffs and bands.
· Use a firm ribbed band to hold the bloused effect.
· Choose a style with a ribbed waist section, threaded with a tie.
· Line the garment.
· Combine silk with other fibres, wool, mohair or cashmere, but not cotton because it will drop as much as silk
· Only use plied silk for knitting because handspun singles have a tendency to shift on the diagonal. This will also happen when one thread is plied fractionally tighter than the other.

Knitting elastic or lycra is sold on small bobbins in a limited range of colours, including clear, natural, beige and black. It is invaluable when knitting bands in silk or cotton, both of which have little elasticity. Try adding it when plying, but it seems to work in more evenly when just knitted in along with the yarn.

Joining the yarn Silk does not look good knotted in the middle of a row. It is better to make the join at the end of the row, but occasionally it must be joined, so use the split thread technique. Take the ends of both the old and new yarns, and split them back about 2 inches into their separate singles. If more than two, or if they are bulky, tease out and discard the third singles from each end. Now, top and tail the yarns and roll one single thread from each yarn together between your palms, and finally roll them both together to re-form into one thread. It will be too fragile to take any strain but it can be knitted and will not show. It is a personal choice as to whether or not you lick your fingers because any dampness may cause the joined silk to show as gray streaks in your knitting that may not come out in the wash, although it will make it easier to roll.

Drawing out a thread because the garment is too long or too short

Use the pulled thread method. Work from the wrong side and choose a row without pattern. Pick up one stitch loop, about three stitches from the edge, at the desired position and gently draw the thread out, moving it right across the knitting until it can be pulled no more. Snip this thread at the far side, and pull it right out. The work can now be gently drawn apart and the stitches picked up.

To finish the garment at this new shorter length, just pick up the stitches and knit the band or cast off.

If the work is to be lengthened, the stitches may be easy to pick up, but they will be lying in an odd way because you will now be working in the opposite direction from when it was first knitted. To disguise the alteration, consider doing a few rows of textured pattern or using a contrasting colour and turning it into a feature before continuing to the required length.

Short lengths of coloured silk yarn

·   Do a multi-colour or knitted patchwork design.

·   Tie the threads all together and knit the ends in as you go for a random effect.

·   Leave the tied ends showing on the right side as a decorative feature.

·   Use the short lengths to over-knit or Swiss darn on the right side to give a Fair Isle look.

·   Chain stitch on the surface, or include embroidery.

·   Short lengths of dyed silk are ideal to make tassels, plaits and cables.

Washing Silk

Silk is washed after it has been spun, plied and skeined to set the twist and condition the fibre. The garment must also be washed after it is knitted. Do it before its final sewing up, because it is apt to drop and adjustments are easier before the final finishing.

Fill a large bowl with hand hot water and add a dash of liquid silk wash or mild detergent to each 4-6 litres of water and stir vigorously to make it sudsy. Drop in the skeins or garment and pat them gently until they are immersed. Don't leave them to soak, but draw them to the side and squeeze them gently, then let out the soapy water. Rinse twice in clear water of the same temperature. To the second rinse add your choice of a little fabric softener, drop of baby oil, lavender oil or vinegar to the water. Squeeze the silk items and roll them in a towel, or place them in a laundry bag and spin them in the washer, just for the last cycle to remove as much water as possible. Shake them out.

They will look really dreadful, and you may fear the worst. When silk is wet, the fibres stick together and they become very stiff and unpleasant. If you have spun the fibre around air, then Secret Number Nine is to give the skeins or garment a really good flick and shake before hanging them out of direct sunlight to dry. Support a heavy garment over a rack, but don't lie it flat on a towel as it will take too long to dry and will become stiff and hard. Finally, a few minutes in the

Handspun silk dyes easily and a Patchwork jacket is a grand way to combine the colours and use up scraps.

tumble drier also helps the fibres to spring back to life. A final gentle pressing on the inside of the garment, with the iron set on silk, or using a damp cloth, will help the gloss to return.

Some final tricks, especially if you just hate sewing up

- To make a pattern easier to read, enlarge on a copier machine, colour in, or draw it again using a child's school quad book.
- Always cast off rib bands in rib.
- If either the plain or purl rows tend to be a bit tight, this will show as a 2-row ridged look on the right side. Using one needle one size larger for the tight rows, should compensate and solve the problem.
- If you have a lot of ends of yarn to sew in at a seam, a flat fell seam will enclose them all and make a perfect finish.
- Knit the front bands at the same time as the garment but consciously knit them tighter, holding the silk more firmly in your hands to give a firmer tension as you knit.
- Knit on neck bands and collars.

Carnival feather jersey, using two types of silk in the stripes; filament silk plyed with handspun silk and handspun throwsters waste. The feathers are knitted in and the jersey is hand washable.

SILK GLOSSARY

Acanthus Stylized pattern of curling acanthus leaves frequently seen on Italian velvets and damasks.

Alamode, a la mode Thin light glossy silk.

All-overs Machine made patterned lace produced as yardage for dressmaking.

Antioch silk Named after the Syrian city famous in the 10-12th centuries as a textile market. General name for rich silks from the East, including a brocaded silk figured with animals, gazelles, birds whose beaks, heads, feet and roundels on the wings are highlighted in gold thread.

Appliqué Method of attaching individual motifs onto another background. Used in stump work, court and ecclesiastical embroidery and to attach lace motifs onto an openwork background.

Arabesques Scroll motifs with interlace and intertwining leaves, branches, curving lines, low relief decoration popular in Rococo embroideries and tapestries of Oriental and Moorish origin.

Armozeen, Armazine, Armoisin Heavy black silk, used for clerical gowns and mourning bands.

Arras Important Flemish weaving centre from 1313, also a rich tapestry fabric.

Attifet Heart shaped bonnet, with a dip in the middle of the forehead identified with Mary Queen of Scots.

Aumoniére (Fr) *aumone*, Bag for coins, alms, worn on the belt by men and women.

Aune (Fr) Old measure, about 1.18 metres.

Balanced yarns Same thickness and twist given to both warp and weft yarns.

Baldachin, baldaquin Rich patterned silk from Baghdad, also silk and gold canopy or tester suspended over a bed.

Baldric Wide sash or band of silk or leather, worn crosswise over the chest and used to carry a sword, horn etc. Embroidered or edged with small bells, later fastened onto the left hip.

Bale Variable weight of raw silk wrapped up in cotton. Shanghai and Japanese bales weigh between 55-65kg, European and Italian bales weigh 90-100kg, (200 lbs), Canton bale 48kgs, Indian bale around 20kgs.

Baleine Whalebone.

Ball warps After the warp has been wound onto the warping mill it is roped and balled in preparation for handweaving.

Basque Extension, like a short skirt attached to the bodice at the waistline.

Baroque Florid 17th century European, heavily ornate style with large scrolls, rich colours, exuberant, lavish use of metal thread work and bold crewel work designs.

Basine Silk fabric with two sets of warps that float over two weft threads and interlace with a third.

Basinetto, Ricotto, Bisou, Bisu, Basin refuse
Waste silk from the innermost part of the cocoon, left over after reeling, made into spun silk.

Basquine, basquina, vasquine Bodice, with tabs or a basque, a wide underskirt worn with a farthingale in 16th century Spain, in England a petticoat.

Bast liquor Acidified soap solution used to degum cocoons and in dyeing to level the colour.

Batten Flat sword shaped piece of wood with one sharp edge, used to beat down the weft on certain looms.

Batting Thick layer of fluffy silk used for quilting and insulation of quilts and jackets etc.

Bavolet 16th century woman's headdress, by the 18th century it was a cap covered with strip of linen that hung behind, over the shoulders also a soft frill attached to the back of a bonnet.

Bedfordshire Maltese Lace Bobbin-made lace in black silk copied from Maltese lace.

Bell Package of Mawata caps, around 500 grams, can be handspun, thigh rolled, used in embroidery, paper, felt.

Bengaline Lustrous all silk or mixed fibre fabric, fine silk warp and thick silk corded weft rib of silk, cotton or wool, originally from Bengal in India, strong, durable, drapes well, used for women clothes and millinery.

Berlin silk High twisted cordonnet or crochet silk thread, made by twisting together 4-8 single yarns with a Z twist and 3 of these with an S twist.

Berretta Cappuccio, brimless hat.

Bertha, berthe Large lace or fine silk collar which formed a cape over the shoulders and ended with lappets tucked into the waistband, popular in 1830s.

Betsie Mid 16th century multi-tiered lace collar, called a cherusse during the first Empire.

Bezants Coins, ornaments stamped in pure gold or silver sewn onto garments for decoration.

Biancheria Underclothes, including shirts, handkerchiefs, stockings, hose, coifs and collars.

Bias   Diagonal line at 45 degrees angle to the grain of the fabric.

Biggin   Close fitting baby's cap, 16th century.

Binding warp   Secondary warp that holds down the weft floats, pattern or brocading.

Bistanclaque   (Fr) Traditional manually operated loom.

Bizarre silks   Exotic woven silk, with non-directional design, Oriental, Indian and Turkish styles fashionable in Europe between late 17th and early 18th century, probably originating in Lyon.

Blackwork   16th century Spanish or Holbein embroidery, black silk usually on linen, stylistically related to Arabic and Moorish designs, small scale, angular repeated motifs, in double running stitch, flowers, birds, animals and insects.

Blaze, Floss   (Fr) spelaia (Italian), short fuzzy fibres on the outside of the cocoon spun first to support the silkworm while it spins its cocoon. Used for spun silks and lightly twisted dyed embroidery thread.

Bleeding   Fault where one colour seeps into another.

Block   Piece of carved wood, loaded with dye and pressed onto the fabric leaving a pattern.

Blonde   18th-19th century natural coloured, continuous silk bobbin lace, using two heavy lustrous silk threads, often dyed black.

Boarding   Process of shaping silk stockings by pulling over a heated metal form after they have been dyed.

Bobbinet   Fine six sided net, originally made with bobbins until John Heathcote in 1808, invented a machine, based on Bucks point ground.

Bodice, Body, 'pair of bodies'   16th century, close fitting upper part of a woman's dress, either belonging to the gown or worn as a separate under bodice, of canvas or stiffened with whalebone. **Bodice en coeur**   Heart-shaped bodice with narrow pleats at the edge of the neckline.

Bodice a l'enfant   Drawstring neckline.

Boiled off cocoons   Unreelable, weak, stained or broken cocoons, opened during the boiling process, separated out as waste for spinning into spun silk.

Bolt   Full length of fabric either rolled or folded onto a tube or card.

Bolting cloth   (Fr), *blutage*, sifting. Fine plain gauze weave ungummed sheer silk cloth, known as millers gauze, also used as a base for screen printing or for embroidery, the warp is high twist organzine, the weft still has sericin.

Bombast   Cotton, tow, rag stuffing used to pad out 16th – 17th century breeches, sleeves and doublets.

Bombazine   19th century black twill weave silk or half silk, fashionable for mourning clothes.

Bombyx mori   Domesticated silkmoth grey-white in colour, feeds on mulberry leaves, lays between 350 and 600 eggs, produces white or pastel coloured cocoons, the basis for most of the world's production of filament silk yarn.

Book of silk   Parcel of raw silk hanks weighing 2 kgms, or 4 – 4 ½ lbs. A bale of Japanese silks contains 30 books of up to 60 skeins. Chinese books were heavier. 18th century 3000 cocoons make one book. Now usually 16-20 skeins of raw silk, packed under pressure into a parcel weighing between 2-2.5kgms.

Book of the Prefect   Valuable source book for the Byzantine silk industry, issued by the Byzantine Emperor Leo VI in 911-12, details the restrictions and activities of the manufacturers and merchants in Constantinople.

Boot hose   Either long or short socks worn inside the boots to protect the embroidered, lacy or decorated wide topped silk stockings. Very popular with 17th century Cavaliers.

Borato   Lightweight silk or silk and wool, produced in England during the 17th century.

Bordadillo   Floral Spanish silk taffeta, used for women's wear.

Bouclé   Yarn with one or more looped threads plied onto the core yarn. In a woven fabric, bouclé texture is achieved through using a looped or metallic secondary yarn in the weft.

Boudoir cap   Lace trimmed cap for wearing indoors often with a negligée.

Bouffant   18th century puffed up style of skirt, also hairstyle.

Bouillon   Bubbly effect on surface of the fabric, 19th century, also gold thread.

Bourette   (Fr) *Bourre de soie*, Dull rough textured silk floss yarn or fabric, plain or twill weave. Made from the waste from the schappe degumming process and the short fibre noils, including discarded and crushed chrysalids that present as black or brown specks. Resistant to wrinkling, but shrinks during first wash, absorbs dyes well, not very colour fast, especially to sunlight, used for clothing and furnishing fabric.

Bourrelet   (Fr) *bourrer*, to stuff. Padded brim of man's hood, or woman's headdress,

Bourse   (Fr)   Purse or pochette for carrying cosmetics, around 1730 referred to a decorative bag which restrained and contained the hair.

Braguette, codpiece Small bag of matching material attached by points to men's breeches.

Braid, Braiding Narrow, flat, round, woven or plaited edging or cord, used for trimming.

Brandenburgs Long loose overcoat with two buttons linked together with decoratively twisted cords, from 17th century, sometimes just fastenings.

Brassieres, brasserolles 15th century bolero jacket, usually black silk or velvet worn under the robe. In 16th - 17th century France a short bodice for negligée wear, modern French a child's vest.

Breeches Polybius says worn by the Gaul in 325BC using the Greek name, *paison*, Persian trousers, seen on coins of Santones and Pictones and on the triumphal arch at Orange. Romans adopted them for their troups, as did Gauls, the Steppe nomads, Sythians, then the Germans and the Celts. In 16th century known as **netherhosen** and **trunkhose**.

Brides Generic term for bars or needle lace links between motifs.

Brigandine Silk brocade, velvet with small repeating pattern of circles, dots enclosing a star.

Brightening Use of an emulsion of olive oil and washing soda to oil the silk before scroping.

Bright silk, Brillante Weavers' term for the glossiness of the silk. Completely degummed thrown silk.

Brin, bave Each filament of silk exuded by the silkworm via the spinneret located under its jaws. Two brins with the gum sericin, harden on exposure to air to form a single silk fibre, a bave.

Broadcloth Silk, cotton or woollen cloth with a dull lustre, tight plain weave, often made of spun silk giving a gentle drape. Solid colours and stripes, or small dobby designs, eg silk shirting cloth and Fuji silk, 1 – 1½ m wide.

Brocade (Latin) *brocare* to figure. Stiff, elaborately patterned, compound weave, gold or silver fabric, used for dress or furnishings with floral and scroll patterns imitating embroidery, not reversible. First produced in China and Japan using twill weave, satin ground in the West. Hand manipulated or used a drawboy who sat above the loom pulling the warp threads to a set pattern, now done on a mechanical or computerized jacquard loom.

Brocatelle, or brocantine Satin or twill figure on a plain satin ground. Unrelated to brocade, similar to a damask weave, usually only one or two colours. Has a double warp that gives a distinctive three-dimensional quilted or blister effect. Now made in wool, cotton, silk or man-made fibres, and used for upholstery or drapery. Lightweight cloths are used for dresses. *Brocatelle ~ passementerie,* made with a cotton warp and wool filling.

Brocarts (Fr) Fabric heavily interwoven with gold and silver threads.

Broché (Fr) Figured, or to sew, silk or cotton fabrics giving an embroidered effect and satin pattern on the surface. *Broché coutils* is a jacquard woven cloth used for corsets, *broché* quilt for bedcovers. The warp has two alternating colours forming both background and pattern, hiding the weft completely.

Broken end Cut or untied warp thread.

Bullion Thick twisted fringe, cord, sometimes made from gold, silver or metallic threads.

Bum-roll, farthingale roll Padded sausage shaped cushion tied to the back waist, to hold the skirt out at a fashionable angle.

Burnt out Printing process used to produce opaque or translucent patterns by applying acid to dissolve the fibres supplementary to the ground fabric.

Busc, busk, buske Long pieces of wood, whalebone, ivory, horn steel etc, placed in the centre front of the corset to keep the body erect.

Bustle, tournure (Fr) Wire or whalebone framework cage, or canvas half-cage worn at the back to hold the skirt out, worn in the 17th century, at their height in 1880.

Butterfly cap 18th century, Small lace cap, wired in a butterfly shape, decorated with lappets, jewels, flowers, court wear.

Byssus Also known as Sea silk or pinna, the fibre secreted by the shellfish *Pinna nobilis*. The short fibres have been spun in Southern Italy and made into gloves and stockings.

Calash Folding, silk covered frame for the vast wigs worn by women in the 18th century.

Calendering Machine with heavy heated rollers, giving the cloth a very smooth finish. Some rollers have an engraved pattern to give a moiré, glazed or watered effect.

Camelot 16th – 17th century brocade.

Camisole Loose bodice worn over the corset, formerly known as a petticoat bodice.

Camlets, Camoca Plain ribbed weave, originally a light rich fabric of silk and camelhair, produced in 12th century Turkey, widely used for cloaks and other outer garments. *Camoquos d'Outremer*, from Jerusalem, possibly silk and wool.

170

Canions	Fabric extension of men's truck hose, not usually knitted, popular mid 1580's.
Cannons	Lace or ribbon knee decorations sometimes attached to men's boot hose, forming flounces, or inner boot lining, worn by Cavaliers in the 17th century.
Cannage	Effect of warp tension on the silk cloth, a defect, or as in taffetas, it forms ripples of high and low lustre.
Cannelé	Weave with a ribbed surface formed by warp floats.
Canton silk	Hand-reeled cocoons from Southern China, tends to be uneven, soft, lustrous, fluffy but rather weak.
Canuts	Colloquial term originally used for the Lyons velvet makers from the area around La Croisse-Rouge, taken from the name of the knife used to cut the velvet pile.
Capella	Silk dress material made with a 2/1 twill weave.
Caraco	Gown fashionable in France, late 1780s, long waisted and fitted with a peplum.
Carding, combing	Processes to straighten out or tidy loose or matted fibres preparatory to spinning. Fibres are drawn between rollers or wooden panels with carding cloth of hooked wires or pins. Aligns the fibres, removes short staples and impurities in preparation for spinning.
Cartoon	Design for embroidery or tapestry, sometimes full sized or monochrome allowing for colour choices.
Cartwright, Edmund	(1743-1823) Inventor of the power loom, 1785-90, and wool combing machine, clergyman, poet, farmer, secretary to the Royal Society of Arts.
Cashmire de Soie	Fine silk woven with a finish to resemble cashmere fabric.
Caul	Decorated gold or silver net, 15th century headdress, the side hair was contained in pouches of reticulated gold mesh, decorated with pearls, 16th century a trellised skull cap, 18th century base for wigs.
Cendal, cendaulx, sendal	Lightweight plain weave silk similar to taffeta, often measured by weight rather than width or length. From Asia Minor, initially an expensive fabric, but by 17th century widely used for linings.
Chambon, Croissure (Fr) **Tavelette** (It)	composed of two groups of filaments which cross between the unreeled cocoons and the distributor on the reeling machine.
Chantilly	Fine matt black or blonde silk bobbin lace, fashionable from c1750-1900 with font chant ground, made near Paris, and at Le Puy.
Chapeau bras	Flat hat, slung over the shoulder by its ties, not designed to be worn.
Chardonnet	Made from two thick soft silk yarns, spun together loosely.
Charmeuse	Satin weave fabric, with a soft lustrous face and dull reverse, drapes well, tightly twisted warp, crepe or spun silk weft, weight ranges from 10 to 18mm, used for lingerie. Variations include sand-washed and crepe backed satin, expensive heavy weight used for evening dresses in the early 20th century.
Chatelaine	Decorative belt with scissors, watch, fan, needlework tools, made of gold silver steel etc, popular between 1740 and 1890.
Chemical Lace	Machine embroidery on silk ground, immersed in chlorine or caustic solution, destroys the background fabric, leaving filigree of lace with distinct fuzzy edges, commercially produced 1880's.
Chemise, Camicia	(Fr). General term for a fine linen or silk undergarment with short sleeves, by 1785-1800 was shirt type garment, later came to mean slim unbelted day dress.
Chemisette	Soft piece of silk with tassels at each corner used to wrap around a precious book. In 18th-19th century was a modesty vest or false front to fill in a low neck.
Chenille (Fr)	Caterpillar, a velvet or tufted yarn, originally silk, introduced around 1770, could be couched onto the material or woven into rich silk brocades, also used for fringes.
Chiffon (Fr)	rag, piece of lace or ribbon. Fine matt gauzy semi-transparent silk muslin, made from high twist silk yarns, ranging from 50-100 twists per inch, gives a crepe feel and appearance, snags easily, includes **crepe, georgette, voile, organdie, grenadine** and **mousselline.**
China silk	From at least 1200BC, soft lightweight plain weave silk, known as **habutai, haj** or **paj, Fuji** or **Jap** silk from Japan, used mainly for linings, lingerie and scarves, frequently vat dyed in a full range of colours, inexpensive.
Chiné	Warp threads printed or dyed before weaving, giving a blurred pattern.
Chirimen	Heavy crepe silk, both plain and woven patterns used for expensive Japanese kimonos.

Chinoiserie   European designs imitated or inspired by Chinese patterns, important after the import of decorative wares from the East in the mid 17th century. Peak period 1760s, the style applied to all forms of decorative arts, including lacquer, furniture, textiles, needlework.

Chitterlings   Linen or lace men's neck frills worn during the late 18th-19th century.

Chopines   Shoes, four to five inches high with a cork or wooden soles.

Chrysalis or pupa   Third stage in the metamorphosis of the silkworm, from egg, to caterpillar, to chrysalis to moth. A firm brown case inside the cocoon, where the caterpillar changes into a silk moth.

Cioppa   Woman's over garment related to the houppelande, in Northern Italy called a **pellanda, copelanda, vesta sacco,** or **vestimento**. Always lined, open down the front, had sleeves, often voluminous displayed borders of fine fur.

Ciré (Fr)   Wax or resin coating applied to silk satins and black silks to give a very shiny surface.

Clavi, clavus   Purple stripes to denote rank and position, sewn or woven vertically on Roman tunics and toga, worn by senate members and other high dignitaries.

Classification   of silk threads by winding them evenly over a board so the defects can be identified and yarn graded against standard photograph, expressed as a percentage. **Cleanness** Could be waste matter, knots, hairiness, bad cast, slubs, loops and loose ends. **Cohesion,** Degree to which the silk fibres stick together. **Neatness** Important overall assessment of the uniformity of the raw silk, noting the number of defects, generally due to poor reeling, leaving fine end loops, loose sections, knots, lumps, ruffling, loose brins etc. **Selection** Separation out of all silk cocoons, that are over or under-sized, doubles, poor colour, stained, compared to the finest cocoons, known as 'royals'. **Uniformity** Measurement indicating the regularity and size of the raw silk fibre.

Clock   Embroidery or decoration running up the side of the stocking from the heel.

Cloqué (Fr)   Blistered, any fabric with a raised embossed or puckered surface, such as seersucker, obtained from weaving a smooth filament yarn together with a highly twisted crepe yarn. Sometimes made with a modified double weave or passed through heated rollers or treated with a special chemical.

Cloth of gold, or silver   Elaborate, extremely expensive woven silk fabric heavily enriched with metallic threads in either or both warp and weft.

Coat of Arms   Arrangement of heraldic emblems often on a shield shape, a major status symbol, indicating an important or distinctive family line, originally worn by knights on their cloaks or mantles, over their armour to identify them in battle.

Cocoon   Protective outer layer of silk fibres spun by the silkworm during the fifth instar of its metamorphosis, when it changes from a caterpillar to a pupa, then a moth. The Bombyx mori cocoon is 2 to 4cm, can be oval or peanut shaped, white, pale green, yellow, cream, or pinkish. Wild tussah moths form much harder and tougher cocoons up to 15cm in length, silk from palest honey to rich treacly browns depending on the breed and amount of tannin in the food source. Cocoon requires gentle boiling in an alkali or soapy solution to soften the sericin so the fibre can be unreeled or spun.

Cocoon strippings   Waste silk from the inside of the cocoon, after the main filament has been reeled.

Codpiece   Decorated bag to conceal front opening and 'privy members' on men's hose, attached by points and laced to the doublet, or buckled to the belt. Could also serve as a pocket to hold money or a handkerchief. Fashionable in the 15th-16th century when doublets became shorter.

Coif coiffe, cale, (Fr) closely fitting cap or fitted linen bonnet, tied under the chin, worn under a helmet during the Middle Ages, often embroidered, still worn by judges, lawyers academics in 17th century.

Colbert, Jean Baptiste (1619-83) Assistant to Cardinal Mazarin, Louis XIV's Controller-General of Fiance from 1665. Favoured a protectionist economic policy, encouraging home production of silk rather than imported items.

Collet monté   Late 16th century ladies wired standup collar edged with lace.

Commode, Palisade   Silk covered wire frame to support fontage head-dress, of ribbons bows, lace etc, between 1680-1710.

Compenzine   Crinkly yarn made by plying together an untwisted yarn with a twisted one, making a tight hard and smooth thread, used for silk stockings.

Compound weave   Complex weave incorporating two or more sets of warp or weft threads, so one set appears on the face and the other on the reverse, eg damask, brocade.

Complex yarns   Fancy yarns, constructed in such a way as to produce a bulky or uneven texture.

Conch   Large head-dress of silk veils over a wire frame, worn in the late sixteenth and early 17th century

Coptic textiles   Egyptian textiles mostly wool and linen, occasionally silk, produced between the introduction of Christianity and the Arab conquest in 640AD.

Cordonnet   Waste silk lightly spun, used for fringes and outlining in bobbin and needle lace to give a raised effect. Could be stiffened with crin, ie horsehair as in Alencon lace or part of the fabric as with Brussels lace.

Corduroy   Cloth with cut pile in ribs or wales running parallel to the selvedge.

Core   Central yarn around which other yarns have been spun.

Cornely Machine   Machine used during the 19-20th c for embroidering net, often in chain stitch using coloured silks.

Corsage   18th century, upper or bodice part of dress.

Couching   Method of attaching threads, often silk, gold or silver by laying them on the surface of the textile, and over-sewing using a fine thread.

Course, row   Horizontal line of loops in knitting,

Couvrechefs   Fine head covering, includes **crispes, cambrey, relusant, cipré, boillez, kerchief** , possibly **veils**.

Crape   Stiff dull silk, usually dyed black, fashionable for mourning clothes.

Cravat, 1692.   Decorative neckwear or scarf tied loosely at the front, possibly from linen neckwear worn by Croatian regiment in 1660s, developed in 17th and 19th c. **Chaconne** Ribbon cravat, popular in the 17th c.

Crepe   Plain weave fabrics made up of tightly twisted yarn twisted specifically in an S or Z manner, and plyed in the same or contrary fashion. All crepe fabrics are treated with concentrated sulphuric acid, woven as raw silk and degummed after weaving to give a very flexible springy fabric with a soft drape and dull matt finish. Variations include **marocain, crepe georgette, Crepe de chine** which usually has 1600 to 2500 twists per metre, made from between 3 to 5 raw silk threads. **Crepon** silk or rayon, heavier weight dress fabric, crepe effect comes in the warp direction, produced by using different amounts of twist in the yarn, or by slackening the warp yarns.

Crimp   Both fibres and yarns, indicates the number of waves in the fibre or twists in the yarn in a unit length.

Crin, gut   Silk glands that have been removed from a mature silkworm before it spins its cocoon, approximately 18-20 inches long and transparent in water, used for the fine leader lines used by fishermen, also in surgery as drainage vessels and sutures.

Crinoline   18th-19th century Latin crinus, hair, (Fr) crin, and linum (Latin) linen. Petticoat stiffened with boning or horsehair to hold the skirt out into the fashionable bell shape in the 1840s. Quilted petticoats reinforced with whalebone were replaced by a light-weight metal cage.

Crompton, Samuel (1753-1827) inventor of the spinning mule, patented in 1779, combing the features of Hargreaves spinning jenny and Arkwrights water frame, was a weaver from Bolton.

Cropping   To trim the pile to an even length or to a pattern, or the surface of a smooth faced fabric to eliminate superfluous threads.

Cul-de-Paris, bustle   Worn to support the skirt when it was pulled up towards the back.

Culottes (Fr) Late 16th and early 17th century men's breeches. **Sans-culottes**, trousers rather than breeches, means 'without breeches', worn by revolutionaries to distinguish them from the aristocrats.

Cut pile velvet Loops formed when making the velvet pile, are later cut. Produced by double weaving or by looping an additional filling thread over the basic weave, then later cut to give tufted effect.

Cut-ups   Stockings or socks cut from machine knitted fabric, rather than shaped on the machine.

Cutwork   Small squares of fabric are removed, edged with buttonhole stitch and the inside used as a frame to rebuild an openwork decorative pattern, 16-17th century.

Damask   Originally a single colour, flat reversible, compound weave fabric of silk, cotton or linen mixture. Combining free floating warp and weft faced satin or twill weaves with plain or taffeta weave, in a complex pattern of flowers, animal and abstract designs, predates brocade, possibly named after the Syrian city of Damascus. Procopius in the 6th century states that damask was woven in Tyrus, Antioch and Berytus, but no mention of Damascus. *Drap de damas de Lucchese* frequently mentioned in inventories from 1350 onwards, but by the 15th century, Venice and Florence had become important silk centres with their own special designs incorporating fruit and flowers. By 16th century, large patterned damasks, showing an oriental influence of meanders, palmettes, lotus flowers, crowns and pomegranates, woven in the French and Spanish textile centres on a drawloom. (Fr) damas or damasse that has silver or gold in the weft, while *damasse Chine* has printed silk warps.

Décolleté, décolletage   Very low cut neckline.

Degumming, Decreusage (Fr) **Discharging** Approximately 20% by weight of raw silk is made up of sericin, that coats and protects the silk fibres while the silkworm is spinning and helps the cocoon to keep its shape while the caterpillar is changing into a pupa, then silkmoth. Sericin can be removed at the spinning, reeling or weaving stage by immersion in hot water with soap or alkali solution. Must be removed before dyeing for the dyes to take successfully. Sometimes sericin is saved, and a portion added back in finishing stages to weight or conditioning the fabric.

Denier Comparative measurement of the thickness of a filament yarn, thread or fibre expressed as the weight in grams to a fixed length of 9,000 metres. The Association International de la Soie sets the weight in demi-decigrams of the length of 450m of silk, the smaller the number the finer the weight of silk. Italian weight standardized at 0.05 grams. **Dtex**, the weight in grams of 10,000 metres of silk thread. **Dram** English equivalent to denier, for thrown silk, 1/16th of an ounce, based on 1,000yards to the dram, or 256,000 yards to the pound weight for size No.1. Dividing 256,000 by any dramage gives the yardage per pound. **Micron** One-thousandth of a millimetre, often written as u (pronounced mew). I micron = 1/25,400th inch. **Momme** Japanese unit of weight equivalent to 3.756gms measured over a piece of fabric 25 yards by 1.49 inches, and denoting the quality of a given woven silk, abbreviated to mm, ie 1mm silk weighs 3.62 grams per square yard, eg habutai is usually 2.5 to 60 mm. The higher the momme, the heavier the fabric. **Metric count** M.C. an indication of number of yards of silk to a given weight, used for spun silks. **Tex** is weight in grams of 1,000 metres.

Dentelle 18th century binding style, also French for lace.

Deshabillé Undress, loose or informal gown.

Diapause Form of hibernation that allows the chrysalis to lie dormant over winter.

Diocletian Edict 3rd century regulations issued by the Emperor Gaius Diocletian in regard to sumptuary laws for the wearing of silk clothes, tailoring of them and weaving silk.

Dormeuse Day cap with a ruched border, puffed up crown, sometimes fastened with ribbons.

Doublet, doubletta, Fasetto Men's quilted upper garment, worn from the fourteenth century and standard wear throughout 16th and 17th centuries, close fitting and waisted, hose attached by points.

Double weave Two layers of fabric, woven together simultaneously.

Doubling, plying, folding Twisting together two or more threads, in the opposite direction forming a stable fibre.

Douppion, Duppion, Duppioni from duo, meaning two cocoons that have fused together during the cocoon spinning process, hand reeled. Firmly woven fabric with a fine warp and heavier slubbed weft, in a variety of weights, often dyed brilliant colours before being woven into plain or shot silks, plaids and stripes used in clothes and furnishings.

Drawing, drafting Process whereby fibres are gently drawn out from the mass to form a finer **sliver** or **roving** so that an even amount can be twisted together in spinning to form a thread.

Drawloom Used for the finest figured silks, from the 8th century onward, came from the Near East, and required a boy to sit on a platform above the loom, pulling the heddles through which the silks were threaded to form the pattern. Lashes attached to the tail cords permit automatic repeats of the complex patterns.

Droguet 18thc silk fabric, with a small repeating pattern.

Ducape Heavy corded silk fabric, widely used from mid 17th century for dresses and outer garments.

Dyes, Acid dyes suitable for dyeing silk. **Anilines** Chemical dyes, based on a colourless oily aromatic fluid, later made from coal tar. The first synthetic dyes were developed by O. Unverdorben in 1826. In 1856 W H Perkins (1837-1907) developed the benzine purples and four years later in 1860, mauverine and magenta. **Reactive dyes** Class of dyes that reacts chemically with the fibre molecules, produces fast bright colours. **Resist dyeing** or **Ikat** dyeing where wax or clay applied to the fabric or fibres tied into tight bundles to stop the dye penetrating in that area.

Dynamited silk Silk that has been seriously overweighted with tin salts.

Echelle Ladder, (Fr) 17th and 18th centuries, rows of ribbon bows down the front of a ladies dress.

Ecru Natural coloured tussah silk thrown or woven before being degummed.

Ell Old measure for fabric, in England c45"or 1.14m, different in other countries.

Embossing Finishing process, where a plain fabric is passed between two heated engraved rollers that imprint the pattern onto the silk, eg. moiré.

End Individual warp thread.

Engageantes Deep, tiered sleeve ruffles worn in late 17th and early 18th century.

En-tout-cas Umbrella or parasol that could equally well be used in rain or shine.

Epingle (Fr) pin, indicating a fine corded effect in either warp or weft, alternating thin and thick ribs sometimes in contrasting colours, used for men's ties and women's wear. **Epingle brocade** is a figured fabric with a ribbed background made on a jacquard loom.

Faconné Figured silk fabric, embellished with small ornaments.

Fagotting Decorative trim to join two edges of fabric, by pulling together small group of horizontal threads from a fabric and gathering the remaining cross threads into an hour glass shape.

Faille (Fr) scarf-style woman's head-dress, also a thick soft plain weave taffeta silk fabric with fine horizontal weft ribs or impressed with a moiré finish.

Falling band Ruff or collar of lace or linen worn in 17th century.

Fardel, torsello Long bale of skeined, raw or woven silk, a quarter of the weight that an animal can carry in each pannier bag, emblem of the Lucchesse silk merchants and the Court of the Merchants.

Farthingale (Fr), **vertugade**, (Sp).
Stiffened woman's underskirt, with radiating hoops of cane, wire, whalebone or rope to hold the skirt in a bell shape, began in 16th century Spain worn throughout Europe.

Fascinator Light soft lacy scarf that covers the top of the head. Has lacy lappets hanging down each side, 1878.

Fashioned, fully fashioned Any garment especially socks and stockings shaped on the knitting machine by either increasing or decreasing.

Ferronerie 18th century Decorative narrow gold or jewelled band worn around the head with centrally placed jewel on the forehead. Also curved design like wrought iron work, often voided on velvet.

Festoon, garland Decorative swag for drapes and skirts. Popular designs for silk fabrics in 18th and 19th centuries.

Fibrillae Specks on the surface of the yarn.

Fibroin Amino acid based compound of extended protein chains forming the core fibre of silk, along with a fine coat of protective sericin gum, constitutes nearly 70 % of the silk fibre. Manufactured in the silk glands of the silkworm and ejected from the two spinerettes on its head. The liquid silk hardens on exposure to air to form a continuous silk filament, insoluble in water.

Fichu Small triangular lace scarf or cape of white silk or cotton, with long ends tied or crossed in the front and tucked in the waist band of the skirt, or draped around the neck, throat and shoulders, originally lace often black, fashionable in the late 18th and early 19th century.

Figured silks Silks where the design is woven into the fabric rather than embroidered on it.

Filament Any continuous thread or fibre, natural or man-made. Silk is reeled off the cocoon, 2,000 to 3,000 feet long. It takes filaments from 4 to 9 cocoons to produce 14 denier silk.

Filature Factory or community based reeling house where silk cocoons are boiled and the silk reeled.

Filé Smooth thread composed of a core of silk with metallic gilded membrane or parchment wound around it.

Filet (Fr) **lacis** handmade knotted net, also a decorative gold band to be worn on the head.

Finishing Treatment given to fabric after weaving to improve its appearance, felting, ironing, washing, sizing.

Flea-fur Elegantly stuffed and decorated small fur animals, sables, martens, weasels, sometimes with precious or semi-precious stones, attached by a gold chain and worn during the 16th century, to attract the fleas from the person.

Float Weft or warp yarn carried over the surface of two or more threads of the weaving, or the back in knitting.

Flounce, Furbelow Gathered strip of fabric, attached to the hem or cuff for decoration.

Flowered silks 18th century sprigged silks from Spitalfields in London.

Fly Ladies cap, often of lace, wired at the sides to form small wings, and decorated with jewels, 1750-60s.

Flyer Part of a spinning wheel or machine that draws the spun fibres on to the reel automatically.

Fontanges Small flat crowed cap on which extremely high and embellished hairstyle and decorations erected over a metal frame and secured with ribbon, added ruffles of lace and jewels, c1680 .

Foulard Light weight 2+2 twill, taffeta or satin woven silk, composed of a raw silk warp and schapped silk weft, pieced dyed and prints well, washes easily, used for handkerchiefs, ties, scarves, linings.

Frame knitting Knitting machine invented by William Lee, 1589 to replace hand knitting, for socks and stockings, later jackets etc.

French Hood Small bonnet type hood made on a stiffened frame.

Frisé	Crinkly thread made up of a fine strip of gilt, leather, parchment or paper wound around a core.
Frisons	Short irregular lengths of silk fibre discarded from the reeling process, including the **floss** drawn off the cocoon before the single filament is reeled off.
Frogs	Loops of braid to form fastenings, sometimes gold or silver popular in 18th century.
Fur, Ermine	Coat of the weasel family turns completely white in winter, except for the tip of its tail, each black spot presumed to be a tip of tail, but usually scrap of black lamb, limited to royalty, but often worn by aristocracy. **Vair, varo, miniver,** mini-vair, White belly of the Russian squirrel, arranged in shield-like rows.
Gabardine	Yarn dyed, solid colours, using fioretto silk, the weft can be passed through a waterproofing solution before the fabric is woven.
Gallants	Small ribbon bows wore by both men and women in their hair and on their clothes.
Galligaskins	Knee Breeches.
Galloon, galon	Silk or metallic braid or ribbons used to trim uniforms, upholstery.
Garde-infante	Late 17th century (Sp) **farthingale,** (Fr) **paniers,** frame for full skirts.
Garnetting	Method of tearing waste fibres or fabrics apart, and reconstituting into a thick filling.
Garters	Band ties under the knee to keep the stockings up. **Garter Stitch** after 1840, every row plain knitting, possibly named because it was used for garters and at the top of stockings.
Garthwhaite, Anna Maria,	(1690-1763)silk textile designer, active from the 1720s to mid 1750s in Spitalfields in London, over 1000 of her designs still survive at the V&A, daughter of a Lincolnshire parson.
Gassing	Process used to pass the fibres swiftly over jets or flames to singe them leaving a smooth thread.
Gaufres	Small ornaments pure gold or silver gilt, stamped in fantastic shapes and sewn onto garments.
Gauge	Number of needles per inch for knitting on the stocking frame.
Gauze, gaze	Very fine sheer stiffened silk, used for millinery, popular in Paris in the early 17th century, possibly from Gaza. Plain, leno or gauze weave, the ends alternatively from right or left to lock the open weave in place.
Georgette	Medium weight chiffon style fabric, less lustrous than crepe de Chine, with a soft drape and handle, woven from tightly twisted two or three ply crepe yarns, snags easily, used for millinery, curtains, dresses and lingerie, named after a French milliner, Madame Georgette de la Plante.
Gilded membrane, parchment	Flat guilded strips, woven or embroidered into garments.
Gimp	Thick thread or cords, spiral wrapped around an inner core, used for outlining in lacemaking, also braid or narrow trim sewn flat on the garment, sometimes silver or gold thread, used for furnishings.
Giubbetto, zuparello, corpetto, farsetto, zupone	Men's doublet, close fitting garment with a low standing collar, usually with sleeves, reaching below the waist, padded and quilted, sometimes rich fabrics.
Glaucus	Grey, greenish or bluish, sometimes yellow colour.
Glacé	Thin plain weave silk fabric with a lustrous surface.
Gloria	Fine canvas, twill or satin weave silk fabric of superb quality to ensure even waterproofing and transparency, mostly used for umbrellas, sometimes silk and wool, **silesienne** (Fr).
Gobelin	Company making tapestries using the high warp or *haute lisse* method near Paris.
Goffering, Gauffrage, Gadroon	16th c pleated edge of ruffs made using an iron or by heated rollers.
Gold thread	Fine gilded strips or membranes of fish skin or animal gut, later wafer thin wire or flat strips of beaten gold wrapped around a silk core, pure gold replaced with silver gilt with a coating of gold made in Cologne.
gonnella, gonna, sottana, gamurra, camora,	(Florence) or a **zupa, zipa, socha** in Northern Italy, a simple unlined gown worn by all women, whatever class, mostly wool sometimes with silk sleeves, worn over a light chemise.
Gossamer	Very fine silk used for veils.
Grain	Smallest unit of weight being $1/5,760^{th}$ pound (Troy) or $1/7,000^{th}$ pound (avoirdupois). Dates from 1542, the weight of the centre of an ear of corn, also the lie of the fabric.
Grainage	(Fr) seed, also the building or group of buildings where DFL (disease free layings) silkworm eggs are produced under scrupulously controlled and hygienic conditions. From the grainages the eggs are either developed to a later stage or sold as certified seed to the growers. **Graine** (Fr) Silkworm seed.
Great Wardrobe	Department of royal household handling clothing and textiles, furnishings dry goods.
Grége (Fr)	**Grey goods** Fabric or raw silk that still contains the gum sericin.
Grenadine	Fine dull highly twisted organzine silk or woollen dress fabric, possibly originally from Grenada in Spain.

Grosgrain (Fr) Gros, large and grain, cord. Plain transverse ribbed silk, with fine closely set warp threads of organzine silk and thick soft weft. Can be moiréed, made into firm stiff ribbons, or bindings, trimming, includes **Gros de Naples, Gros de Tours.**

Grotesques Fanciful or fantastic human and animal forms often interwoven with foliage masks, bird, flower and animal motifs used in Medieval manuscript illuminations and Renaissance tapestries in the 17ᵗʰ and 18ᵗʰ centuries.

Ground Background of the design or pattern.

Gynaeceum Women's weaving quarters, during Roman and Byzantium period, later not exclusively feminine.

Habutai, Habutae, Habotai, Paj Lightweight Chinese plain weave silk, 5-10 mm or 20-24grams. various widths popular for scarves and linings, takes dyes brilliantly, used by magicians. Also **Jap silk.**

Hand Feel or handle of fabric, the way its drapes.

Handrun lace Machine made lace, finished by adding heavy outlines of cordonnet threaded through by hand to outline the motifs, to give the appearance of being totally handmade.

Hantong, Honan, Hunan, Antung, Pongee, (Ch) *pen-chi* 'handwoven at home'.Chinese plain weave medium weight wild silk, natural pale creamy colour, often incorporating both domesticated silk for the warp and wild silk for the weft. Can be piece dyed or printed, the bombyx mori and tussah silks absorb dyes slightly differently, giving a subtle, distinctive finish.

Hank Skein of silk tied in a number of places, twisted into a figure of eight for storage or transporting. Spun silk is given a number based on the number of hanks of 840 yards in length, per pound.

Hargreaves, James invented the spinning jenny in 1764, linking several spindles together and manned by one person.

Hoop-petticoat, 'Improver' 18ᵗʰ century England panniers or whaleboned petticoat.

Hose Long tailored fabric stockings of velvet, silk or other cloth, striped or parti-coloured, fur lined in winter, foot portion soled making indoors shoes unnecessary. Begun as chausses or separate stockings, became longer and braises shorter. By 1370-80 had become tights attached to tunic by laces and eyelet holes requiring a braguette or codpiece.

Jabot 17ᵗʰ century neck opening of the chemise, trimmed with lace, later the falling neck ruffle of silk, linen or lace worn by both men and women.

Jacquard Series of punched cards laced together and attached to a loom that enabled complex patterns such as damask and brocade weaves to be produced. Developed in France in 1801-10 by Joseph-Marie Jacquard (1752-1834). No longer required a drawboy to sit on top of the loom lifting the threads to make the pattern, now computerized.

Jerkin 16ᵗʰ and 17ᵗʰ century outer doublet, generally sleeveless.

Journeyman Man or woman who had completed their apprenticeship and now qualified and free to work for wages.

Justaucorps Originally a military garment, replaced the jacket later 17th and 18ᵗʰ century.

Kay, John, (1704-64) inventor of the flying shuttle that allowed the weaver to weave a width of more than 35 inches. Patented in 1733.

Kekolymena Highest grade of Byzantine silk, manufactured in the Imperial Workshop for the use of the Emperor or as state gifts. These 'forbidden cloths' only available to selected people, attracted heavy penalties.

Kermes Shield louse that lives on a sub-tropical species of oak. The pregnant females are dried and ground up and yield a brilliant scarlet colour fast dye.

Kincob Metal brocade of Persian or Indian origin, speciality of Benares. Chin in Chinese means gold.

Kirtle 14ᵗʰ to 17ᵗʰ century women's chemise, petticoat, an inner garment worn over the shirt or smock.

Knitting stick Wooden, metal or bone stick with a cleft or eyelet for holding one knitting needle firm.

Knotless netting Ancient netting technique worked with one needle, producing strong and compact fabric.

Kufic Script of the early Korans and other Moslim groups, thick, compressed and angular.

Lace, Bobbin or Pillow Lace Generic term for lace made by plaiting and twisting many threads, pinned onto a pillow, each thread weighted with a bone bobbin (bone lace) so they can be manipulated without actually touching the fine threads. **Needle lace** Generic term for lace built up using buttonhole stitch, usually on a framework of threads pinned to parchment, pricked pattern.

Lacemen Middlemen, merchants and dealers who bought together the lacemaker and the customer.

Ladder   Where a knitted stitch has been dropped or through error travelled back down through the work.

Lamé   Rich fabric where most of the pattern is made up with gold or silver threads.

Lampas, Diasper Compound weave where the glossy weft forms the pattern against the plain ground, composed of weft floats held in place by a binding warp on a ground of tabby, twill, satin or damask weave. Small all-over repeat checkered, diamond or hatched background, figured silk fabric, with a brocade effect.

La Modesta   Little piece of lace inserted in the low neck of the bodice in 18th century.

Lappets   Long narrow fabric attached to a band and worn by women around the upper arm, 14th century. In 17th to 19th centuries lace lappets were attached to the coif, cap or headcovering and hung down the back or over the ears.

Lasalles, Philippe de, (1723-1805) Important Lyon silk designer and manufacturer, trained under Boucher in Paris.

Lashes   Group of cords that enable the drawboy to control the raising of the threads on a draw loom.

Laventine   Very fine silk and cotton mix only used for umbrella covers.

Leavers   Lace making machine invented by John Leavers, Nottingham in 1813 capable of making extremely complicated designs.

Lee, William (c1556-1610) Inventor of the hand frame knitting machine in 1589.

Lisse   Fine silk gauze fabric, used in France on a high warp loom 'haute-lisse', a low warp loom is a 'basse-lisse'.

Loading, weighting Addition of metal salts to stiffen silk and replace the weight lost by the removal of the sericin.

Looms   Cylinder attached to the loom on which the warp is wound. **Beater** Swinging frame through which the warp threads pass. It compacts the weft threads against the warp when it is drawn back and forward between pics. **Cloth beam** Back roller on which the completed cloth is rolled. **Dobby** loom attachment controls the shedding of the harness as compared to the Jacquard arrangement which controls individual heddles, used for small geometric designs. **Harness** General term for all the shafts on a loom. **Heddle** Set of parallel strings or wires, with a central eye, threaded in a particular pattern sequence, for separating and guiding the warp threads on the loom. Raising an alternating group of heddles provides a shed through which the weft threads can pass, thus forming the pattern. **Shed** Space formed when the heddles are raised or lowered allowing the shuttle to pass with the weft threads.

Lousy silk   Woven silk fabric with light coloured specks and curled little knots on the surface.

Lucca   Italian city in Tuscany, major Medieval silk centre in 13th c first town in Italy to admit Muslim silk weavers.

Lustring, lutestring Speciality silk of Nimes and Lyon, a glossy plain weave silk taffeta used for dresses or ribbon. It is stretched and pressed between heated rollers, then steamed to set the fibres. Royal Lustring Company founded in England 1680, all imported lustrings were banned in England after 1692.

Lyons   Major French silk centre, and market for Italian silks. Production and weaving heavily promoted by Louis XI, expanded under his Minster Colbert, who in 1667 imposed a ban on the importation of foreign silks, to foster the local product, by 1780's had 20,000 craftsmen.

Macaroni   Derogatory term in 1760s for a group of young fashionably dressed men, considered effeminate and fussy.

Machine lace and nets Bobbin net machine invented in 1809 by John Heathcote, producing twist net. Pusher lace machine invented 1820, lace mainly finished by hand. Square mesh net for curtains invented by John Liversey 1846.

Magnanerie (Fr) Silk rearing house.

Maheutres   Decorative padded rolls attached to the shoulder and armhole seam on jackets in the mid 15th and early 16th century to emphasise broad shoulders.

Maltese bobbin lace Heavy silk, usually cream ie blonde, sometimes black, often with wheatears and nearly always with Maltese Cross incorporated in the design.

Manches, manicottoli Sleeves.

Mantua   Possibly from (Fr) manteau, silk gown or petticoat or Mantua in Italy. Has a loose unbuttoned bodice, with a train, open in the front to show the decorative underskirt.

Marlotte   Short coat open at the front worn by women in the 16th century, falling in deep folds, puff sleeves and a standing collar which sometimes supported a ruff.

Marquisette (Fr) an entrance, used as mosquito netting, made in leno or gauze weave, for dresses, children's clothes or curtains.

Matelassé (Fr) Double, quilted, padded or stuffed cloth, a puffy effect against a plain or twill ground, woven on a jacquard or dobby loom, the two layers woven under different tensions and shrunk after weaving, causing one layer to tighten up and the other to stand proud of the surface.

Mawata Pierced cocoons, soaked in hot water to soften the sericin, opened up and stretched over a dome or square frame, and left to dry. A cap is made up of 8-15 single layers, a bell around 30. Thigh rolled, spindle or wheel spun, dyed.

Medici collar Named after Marie de Medici, fan shaped standup collar, supported by wires.

Milanese fabric Lightweight sheer ladder resistant warp knitted silk fabric, constructed from two sets of threads crossing over, leaving characteristic diamond or diagonal effect on the back of the fabric, used for lingerie and gloves.

Mille Fleurs Design with thousands of flowers, used in tapestry and illuminated manuscript, typical of the courtly International Gothic style, 15-16th century, famous set of tapestries in the Musee de Cluny, *La Dame a la Licorne.*

Mixed silk Woven fabric, less than 100 % pure silk, can include linen, cotton, wool, ramie in the weave or spun with the silk.

Moches Bale of imported raw silk.

Mockado 16th and 17th century cloth of imitation velvet, made in silk or wool.

Moiré (Fr) Process whereby silk taffeta or ribbed silk was drawn through heated and ridged rollers, that flattens parts of the ribs and imprints a wavy watered pattern that reflects the light in different ways. Dress weight or heavier for furnishing. Others include faille or *poult de soie*, or *moiré d'Angleterre.*

Monovoltine Silkworm species that produces one generation per year. **Bivoltine** A non-hibernating silkmoth that produces two generations per year. The seed hatches after it has been laid, and a second batch is chilled and held over until the next season. **Multivoltine, polyvoltine** Silkworm species that produce a number of generations each year, all of the eggs are non-hibernating.

Mordant Chemical added to the yarn or dye-bath to assist the dye to penetrate the silk and help it remain colour fast.

Moriculture Cultivation of mulberry orchards.

Morning Gown Informal long loose coat with a sash or girdle around the waist, 18th century.

Morocain Heavy weight crepe fabric with slightly wavy cross ribs, possibly associated with French Morocco.

Mouche Small black patches worn on the face for decoration, or to hide disfigurements.

Mousseline Lightweight plain weave silk muslin, similar to chiffon, but more closely woven, usually piece dyed.

Napping Method of raising the surface of a fabric.

Negligée, Nightgown, Undress, morning dress demi-toilette, déshabillé, more relaxed, less formal gown.

Netting Manipulation of a single thread using a gauge and narrow shuttle to produce a fabric of square or diamond shaped meshes, knotted at each corner.

Nett silk Continuous thread filament silk drawn off or reeled from the cocoon.

Nib Lump of raw silk, formed by the collection of waste from boiling the cocoons.

Noil Rough knotty short lengths silk fibre, the final discard from carding, spins or weaves into soft hardwearing fabric, usually piece dyed, sometimes the natural colour of the fabric shows up at the cut edges, not always colour fast, especially to sunlight. It may contain black flecks from the last skin that was shed inside the cocoon.

Nub, knub, nep, nepp, frison Little knots or bits of silk that sit on the surface of an otherwise smooth fabric. **Slub, Bouchon** small irregular knobs in the thread, usually in weft but can be also in warp threads. Result of poor reeling or poor quality silk. It can also be a choice to give a textured silk.

Organdie Very light, stiff, translucent plain weave fabric, silk, cotton or other fibres, used for millinery, children's party dresses, evening wear. Woven with a low density count of 40 threads per cm, piece dyed, sometimes printed or 'cold' dyed to increase the stiffness. **Organza**, similar but softer fabric using tightly twisted yarns having 10-20 turns per inch. The fabric is strong, stable with a smooth texture, dyed in the yarn before the gum is removed.

Organzine High twist fine yarn, used for silk warps. Raw silk threads twisted in one direction 14-16 times, doubled, and given a reverse twist 12 times, to make a strong elastic thread.

Ottoman	Firm lustrous furnishing weight silk with thick weft ribs heavier than faille, originally woven in Turkey.
Pall	Elaborate cover often embroidered and fringed to go over a coffin during the funeral ceremonies.
Palmette	Flower design, cut in half to reveal its inner structure and formalised into a decorative design.
Pane(s)	Strips of fabrics, joined for hangings or a counterpane, also in the 16th century the long slashes allowed the underlying fabric to be seen or pulled through to decorative effect.
Paniers	18th c hoop petticoat, whalebone or reed cages tied at the waist and worn under the skirt to hold it out to the sides, for a fashionable shape displaying the gorgeous material of the skirt to best advantage.
Panné velvet	(Fr) Shag, velvet or velour where the pile is heat set to lie diagonally, creating a lustrous surface.
Parti-colour	Half or quartered garment in different colours or designs.
Partlet	Sleeveless jacket or detachable collar or yoke, white embroidered or jewelled to fill in a very low neck.
Par Weighting	Finished weight of silk with the gum or other salts returned so that it is the same weight as it was before the gum removed. **Conditioning** Replacement of 11% moisture into the silk fibre.
Passementarie, Passement	(Fr) Braids and tassels, trimmings and woven decorative items, pulls etc, including early 16th century metal thread lace, laid on top of silk, appliqué decoration, beads, fringe or cord.
Paste	Sticky substance, usually made with flour and water, used to stiffen material for corsets and petticoats.
Pattens	Wooden or cork overshoes for wearing outside, held onto the foot by strap or buckles, with ridges underneath to raise the wearer above the mud and filth of the streets and protect the soft leather soles of hose.
Peasecod belly	(Sp) Padded belly effect to the doublet, to give a paunch shape, second half 16th century.
Peau de soie	(Fr) 'skin of silk', expensive medium weight smooth lustrous fabric, originally made in Padua in Italy, similar to medium weight satin, but made from a tightly packed plain weave, with very fine crossways ribs.
Pebrine	Disastrous silkworm disease that almost wiped out the industry all over Europe and the Near East in the mid 19th c, only controlled when Louis Pasteur discovered the hereditary cause.
Pecia	Measure of silk cloth, cf *pannus*, for woollen cloth.
Pekin	Dress-weight silk of Chinese origin, with alternating lengthwise stripes of plain and satin velvet.
Pelerine	Short cloak or shoulder cape with long ties in the front, made from silk, lace, fur or velvet.
Peplum	Short flounce attached to a fitted bodice.
Petersham	Silk ribbon, stiff weft-ribbed or corded used for hats and waistbands.
Petticoat	(Fr) cote, could be either a richly decorated and embroidered underskirt often visible through split upper skirt, made of silk, quilted, decorated with lace, or a warm underskirt, the number of layers sometimes set by legislation.
Petticoat breeches, Rhinegraves	(1650-75) short wide breeches decorated just above knee and at waist with excessive ribbons ruffles and lace.
Picadils, Wings	Crescent shaped padded protrusions around the join of the sleeve to the shoulder. Scalloped or tabbed edge, fashionable in late 16th early 17th century. Piccadilly called after the tailor who made the fashion.
Piece	Length of silk or ribbon, usually 10 yards, and woven silks between 10 and 60 yards depending on the weight.
Piéce	(Fr) Small piece of cloth, often velvet or satin, worn across the chest for warmth or modesty.
Piece dyeing	Length of fabric dyed after weaving.
Pierced cocoons	Cocoons where the moth has broken through the layers of fibre to emerge.
Picots	Decorative little loops along the edge of lace or ribbon, a crenellated edge on knitting, made by knitting rows of holes, folded over to make an edging of tiny bumps or arches.
Pinking	Method of cutting zig-zag edges or punching holes for a decorative effect or to stop fraying.
Pinner	Apron, or at times the lappets on a headdress or fill-in for a low décolletage.
Plastron	Metal breastplate in armour, then name given to fur neck infills, and later decorative stomacher and lace shape to cover the front opening on the bodice.
Plissé	Puckered effect formed by shrinking the fabric in a selected way, with heat.
Plumpers	Small rounded pieces of cork, worn in the mouth to plump out the cheeks.
Plush	Soft, heavy fabric with an even pile, like velvet or velour, silk, cotton, rayon or wool.
Ply, Plying	Twisting together of two or more spun threads, usually in the opposite direction, to make a stable yarn.
Points, laces	Metal tipped laces for attaching hose to breeches, doublet to hose, sleeves to doublet.

Polonaise   Late 18th century gown, boned bodice, skirt open in the front to show the underskirt. The overskirt was drawn up into three puffy sections by gathering strings, the tight sleeves ended in ruffles.

Pomander (Fr) *pomme d'ambre*. Mixture of aromatic herbs and spices with ambergris, contained in a small fabric bag, or metal filigree ball hung from the ladies girdle, or carried by fashionable man to ward off diseases and mask unpleasant smells.

Poult   From paduasoy, a silk cloth from Padua in Italy, similar to grosgrain or faille, with a finer warp and slightly heavier weft, used for dresses and linings.

Pounce   Method of pricking out a design from a piece of paper or parchment, so that the charcoal or other dust goes through the holes and outlines the pattern on the fabric underneath.

Pourpoint, gipon, aketon (Fr) Garment became the doublet or padded vest, implied military use, became shorter when a tight waist became fashionable with the fullness radiating above and below the belt, high neckline under the ears, trimmed with fur. Variety of sleeves, very wide at the wrist, turned back to show the fur or contrasting silk lining, often dagged, others full at the lower part but gathered tightly into the wrist.

Point rentré   Weavers method of obtaining *chiarascuro* shaddows and three dimensional form, by interlocking threads of contrasting colours to create an impression of relief, developed by Jean Revel textile designer, early 18th century.

Prin, quill   Two prins or spools with the yarn wound on each are held in the shuttle for weaving,

Printing   Various method of adding a pattern and colour to the surface of cloth, using blocks, screen, lithographic rollers, transfer, etc.

Properties, Crease resistance Fabric given a resin finish, heat set, ability to resist and recover from crushing. **Colour fastness** Resistance of fabrics to the loss of colour, usually because of poor or unmordanted dyes, sunlight, moisture or perspiration. **Lustre** Reflection of light from the surface of the fibre or yarn, directly proportional to the straightness of the fibres and tightness or looseness of the spinning and plying. Lustre reduced by unevenness of the fibre or poor finishing.

Pure silk   100 % silk fabric, no other fibres added or extra weighting salts, except those permitted for dyeing. Produced by various domesticated and wild silkmoths. Known as see-Chinese, soie-French, seide-German, serikon-Greek, seta-Italian, sir-Korean, sericum-Latin, seda-Spanish, sheolk-Russian.

Purling   Made with a needle and often of gold thread, it forms the edge to coifs and ruffs, 16th century.

Purpura   Various shades of red to purple dye retrieved from the Murex shellfish. Difficult to obtain, the intense royal colour led to purpura signifying a very precious silk fabric.

Pusher   Machine invented to produce Chantilly lace, to make a twist net and shawls in the 1850s-60s.

Rabato, Rebato (Sp) Starched or wired support for a ruff, and tipped it forward, 16th century.

Ratiné   Novelty yarn made by twisting a heavy yarn round a fine one, or plain weave fabric with a ratiné yarn.

Raw silk   General term for all silk yarn or fabric with the sericin gum still in it and still unprocessed, making it feel stiff and dull and retards the acceptance of dye. Soupling retains most of the gum, but leaves the silk soft. Raw silk is not the same as wild silk which is generally non-mulberry, undomesticated or one of the tussah silks.

Redingote (Fr), riding or travelling coat, worn in England, early 18th c, full with large collar and reveres. 18th c, women's highwaisted coat dress, with collar and reveres, and open down the front.

Reeling   Drawing off or unwinding the baves, or twin filaments from a number of silk cocoons onto a large reel or wheel, later wound into skeins. **Reeled silk** from each cocoon c350 and 1500m in length.

Renditta   Term used to determine the weight in kilogrammes of cocoons needed to reel 1 kg of raw silk.

Reps   Can have either lengthwise or transverse ribs, thick ribs on a plain weave base. Silk rep has a vertical rib formed by loosening the weft.

Residue   Discarded silk waste from which spun silk fibres are made, later woven into spun silk fabrics.

Reticule   Dainty handbag, Directoire and First Empire period.

Rewinding   Secondary process used to clean the yarn by passing it once again through slub catchers.

Riband, ribbon Continuous length of silk, up to 18 inches wide, used for decorating clothes.

Rigattiere   Secondhand clothes dealers.

Robe   Set of three, four, five or six matching garments, including tunics, mantles, cloaks, later in 18th-19th century meant a gown or dress with an overdress, open in front, long behind. **Robe battante, Robe a l'anglaise, sacque** 18th century dress with two large box pleats hanging from the shoulders.

Rococco	18th century Flamboyant European artistic style, featuring scrolls, shell motifs and counter-curves.
Ropa (Sp)	fashionable in England, 1560-1720, a woman's outer garment, with puff sleeves and high collar, made in velvet with fur or jewelled trimming, fastened at the throat, open down the front.
Round gown	Bodice and skirt all in one, without a train.
Roving, Sliver, Rove, Rolag, Tops	Loose untwisted fibres prepared by carding, combing, or some mechanical means in preparation for spinning.
Ruche, ruching	Narrow strip of fabric finely gathered crimped or fluted , developed into the 16th century ruff.
Ruff, Band	Stiffly starched fluted and pleated multi-layers of linen or silk, sewn onto a band and worn around the neck, the largest and most extreme up to eighteen inches wide called a cartwheel ruff. Needed supporting on wire or wooden frames, late 16th and early 17th century.
Sendal, sandeli, cendal, samite	Rich, heavy satin silks, weft faced compound twill, occasionally patterned, often interwoven with threads of gold and silver, originally produced in the east and used for royal robes, ecclesiastical garments, clothing, furnishings, funeral palls. Widely used strong plain weave taffeta for banners, finer for headdresses, specially during the Middle Ages.
Sarsenet	Fine light silk used for veils, appearing in old inventories, said to have been made originally by the Saracens in 13th century, fashionable in the West from the 15th century for dresses and trimmings.
Satin	Highly lustrous smooth-faced silk fabric, twill weave based on four, five or eight ends, the number of picks equal to or a multiple of the number of ends. Piece or yarn dyed, twill, taffeta or crepe on the reverse. Used for fine lingerie to heavy duchesse satin for wedding gowns and furnishings. **Duchesse mouseline** a variation woven in a fancy twill weave.
Scarlet, escarlate	Top quality woollen cloth, became the brilliant expensive red colour it was dyed.
Schappe, Souple	Rather smelly process to remove the gum from the silk by the process of fermentation, produced a soft dull finish. Waste silk is piled high in deep warm place, gum begins to ferment, and can be washed off.
Scouring	Method of subjecting fibres, yarn or fabric to an aqueous solution, with or without additives, soaps or alkalis to remove extraneous dirt and grease or natural impurities like wax or oil.
Screen printing	Relatively expensive method of adding colour and pattern to fabric, ideal for expensive or short run items. The fabric is stretched on long tables, a squeegee is used to force the dye through the prepared screen, a separate one for each colour. Screens originally made of silk.
Sericin	Protein based gum which unites the two filaments, the brins of silk, exuded by the silkworm when spinning its cocoon. Sericin makes up 25-30% of raw silk, and is removed by gentle boiling in soapy water, alkaline solution or fermentation by the schappe method.
Sericulture	Cultivation of mulberry trees and the care and nurture of silkworms to produce cocoons and reelable silk.
Shantung	Northern province in China, known for its development of a hand reeled wild tussah silk. It is a tough comfortable fabric, with low lustre and horizontal slubs.
Shoddy	Web of loosely woven fabric
Shoe rose	16th and 17th century ornamental rosette covering the shoe fastening, often expensive lace or ribbons.
Shot silk	Stiff plain weave silk fabric, like taffeta, woven from two contrasting colours in the weft and warp, giving an iridescent quality and sparkle.
Shuttle	Carrier of a spool or quill of yarn, shot from one side to the other carrying the weft, during weaving.
Siglatons	Plain silks from the Cyclades.
Sircotys	Over tunic with hanging sleeves.
Sizing	Addition of a fine film, usually starch, added to the warp yarns before weaving to protect and make them more durable during the weaving process. Sometimes added to silk fabric to stiffen it. Some are water soluble and can be washed out, leaving fabric limp.
Skein	Hank or coil of yarn, often dyed in this state.
Slashing	Fashion for making decorative cuts in fabrics so the contrasting under garment shows through.
Slips	Motifs appliquéd onto the main fabric, used on heavy silk, velvet hangings, lace or vestments.
Slops	Short breeches ending just above the knee.
Singles	First yarn spun for a thread.
Solitaire	Little black ribbon tied to the wig at the nape of the neck, bought forward and fastened in the front, 18th century
Space dyed	Controlled absorption of vary coloured dye.

Spangle	Small shiny glittering objects of various materials sewn onto fabric to give a sparkly effect.
Spanish lace	Hand or machine made black or cream silk lace with bold dense pattern.
Spencer	1803, short waist length jacket for men with rolled collar and cuffed sleeves. For ladies, short fitted waist length jacket, could be sleeveless, possibly from Second Earl Spencer (1758-1834) who wore a double breasted fitted shortwaisted coat.
Spinning	Process of using a wheel, spindle or appropriate machine to draw out fibres and give them sufficient twist to hold together to form a single thread. **Spindle** Thin stick, weighted at one end so when fibres are attached and the stick is twirled by the spinner, the fibres are drawn out and twisted together and form a thread which is wound onto the spindle shank.
Spitalfields	Area in East End of London settled by Huguenot silk weavers during the 17th and 18th century after they had fled from France and persecution after the Revocation of the Edicts of Nantes in 1685, also a special silk fabric.
Spider silk	Can be raised to produce usable silk for weaving or knitting, more often used for its fineness as lines on telescopes and optical instruments, only thread drawn from molten rock crystal is finer. Spiders are carnivores so not practical to raise them commercially, costly and difficult. Common black garden spider can produce silk.
Spooling	Winding the silk filament yarn onto a spool or bobbin after it has been thrown, or onto a prin which is inserted into a weavers shuttle.
Sprang	Ancient form of pre-knitting, to make a decorative mesh fabric.
Spun silk	Short lengths of waste or non-filament silk that cannot be reeled, are carded, combed and spun to form a silk fibre. Most wild or tussar silks and all domesticated bombyx mori cocoons where the moth has been used for breeding, or has died, stuck together etc are spun. Prepared by carding to lay the fibres parallel, then cut into usable lengths 2-8 inches for spinning.
Staples	Fibres short enough to measured in inches or centimetres.
Stays, Corset, corsettus	(Fr) corps, body, close fitting bodice, stiffened with whalebone etc. Initially made by armourers, to be worn under armour, later by tailors or special craftsmen. An undergarment worn to control shape of figure to the current fashion. The Spanish corset compressed the bust, was stiffened and laced, worn with the farthingale, panniers, crinoline, often highly decorated and covered with rich material. In the 17th century, it was shortwaisted but by the 18th century was longer and pointed. It almost disappeared during the French revolution.
Steaming	Heating the silk threads by steam to fix the twist in the yarn.
Steinkirk	Long, lace edged cravat, ends passed through a buttonhole on one side to anchor it, so called after the Battle of Steinkirk. **Stock** 18th century, folded white linen neckwear that replaced the cravat.
Stencil	Method of imprinting a pattern on fabric, used by the Chinese and Japanese since 500AD.
Stifle	Method of killing pupa or silkmoth by steam, before it breaks through and emerges from the cocoon.
Stomacher, Placart	Ornamental panel stiffened with whalebone, starched canvas, even wood, often highly decorated to fill in the gap between the low décolletage and the waistline.
Stripping	Removal of the gum sericin from the silk.
Strutt, Jedediah	(1726-1797) invented a device for doing rib on the knitted stocking frame in 1758, later known as the Derbyshire patented rib, in partnership with William Arkwright from 1769-1782, developing the spinning frame.
Stuff	General term for silk blended with another fibre in the weaving and manufacture of fabric, partly to reduce the cost, incorporate novelty yarns and effects, some more accurately called union cloths.
Stumpwork	Pictorial embroidery method involving raised and padded scenes and figures, appliqué and beadwork, often decorating boxes, picture frames etc, derived from stamps or engravings, popular in the mid 17th century.
Sumptuary laws	Laws designed to regulate expenditure, and what people could wear, so their position and rank were clearly defined, and prevent luxurious or flamboyant living especially in the lower orders of society.
Surah	Glossy heavier silk, often twill weave, used for ties and women's dresses, similar to foulard, initially from India and named after the town of Surat. Often yarn dyed threads woven in stripes, bars or checks, paisley designs, the warp being finer and closer set than the weft.
S-spin, Z-spin	Direction that fibres are spun, right to left in S, or left to right in Z, to form a continuous thread.
Swift	Simple frame with extending arms, used to wind threads into a skein.

Tabard	Sleeveless or short-sleeved tunic worn over armour to deflect the sun, often highly decorated for ceremonial occasions, with coats of arms and heraldic devices.
Tabbi, Tabby	Simplest plain weave fabric, could be a corruption of Attabi, a textile district in Baghdad where striped and ikat silk, muslin and canvas were made. Yarn or piece dyed, sometimes striped or watered, a base for printed designs. In England also a taffeta silk with a wavy, watered or moiréd appearance.
Tabs, Tasset	Short square or oblong shaped pieces of material, hanging from the bottom of the bodice, or 17th century doublet to give more freedom of movement and allow for the shape of the hips.
Taffeta, taftah, taftan	Possibly from Persian taftan, glossy twist. Taffatie and taffety, exported from Bengal in India, to Europe in the 17th century. Smooth, crisp, tightly woven plain weave silk, warp finer than weft, giving a slightly ribbed effect. Sometimes moiréed, yarn dyed and stiffened by the addition of metallic salts which give a papery feel and cause it to rustle, called scroop. Chemical treatments now controlled because some rot the silk causing it to crumble into a powder. Used in the 17th century for doublets, 19th century for full skirts and mourning clothes. Can be an impermeable oiled plain weave, used for umbrellas also dresses, curtains and upholstery.
Tambouring	Chain stitch worked with a small hook over a tambour or drum frame, introduced from the East in the mid 18th century, most often used in whitework, lace and bead embroidery.
Tartar cloth	Silk from Tartary or old China, by the 14th century used to describe figured exotic silks patterned in gold with birds animals and mythical beasts. Tartarine, ancient silk fabric, from Tartary.
Tatting	Circular lace-like motifs linked together with picot stitch using a shuttle and single thread, looped and knotted between the fingers.
Tease	To open out entangled fibres prior to carding.
Tender silk	Woven fabrics, fragile through improper dyeing or weaving.
Tension	Tightness or looseness of the knitting or the amount of stretch in the fabric knitted or woven.
Tentering	Process whereby both selvedges of the cloth are held with wire clips to keep the fabric at a standard width while the cloth is heatset.
Textile	Any flexible cloth, plain or decorated, made from fibres through weaving, felting, knitting, lacemaking.
Texturising	Process that puts a permanent crimp, coils or loops along the length of the fibres, resulting in bulky fabrics, some with insulating, moisture absorbing, or stretch.
Thread	Two or more single fibres twisted or plied together usually in the opposite direction to the first spin. Used to describes all smooth even fibres to sew or weave. **Thread count** Number of warps per unit width, or weft per unit length to form a fabric.
Throwing	Second major process after reeling groups of three to ten silk filament off the cocoons. From Anglo-Saxon word *thrawan*, to twist. Initially done by hand by a **throwster,** later in throwing mill, the raw untwisted silk fibre is twisted and doubled together to make a more durable yarn of a specified twist and character.
Thrums	Waste silk warp fibres too short to weave, cut from loom ends after the weaving is complete.
Tippet, typeitis	Long hanging pendant streamer strips attached to upper arm of sleeves. Also used to attached to a hat, slung over the shoulder, called a chapeau bras not designed to be worn and Victorian name for small shoulder cape, usually fur.
Tiraz	Arabic and Spanish Moslem textile workshops, also the decorative woven bands made there, sometimes with Kufic inscription usually religious or the names of Sultans or noblemen, woven in gold or coloured thread.
Tricolette, Tricot	(Fr) Knitted fabric, originally only silk, now cotton or man made fibre, similar to jersey, light weight, warp knitted with vertical wales on the face of the fabric, crosswise ribs on the reverse, run and ladder resistant.
Tissage (Fr)	weaving.
Toile	Fabric-like part of lace design, or plain coarse twill woven fabric.
Toledo	Important Christian Spanish silk centre, from before the city was captured by the Christians in 1085 until the 16th century, produced velvets, damasks, and figured silks.
Tours	French silk centre, since the 15th century, patronized by Cardinal Richlieau who introduced protectionist laws to limit the importation of silk from Italy.
Tram	Thick yarn composed of 2-3 silk yarns, barely twisted (100-150 tpm) in one direction only, used in embroidery for the preparatory laid threads on the canvas and in weaving in the weft for filling to give a ribbed effect.

Traverse	Controlled layering onto a skein or bobbin in a criss-cross way, so that the yarn lies smoothly and can be unwound evenly.
Trunk-hose	Medieval garment from the waist to the knee, later known as breeches.
Tucker	Frilled edging in soft material, lace or tulle, to fill in the low neckline.
Tufttaffeta	16-17th century, fashionable silk with a plain weave taffeta base and tuffted pile.
Tulle	Very fine machine made hexagonal netted silk, used for veils, decoration, millinery, possibly originated in Nottingham in 1768 or named after the town of Tulle in France, who perfected this invention.
Tussah, Tusore, Tasar	Wild semi or undomesticated silkmoths. Darker and coarser than bombyx mori, more ribbon-like in cross section, more difficult to dye or bleach because of its courser texture. Colour ranges from pale cream to treacly brown, result of eating leaves with tannin. Three main types: the Saturniidae giant silkworms, Attacus Tasar, Muga, and Eri. Three species of the genera Antheraea and Philosamia are grown for commercial production of tussah silk. The Antheraea mylitta found in India, the A. yamamai from Japan, and the A. pernyii, from China. The Muga silkworms, A. assama, from Assam in Northern India produce golden yellow silk. The eri silkworm, Philosamia ricini and Samia cynthia from Northern India, feeds on Castor oil plant, spins a very loose flossy cocoon, orange-red or white. Large brown moths have an 'eye' on the wings. Large tough cocoons have a hook, or pentacle so they hang like fruit from the trees. Some species build a community nest with poisonous spines. The cocoons produce less reelable filament yarn, though much can be carded and spun, used in **pongee, shantung** etc for blouses, clothes, furnishings.
Twill	Weave based on three or more ends and picks, over one and under two, offset, to give a diagonal effect, used for surahs, herringbone and diamond patterns.
Twist	Sewing silk thread.
Vegetable silk	Plant product with fine fibres, like those in the Kapoc plant.
Velours	Tightly set with the nap lying in one direction, *Velours de Gene* a polychrome floral voided velvet from Genoa, *Velours de Venice* and *Velours de Florence*.
Velvet	(Latin) *vellus*, fleece. Pile silk, used for clothing and furnishings, extra warp threads form loops when laid over wires and later cut. Pile can be voided, of different heights to give a sculptural effect as in *alto-e-basso* or pile on pile velvet, areas can be plain, satin or brocaded, with metallic and gold threads used to heighten the design. New method devised in Lyon 1830 where two cloths woven simultaneously, and the connecting threads cut to separate the two fabrics, leaving both with a pile. Quality determined by the closeness of the pile, complexity of the weave and decoration, almost priceless when richly woven with gold thread. Can be combined to make chiffon velvet, panné velvet, brocaded velvet, or the pattern chemically burnt out known as faconné velvet. Most are dry-cleaned. Velveteen is cotton velvet, close short pile sometimes corded, crushed. Today most silk velvet is 18% silk and 82 % rayon. **Ciselé velvet** Pattern formed by cut and uncut pile of different heights giving a rich three dimensional effect. **Raso vellutato** Voided velvet. **Stamped velvet** with a pattern engraved by feeding it through incised heated rollers.
Venetians	Late 16th-18th century, wide baggy balloon shaped knee breeches, padded around the hips.
Verdugo, vertugade	(Fr.) farthingale, has pliant wooden bands inserted into petticoat structure.
Voile	Fine silk, cotton or wool semi-transparent balanced weave fabric woven loosely with hard twisted double or triple threads. Can be solid colour, patterned, printed flocked, striped.
Wales	Vertical columns of knitted stitches.
Warp	Lengthwise threads laid on the loom to weave a fabric. **Warp-faced** fabric, the warp threads predominate or additional warp threads are incorporated so that the weft threads are completely covered.
Waste silk	General term for all silk fibres other than reeled filament threads. Includes all spun silks floss from the outside of the cocoon, innermost weak threads, unreelable cocoons, double cocoons, ends from weaving, throwing and reeling.
Watteau Gown	Sack Dress, Named after Jean-Antoine Watteau the painter who included many women in his paintings wearing this gown. Bodice fitted in the front, often with a decorated stomacher, but having two large box pleats dropping to the floor from the shoulders at the back.
Weft	Crosswise threads laid in between alternating warp threads to form the fabric, also called woof, picks, or filling threads, usually laid in using a shuttle. **Weft-faced cloth,** has a finer and closer set warp, the weft or filling yarns are packed down to completely cover the warp threads.

Weighting	Chemicals or metallic salts, gums, or sugars added to silk, or returned to silk after scouring, to improve appearance, handle, add density or for special effects.
Welt	Fitted top or bottom hem of a stocking, or garment.
Wheatears	Small bobbin lace motifs common on Maltese lace.
Whisk	Broad, lace trimmed falling collar.
Wigs, Bag-wig	18th century powdered wig with the ends tied into a black silk bag, so the powder does not fall on the wearers coat. **Cadogan,** 1770s worn by men and women where the back hair was looped up and tied, often with a black ribbon. **Campaign wig** Bushy curly wig, short queue at the back. **Full-bottomed wig** Shoulder length wig with centre parting, curls framing the face made of horse or natural hair. **Periwig** (Fr) perruque, peruke, English perwyke, 17th c full bottomed wig.
Wild silk	Silk from semi or undomesticated silkworms from the Saturniidae family, including all the tussah silk fabrics, pongee, shantung etc. Colour varies from pale cream, off white, beige, dark treacle and grey. Silkworms live in the jungle and feed on local trees and shrubs, oak or quercus varieties, castor oil, plum, jujube, most contain tannin which gives colour to the silk. Harvested by peasants who jealously guard their traditional way of life. Wild silks are usually tougher and stronger in texture, harder to reel, usually spun and gum must be removed before bleaching or dyeing. Some have single cocoons, others build colonies, have poisonous spines and distinctive smell. Assam or Muga produces the lightest and most delicate silk, feeds off the champaca tree. Yamamai silks of Japan have green cocoons and are the strongest and most elastic.
Winding	Process of transferring yarn from a skein to a spool or bobbin before the twisting process.

Bibliography

Anquetil, Jacques, *Soie en Occident,* (Flammarion, Paris & New York, 1995)

Arizzoli-Clementel, Pierre, *The Textile Museum, Lyon,* (Foundation Paribas, 1990)

Aruga, Hisao, *Principles of Sericulture,* Translated from the Japanese, (New Age International)

Ball, J N, *Merchants and Merchandise, The Expansion of Trade In Europe, 1500-1630,* (Croom Helm, London, 1977)

Black, J Anderson, Madge Garland and Frances Kennett, *A History of Fashion,* (Orbis, 1983)

Balfour-Paul, Jenny, *Indigo,* (British Museum Press, 1999)

Barfoot, Audrey, *Everyday Costume in Britain,* (B T Batsford, London, 1961)

Baricco, Alessandro, *Silk,* (Panther, 1997)

Baines, Patricia, *Spinning Wheels, Spinners and Spinning,* (B T Batsford, London, 1991)

Barham, Henry, *An Essay Upon the Silkworm,* (1719)

Barron, Caroline, & Nigel Saul, *England and the Low Countries in the Late Middle Ages,* (Sutton Publishing, 1998)

Beck, S William, *Gloves, Their Annals and Associations,* (Hamilton Adams & Co, London, 1883) reissued by (Singing Tree Press, Book Tower, 1969)

Belfanti, Carlo Marco, *Fashion and Innovation, The Origins of the Italian Hosiery Industry in the 16th and 17th century,* Vol. 27 (2), (1996)

Benedict, Philip, *Cities and Social Change in Early Modern France,* (Unwin & Hymen, London, 1989)

Bennett, Frances, *Macclesfield Buttons,* (monograph, ex Macclesfield library)

Bermont, C, *Profitable Strangers, A Point of Arrival, London's East End,* (Eyre Methuen)

Birbari, Elizabeth, *Dress in Italian Painting, 1460-1500,* (John Murray, 1975)

Bonds, William N, 'Genoese Nobelwomen and Gold Thread Manufacture', in *Medievalia et Humanista,* Vol 17

Bone, Quentin, *Henrietta Maria, Queen of the Cavaliers,* (Peter Owen, London, 1973)

Born, W, *The Spinning Wheel,* (Ciba Review No 28, 1939)

Bradfield, N, *Historical Costumes of England 1066-1968,* (Eric Dobby Publishing, 1970)

Branca, Patricia, *Women in Europe since 1750,* (Croom Helm, London, 1978)

Brooke, Iris, *A History of English Costume,* (Methuen, London, 1988)

Broudy, Eric, *The Book of Looms,* (Studio Vista, London, 1979)

Brown, Judith, *In the Shadow of Florence, Pescia, Renaissance Silks.*

Brown, Judith C and Jordan Goodman, 'Women and Industry in Florence', in the *Journal of Economic History* No 40, (1980)

Buckton, David, ed. *Byzantium, Treasures of Byzantine Art & Culture,* (Published for the Trustees of the British Museum, by the British Museum Press, 1994)

Bull, Anna and Paul Corner, *From Peasant to Entrepreneur, the Survival of the family in Italy,* (Berg, Oxford, Providence, 1993)

Cansdale, C H C, *Cocoon Silk, A Manual for those employed in the Silk Industry and for Textile Students,* (Sir Isaac Pitman & Sons, Ltd, London, 1937)

Carter, F W, 'Cracow's Transit Textile Trade 1390-1795', *Textile History* Vol. 19 (1) Spring, (1988)

Carus-Wilson, E M, *Essays in Economic History,* (Edward Arnold, London, 1955)

Chapman, John and Stanley, 'Four Centuries of Machine Knitting Commemorating William Lees Invention of the stocking Frame, 1589', in *Textile History* 21(1) & (2) Spring, (1990)

Cipolla, Carlo, *Before the Industrial Revolution: European Society and Economy 1000-1700,* Third Edition, (Routledge London, 1993)

Clayburn la Force jr. James, *Development of the Spanish Textile Industry 1750-1800 ,* (1965)

Clark, Alice, *Working Life of Women in the 17th Century,* (Routledge & Kegan Paul, London, 1982)

Collins, Louanne, *Silk Museums in Macclesfield,*

Compton, Rae, *The Illustrated Dictionary of Knitting,* (B T Batsford, 1988)

Consitt, Frances, *The London Weavers Company, Vol.1 12-16th century,* (OUP, 1933)

Contini, Mila, *Fashion from Ancient Egypt to the Present Day,* (Paul Hamblyn London, 1965)

Cormack, Robin, *Writing in Gold, Byzantine Society and its Icons,* (George Philip, London, 1985)

Coward, Barry, *The Stuart Age, England 1603-1714,* 2nd edit. (Longman, London & NY, 1980)

Crawford, Patricia and Laura Gowing, *Women's Work in 17th Century England,* (Routledge, 2000)

Cunnington, Phillis, & Catherine Lucas, *Costumes for Births Marriages and Deaths,* (Adam & Charles Black, London, 1978)

D'Assailly, Gisele, *Ages of Elegance, Five Thousand years of Fashion and Frivolity,* (MacDonald London, 1968)

Davies, C Stella, 'The Silk Industry', in *A History of Macclesfield,* (MUP, 1961)

Davis, Nathalie Zemon, Women & Crafts 16th Century Lyon, *Feminist Studies* No. 1 Vol. 8 Spring. (1982)

Davis, Ralph, *Traders in the Levant in the Eighteenth century, Persian and Syrian Silk.*

Dean, Jenny, *Creating Designs and Patterns for Handknitted Garments,* (Jenny Dean, 1997)

Dean, Jenny, *Wild Colour, How to grow, prepare and use natural plant dyes,* (Mitchell Beazley, 1999)

de Francesco, G , 'Venetian Silks', (Ciba Review No 29, 1940)

de Roover, Edleide, 'Lucchese Silks', (Ciba Review No 80, 1950)

Dollinger, Philippe, transl. D S Ault & S H Steinberg, *The German Hanse,* (Macmillan, 1970)

Driesson, L A, *The History of the Textile Crafts in Holland,* (Ciba Review No 48, 1944)

Dunkerton, Jill, Susan Foster, Dillian Gordon, Nicholas Penny*, Giotto to Durer, Early Renaissance Painting in the National Gallery,* (Trustees of the National Gallery, 1991)

Eales, Jacqueline, *Women in Early Modern England, 1500-1700,* (UCL Press, 1998)

Earle, Peter, *Essays in European Economic History 1500-1800* , (Clarendon Press Oxford, 1974)

Earle, Peter, *A City full of People, London 1650-1750,* (Methuen)

Earnshaw, Pat, *The Identification of Lace,* (Shire Publications, 1980)

Earnshaw, Pat, *Lace Machines and Machine Laces,* (Gorse Publications, Guildford, 1995)

Earnshaw, Pat, *Lace in Fashion, From the Sixteenth to the Twentieth Centuries,* (Gorse, Guildford, 1991)

Earnshaw, Pat, *Threads of Lace, From Source to Sink,* (Gorse Publications, Guildford, 1989)

Ellen, Alison, *The Handknitters Design Book,* (David & Charles, 1992)

Elliott, J H, *Imperial Spain, 1469-1716,* (Penguin Books, 1963)

Endrei, Walter and Geoff Egan, 'The Sealing of Cloth in Europe, with Special Reference to English Evidence'

Epstein, Stephen, 'Textiles, 1300-1500, Sicily' in *Journal of Medieval History,* No 2 June, (1989)

Epstein, Stephen, 'Silk Production and Manufacture' in *An Island for Itself: Economic development and Social Change in Late Medieval Sicily,* (CUP, 1992)

Erlanger, Philippe, *The Age of Courts and Kings, Manner and Moral 1558-1715,* (W&N, London 1967)

Farrell, Jeremy, Gen. Ed, Dr Aileen Ribeiro, *Socks and Stockings,* (B T Batsford, 1992)

Farrell, Jeremy, Gen. Ed, Dr Aileen Ribeiro, *Umbrellas and Parasols,* (B T Batsford, London, 1985)

Falkus, Christopher, *The Life and Times of Charles II* , (BCA, 1972)

Feltwell, Dr John, *The Story of Silk,* (Alan Sutton, 1990)

Firmin, F, *Some Proposals for the employment of the Poor,* (London, 1681)

Flanagan, J F, *Spitalfields Silks of the 18th & 19th centuries,* (F Lewis, Leigh-on-Sea, 1954)

Fletcher, Joan, *Silk in New Zealand,* (NZSW & Woolcrafts Soc. Inc)

Floud, Roderick & Donald McCloskey, *The Economic History of Britain Since 1700,* Sec. ed. (1994)

Forbes, R J, 'Studies in ancient Technology', Vol IV *Textiles,* (Leiden, 1959)

Fraser, Antonia, ed. *The Lives of the Kings and Queens of England,* (W & N, London, 1993)

Fraser, Antonia, *The Six Wives of Henry VIII,* (W & N, 1992)

Fraser, Antonia, *Mary Queen of Scots,* (Panther, 1970)

Friedlander, Max J, *From Van Eyke to Bruegel,* ed. F Crossman, (Phaidon, 1969)

Frost, Patricia, 'Lace' in *Illustrated History of Textiles* by Madeleine Ginsburg, (Studio Editions, London, 1991)

Garfield, Simon, *Mauve,* (Faber & Faber, 2000)

Gies, Joseph and Frances, *Merchants and Moneymen, The Commercial Revolution, 1000-1500,* (Arthur Barker Ltd, London, 1972)

Ginsburg , Madeleine ed. *Illustrated History of Textiles,* (Studio Editions, London, 1991)

Goffin, Judith, 'Gender and the Guild Order: The Garment Trades in Eighteenth Century Paris, in *The Journal of Economic History,* No 54. (1994)

Gombrich, E H, *The Story of Art,* 13th ed. (Phaidon, 1983)

Goodwin, Jill, *A Dyers Manual,* (Pelham Books London, 1982)

Grassby, Richard, 'Smyrna and Constantinople', from *The English Gentleman in Trade, Life and Work of Dudley North 1641-91*

Green, Bertha de Vere, *The Collector's Guide to Fans over the Ages,* (Frederick Muller, London 1975)

Gwynn, Robin D, *The History and contribution of the Huguenots in Britain, Huguenot Heritage,* (Routledge & Kegan Paul, London, 1985)

Hafter, Daryl, 'Women Who Wove in the Eighteenth Century Silk Industry of Lyon', *European Women in Pre-Industrial Craft,* (Indiana University Press, Bloomington & Indianapolis, 1995)

Hanawalt, Barbara A, ed. *Women and Work in Preindustiral Europe.* (Indiana University Press, Bloomington, 1986)

Harlow, Eve, ed. *The Art of Knitting, Garments for today from patterns of the past,* (Collins, Glascow & London, 1983)

Harris, Jonathan, 'Two Byzantine Craftsmen in Fifteenth Century London', *Journal of Medieval History* 21, (1995)

Harris, Jennifer, ed. *5000 Years of Textiles,* (The Trustees of the British Museum, London, 1993)

Harte, N B & K G Ponting, *Cloth & Clothing in Medieval Europe, Essays in Memory of Professor E M Carus-Wilson,* Pasold Studies in Textile History, 2.(Heinemann Educational Books, London, 1983)

Harte, N B & K G Ponting, ed. *Textile History and Economic History, Essays in Honour of Julia de Lacy Mann,* (Manchester University Press, 1973)

Harte, N B 'The Economics of clothing in the Late 17th century', *Textile History* (Vol. 22 (1), 1991)

Harvey, Michael, *Patons: The Story of Hand Knitting,* (Springwood Books, Ascot, 1985)

Hauser, Arnold, *The Social History of Art, Vol. 3 Rococo, Classicism, Romanticism,* (Vintage, Random House, 1951)

Hayward, Maria, 'The Packing and Transportation of the Possessions of Henry VIII with particular reference to the 1547 Inventory', *Costume* (Vol. 31. 1997)

Haywood, Maria, 'Repositories of Splendour: Henry VIII Wardrobes of the Robes and Beds',

Hegyi, Klara, *The Ottoman Empire in Europe,* (Corvina, 1986)

Herald, Jacqueline, 'Cloth of Gold', in *Renaissance Dress in Italy 1400-1500,* History of Dress Series, (Bell and Hyman London, 1981)

Herrin, Judith, *Women in Purple, Rulers of Medieval Byzantium,* (Phoenix, 2001)

Higgins, Clare, *The Spitalfields Silk Industry in the mid 19th century,* (MA Thesis, May, 1989)

Hill, Christopher, *Reformation in the Industrial Revolution, A Social and Economic History of Britain, 1530-1780,* (W&N, London, 1967)

Hogarth Sylvia and Christopher Webb, 'The Account Book of the York Company of Silkweavers, 1611-1700', in the *Yorkshire Archaeological Journal* Vol. 66, (1994)

Howell, Martha C, *Women, Production and Patriarchy in Late Medieval Cities.*(University of Chicago Press, 1986)

Hufton, Olwen, *The Prospect Before Her, A History of Women in Western Europe, Vol. 1, 1500-1800,* (Fontana Press, London, 1997)

Huyghe, Rene, gen.ed. *The Larousse Encyclopedia of Byzantine & Medieval Art,* (Paul Hamlyn, 1958)

Inalcit, Halil with Donald Quataert, ed *An Economic and Social History of the Ottoman Empire 1300-1914* (1994)

Ingram, Elizabeth, ed, *Threads of Gold, Embroideries and Textiles in York Minster,* (Pitkin Pictorials, Andover, 1987)

Jacoby, David, *Trade Commodities and Shipping in the Medieval Mediterranean,* (1997)

Jacques, Anne, *The Wardle Story, A Victorian Enterprise,* (Churnet Valley Books, 1996)

Jardine, Lisa, *Worldly Goods, A New History of the Renaissance,* (Macmillan, 1996)

Jenkins, Elizabeth, *Elizabeth the Great,* (Victor Gollancz, 1958)

Jones, Brian, 'British silk Industry 1700-1870', *Journal of Economic History*, Vol 47, (1987)

Kalavrezou, Ioli, *Byzantine Women and Their World,* (Harvard U Art Museums, 2002)

Kamen, Henry, *Spain in the Later Seventeenth century, 1665-1700,* (Longman, 1983)

Kellenbenz, Hermann, 'Rural Industries' in *Essays in European History 1500-1800,* ed. Peter Earle,

Kemper, Rachel, H. *A History of Costume,* (Newsweek Books NY, 1979)

Kenyon, J P, *The Stuarts,* (Fontana Library, Collins, 1966)

Kerridge, Eric, *Textile Manufacturers in Early Modern England,* (Manchester UP, 1985)

Kisch, Herbert, *From Domestic Manufacturing to Industrial Revolution, Rheinland Textiles, 16th century,*

Kisch, Herbert, 'Wupper valley Textile Trades', *Journal of European Economic History* Vol. 1 (1972)

Knights, Derek, 'Medieval Fairs of Champagne' in *Medieval History,* Vol. 2, No 3, (1992)

Kohler, Carl, *A History of Costume,* (Dover Publications, NY, 1963)

Kolander, Cheryl, *A Silkworkers Notebook,* (Interweave Press, 1985)

Kurella, Elizabeth, *The Complete Guide to Vintage Textiles,* (1999)

Lacy, Kay, 'The Production of 'Narrow Ware by Silkwomen in Fourteenth and Fifteenth Century England', Textile History, 18 (2) (1987)

Larkin, James and Paul Hughes, *Stuart Royal Proclamations* Vol.1 & II

La Seta in Europe, Secc XIII-XX, incl. articles by Donald King (V&A, 1993)

Laver, James, *A Concise History of Costume,* World of Art Library, (Thames and Hudson, 1979)

Leix, A, *Trade Routes and Dye Markets in the Middle Ages,* (Ciba Review, No.10, 1938)

Lemire, Beverley, 'Peddling Fashion: Salesmen, Pawnbrokers, Taylors, Thieves, and the second hand clothes trade in England c1700-1800' *Textile History,* Vol. 22 (1), (1991)

Lemire, Beverley, 'Developing consumerism and readymade clothing trade in Britain 1750-1800' *Textile History,* 15 (1) (1984)

Lemon, H, 'The Development of Handspinning wheels', *Textile History* Vol. 1, (1968)

Le Ver de soie, BT Nature, (PEMP, France, 1994)

Levey, Santina, *Lace: A History,* (V&A, 1883)

Levy, Michael, *Rococo to Revolution,* (World of Art, T&H, 1966)

Levy, Michael*, A History of Western Art,* World of Art, (T&H, London, 1968)

Levy, Michael, *From Giotto to Cézanne,* (T&H, 1966)

Llewellyn, Sasha,. 'Inventory of Her Graces Things, 1747 The Dress Inventory of Mary Churchill, 2nd Duchess of Montagau', *Costume,* 31, (1997)

Lewis, Peta, 'William Lees Stocking Frame: Technical Evolution and Economic viability 1589-1750' Vol. 17 (2) Autumn, (1986)

Lister, Margot, *Costumes of Everyday Life, 900-1910* (Barrie & Jenkins, London, 1972)

Lofts, Norah, *Domestic Life in England,* (Book Club Associates, 1976)

Lopez, Robert, *Medieval Trade in the Mediterranean World,* NY, (1955)

Lopez, Robert, 'European Merchants in the Medieval Indies: The Evidence of Commercial Documents', *Journal of Economic History* Vol. 3-4 (1943-4)

Lubell, Cecil, *Textile Collections of the World,* Vol 2. UK & Ireland, (Studio Vista, 1976)

Mallet, Michael, *The Florentine Galleys of the Fifteenth Century,* OUP.

Mango, Cyril, *The Oxford History of Byzantium,* (OUP, 2002)

Mansell, Philip, *Constantinople, City of the World's Desire, 1453-1924,* (John Murray, 1995)

Marschner, Joanna, 'Queen Caroline of Ansbach: Attitudes to clothes and Cleanliness 1727-37', *Costume,* 31, (1997)

Marlow, Joyce, *Kings and Queens of Britain,* (Artus, 1977)

Marshall, Dorothy, *The English Poor in the 18th Century,* (London 1926, revized 1969)

Mendleson, Sara & Patricia Crawford, *Women in Early Modern England, 1550-1720* (Clarendon Press, Oxford, 1998)

Merrill, John, ed. Oxford Illustrated History of the Tudors and Stuarts in Britain, (Oxford, 1996)

Morgan, Kenneth, *The Oxford History of Britain, The Tudors and the Stuarts,* Vol III, OUP, 1992)

Mosher, Ron, 'The Sidney M Edelstein Collection of the History of Dyeing, Bleaching and Drycleaning Textiles', *Textile History,* Vol. 12, (1981),

M T & H T, *Knitting in Silks,* (Published by James Pearsall & Co London 1900, V&A)

Muthesius, Anna, 'Byzantine Silk Industry: Lopez and Beyond', *Journal of Medieval History* 19 (1993)

Muthesius, Anna, 'From Seed to Samite: Aspects of Byzantine silk Production', *Textile History* Vol. 20 (2), (1989)

Nunn, Joan, *Fashion and Costume 1200-1980,* (The Herbert Press, London, 1985)

Olsen, Kirsten, *Daily Life in 18th Century England,* (Greenwood Press, 1999)

Origo, Iris, *The Merchant of Prato,* (The Reprint Society of London, 1959)

Ortolja-Baird, Ljiljana, ed. *National Gallery, Costumes in Art,* (W&N, 1998)

Parker, Julie, *All about silk, A fabric Dictionary and Swatchbook,* (Rain City Publishing, 1991)

Parker, Rozsika, *The Subversive Stitch, Embroidery and the making of the Feminine,* (The Women's Press Ltd, 1984)

Paulinyi, Akos, 'Development of John Keys flying shuttle', in *Textile History* 17 (2), (1986)

Payne, Blanche, *History of Costume, From the Ancient Egyptians to the Twentieth Century,* (Harper and Row, Publishers, NY, 1965)

Perez, Jose Ignacio Fortea, 'The Textile Industry in the economy of Cordoba at the end of the seventeenth and the start of the eighteenth centuries: a frustrated recovery' in *The Castillian Crisis of the Seventeeth Century* ed. Thompson and Casakilla

Perry, Mary Elizabeth, 'Behind the Veil: Moriscas and the Politics of Resistance and Survival' in *Spanish Women in the Golden Age,* by Sanchez and Saint-Saens

Phillips, Barty, *Tapestry,* (Phaidon, 2000)

Planche, J R, *A History of British Costume, From Ancient Times to the Eighteenth Century,* (Senate Reprint, 2001)

Plowden Alison, *Elizabethan England,* (Readers Digest, 1982)

Plumb, J H, *England in the Eighteenth Century,* The Pelican History of England 7, (1974)

Plummer, Alfred, *The London Weavers Company 1600-1970,* (1972)

Ponting, K G, *A Dictionary of Dyes and Dyeing,* (Mills and Boon Ltd, London, 1980)

Rapley, Jane, Handframe Knitting: The Development of Patterning and Shaping, in *Fashion Development in the Seventeenth Century*

Reininger, W, 'The Textile Trades in Medieval Florence', (Ciba Review No. 27, 1939)

Remi-Constable, Olivia, *Trade and Traders in Muslim Spain,* (1995)

Reyerson, Kathryn, 'Medieval silks in Montpellier: The Silk Market ca 1250-1350', in the *Journal of European Economic History* (No. 11, 1982)

Reyerson, Kathryn, 'Montpellier & Genoa' in the *Journal of Medieval History*, Vol. 20

Ribeiro, Aileen, *Dress and Morality,* (B T Batsford, London, 1986)

Rice, Tamara Talbot, *Everyday Life in Byzantium,* (B T Batsford, 1967)

Rice, David Talbot, *Constantinople, Byzantium –Istanbul,* (Elek Books Ltd London, 1965)

Ridley, Jasper, *Costume and Fashion, The Tudor Age* , (Constable, 1988)

Rogers, Alan, *Rural Industry and Structure: The Framework Knitting Industry of South Nottingham 1670-1840*

Rothstein. Natalie, 'Canterbury and London The Silk Industry in the Late 17th Century', (Vol. 20 (1) 1989)

Rothstein, Natalie, 'Planning a Careless Air, Rococo Silk Design', in *Country Life,*

Ruddock, Alwyn A *The Commodities of Trade in Italian Merchants and Shipping in Southampton 1270-1600,* (1951)

Rutt, Richard, Bishop of Leicester, *A History of Handknitting,* (B T Batsford, London, 1987)

Scott, Philippa, *The Book of Silk,* (Thames & Hudson, London, 1993)

Scott, Margaret, *Late Gothic Europe 1400-1500*, The History of Dress Series*,* (Humanities Press, NJ. 1980)

Scouville, Warren, *The Persecution of the Huguenots and French Economic Development 1680-1720,* (1960)

Sherrard, Philip, *Byzantium*, The Great Ages of Man series, (Time-Life International, 1967)

Sichel, Marion, *Jacobean. Stuart and Restoration*, Costume Reference 3, (B T Batsford London, 1977)

     The Eighteenth Century, Costume Reference 4, (B T Batsford, London, 1977)

     The Regency, Costume Reference 5, (B T Batsford, London ,1978)

Sim, Alison, *The Tudor Housewife,* (Sutton, 1996)

Staley, Edgcumbe, *The Guilds of Florence,* (Methuen, 1906)

Staniland, Kay, *Embroiderers, Medieval Craftsmen*, (British Museum Press, London, 1994)

Stanley, Montse, *The Handknitters Handbook,* (David & Charles, 1994)

Stove, Margaret, *Creating Original Handknitted Lace*, (Caxton Press, Christchurch, 1995)

Swann, June, *Shoes,* The Costume Accessory Series, (B T Batsford, London, 1982)

Sweets, John F 'Lacemakers of Le Puy in the Nineteenth Century', in *European Women and preindustrial Craft*, ed.Daryl Hafter, (Indianna, UP, 1995)

Synge, Lanto, *Antique Needlework* (Blandford, Poole, 1982)

Synge, Lanto, *The Royal School of Needlework. Book of Needlework and Embroidery*, (Collins, 1986)

Szostak, Rick, *The Role of Transportation in the Industrial Revolution, a Comparison of England and France,* 1000-1700, McGill-Queens UP, 1991)

Taylor, G W, 'New Light on the Insect Red Dyes of the ancient Middle East', in *Textile History* (Vol. 18 (2), 1987)

Thirsk, Joan, 'The Fantastical Folly of Fashion, The English Stocking Industry 1500-1700', *Textile History and Economic History* , (Manchester, 1973)

Thompson, E P *The Making of the English Working Class,* (Penguin Books, 1986)

Tilly, Louise, *Politics and Class in Milan 1881-1901*

Tomalin, Claire, *Samuel Pepys, The Unequalled Self,* (W F Howes, Ltd, 2002)

Tommer, Heather, *Lace: A Guide to Identification of Old Lace Types and Techniques*, (B T Bats(ford, London, 1989)

Traupel, R. *Spun Silk* (Ciba Review No. 111, 1955)

Trevalyan, G M, *English Social History, A Survey of Six Centuries from Chaucer to Queen Victoria,* (Longmans, Green & Co, 1946)

Truman, Nevil, *Historic Costuming,* (Sir Isaac Pitman, London, 1947)

Turnau, Irena, The Diffusion of Knitting in Medieval Europe, in *Cloth and Clothing in Medieval Europe*, translated by Maria Starowieyska

Turnau, Irena *History of Knitting before Mass Production*, Translated by Agnioszka Szonert, (Warszawa, 1991)

Turnau, Irene, 'Knitting', in *The Illustrated History of Textiles,* ed. Madeleine Ginsburg, (Studio Editions, London, 1991)

Turnau Irene 'Consumption of Clothes in Europe between the XVIth and XVIIIth Centuries', *Journal of European Economics History* Vol. 5 (1976)

Uitz, Erika, *The Legend of Good Women, The Liberation of Women in Medieval Cities*, (Moyer Bell, 1994)

Van Houtte, J A, *An Economic History of the Low Countries 800-1800,* World Economic History, W& N
Vassberg, David, *Village in the Outside World in the Golden Age of Castille*, (CUP, 1996)
Volbach, W Fritz, *Early Decorative Textiles,* (Paul Hamlyn, London, 1969)

Waller, Maureen, *1700, Scenes from London Life*, (Hodder & Stoughton, 2001)
Wardle, Patricia, 'The Kings Embroiderer Edmund Harrison (1590-1667) The Man and His Melieu' Vol 25(1), 1994)
Wardle, Patricia, *Victorian Lace,* (Herbert Jenkins, London, 1968)
Warner, Sir Frank, *The Silk Industry of the United Kingdom, Its Origin and Development*, (Drane's London, 1911)
Warner, Pamela, *Embroidery, A History,* (B T Batsford, London, 1991)
Wensky, Margret, 'Women's Guilds in Cologne in the Later Middle Ages', in the *Journal of European Economic History*, No. 11, (1982)
Wiesner, Merry E, 'Male Bonding and Women's Work in Early Modern Germany', in *Gender and History* Vol 1 No 2 Summer, (1989)
Williams, Neville, *The Life and Times of Henry VII,* (Book Club Associates, London, 1973)
Wittlin, A, 'The Development of the Textile Crafts in Spain', (Ciba Review No 20, 1939)

Yallop, H J, *History of Honiton Lace Industry, Textile History*, Vol. 14 (2), (1983)

Index

For additional references see Glossary

A

Abbot, Peter de Courpalay, 85
Accessories, 9,103, aprons, 87, garters 87, ruffles, 104
Africa, 19, 22
Agents, 11, 34, 48, 78, 102,
Aleppo, 14-15
Alexander the Great, 57, 84
Alexandria, 6, 36
Almeria, 18-19
Alum, 40-41, 61
Ambassadors, 6
Ambrogio Lorenzetti, 83
America, 43, 60, 79
Ancona, 22,
Andalusia,18-19,
Andros, 9,34,
Antioch, 35
Antwerp, 26, 65, 102
Americas, 20, 72
Antwerp, 48
Apprentice, 19, 21,31, 72, 107, 122, 125
Arabs, Arabia, 17-18, 22, 29
Aristotle, 57
Arkwright, Richard 120
Armenia, 14
Arras, 66, 70
Athens, 9
Avignon, 28-29, 92
Avlona, 10
Augsburg, 51
Austria, 87, 92

B

Baghdad, 11, 36
Bales 10,22-23,36,49, 117
Bankers,10, 20, 29, 44-45, 53
Banners, 23
Barcelona, 21
Bardi, 53

Basel, 43
Basil, 7
Basinghall Street, 75
Bayeaux, 106
Baynard's Castle, 135
Beggars, 21, 43
Belgium, 100, 107
Benjamin of Tudela, 8-9
Bertin, Rose, 147
Bethnel Green, 75, 78
Bezants 34, 44
Bishops, 40, 67, 85-86
Bishop of Cremona, 6
Black Death, 28, 36
Black Prince, 52
Black Sea, 36
Bleaching, 13,
Blonde, 103-104, 113
Blount, Bessie, 135
Bobbins, 29, 83, 99, 106, 111, winders 25, 121
Bologna, 23-24,48 , 82
Book of Ceremonies, 4
Book of the Prefect, 5
Brabant, 43, 62, 70
Braid , 52, 99, 115, 127, 132, 141
Brazilwood, 60-61, 63
Bribes, 10
Broadloom, 115
Brocklehurst, 125-126
Bruges, 43
Brussels, 110
Buckinghamshire, 107, 111
Bullion, 20
Bursa, 10-13
Buttons, 53, 95, 123-6, 141, 147
Buxtehude Madonna, 84
Byzantine Empire, 2,6, 35
Byzantium, 1-4,9, 47, 57-58

C

Cabanis brothers, 46
Caen, 106-107
Cairo, 34
Calenders, 59, 70
Calvaleri, 47

Canterbury, 52, 65-71, 77, 124
Capital, 4,13,24-25,38-39
Caravan, 12, 15,33,
Caravanserai, 11
Cardinal's Purple, 58
Carding, Combing, 21, 119-120
Carpets, rugs, 6,8,18, 87,
Carriages, 3
Caspian, 12, 27
Castille, 21, 43
Catholicism, 19-20, 28, 72, 108, 132, 134, 139, 142
Cechi, Jan, 48
Chantilly, 104-107, 110
Chapmen, 38
Charities, 78
Charlton House, 70
Children, 19, 31, 123, 142
China, 1,11,24,46, 71, 74, 103, 113, 118-119, 143
Chinoiserie, 103,
Chintamarni, 12
Church, 39, 45-46, 48, 53, 85, 132
Christ Church, 77,
Christians, 10, 18-19, 22,28, 58
Cleopatra , 57
Clocks, 93,
Cloth of gold, 26, 49, 51-54, 75, 134
Clothes, 3-4,7, 42. 78, 106, 115, 146, 148, Breeches, 87, 131-136, 141, Chemise, 141, Doublet, 26, 66-68, 131-132, 134-135, 138, Farthingale , 132,134, 140 Gown, Jackets 94, Kirtle, 66, Mantua, 143, Petticoats 97, 120, 134, 141-145, Polonaise, 146, Waistcoats, 93,
Coats of Arms, 52
Codpiece, 137-138
Cochineal , 42, 60
Cocoons, 9,18, 22,29-30, 36,43
Colchester, 77, 125
Cologne, 30-31,38, 43,51,

Colonies, 11, 48
Congleton, 118, 124
Constantinople, 1-3,5-6,8-9,
34-36,58
Consul, 25,
Contracts, 18,
Convents, 31,
Coptic, 58
Cordoba, 47, 93
Corinth, 9-10,34
Cortes 20-21,
Cotton, 10
Cottage Industry, 18
Court, 2,4, 52-54, 137
Courtaulds, 77
Coventry, 124-126, 128,
Cracow, 48-49,
Crafts, Craftsmen, 2,7, 22,30,
52, 66-67, 97, 125
Credit,10, 44-45,78
Crete, 48, 56-57
Crocheteuse 111,
Cromwell, Oliver, 92, 95
Crusades, 34-35,
Cushion, 70, 81, 87, 135,
Customs, 12, 56
Cyprus, 38 67

D

Damascus, 6, 36
Danielis,7-8, 35
Darius of Persia, 57
Debt,10,38,49,78,122,125,135
Denarii, 7,
Derby, 95, 109, 115, 117,
Designs 119,
Diderot, Denis, 92
Dolls, 143
Dowry, 9, 20, 23,
Drawlooms, 24 , 120, 122
Dutch, 49, 68, 77, 91, 127
Duties, 33
Dyes, Dyeing, 4,18, 23, 25,
29, 33, 36, 40-42, 47, 56-63,
72, 76,78, 113, 121

E

Eagles, 4, 29,
East Anglia, 79
East India Company, 15
Edict of Nantes, 68, 90
Egypt, 6,9, 18,58,81,
Eleanor of Toledo, 88, of
Castille 46
Elector of Saxony, 88
Embroiderers,7, 26
Embroidery, 17, 51-52, 55,75,
85, 99, 115, 132, 134, 141,
143, 148
Employment, 21
Emperor, 4, 8-9, Aurelian, 57,
Justinian,3   Manuel
Comnenus, 22, Napoleon, 104,
Empress Eugenie, 107
England, 15, 36, 41, 61, 69,
72, 95,110, 113, 115-116, 132
Eunuchs, 13
Europe, 19-20, 23
Eunuchs, 8,
Europe, 35, 37, 49, 81,91,123
Exhibition, 107, 112

F

Factories, 21, 95, 106, 118, 120
Fairs, 8, 22-23,38-45, 124,
126, 143
Fans, 139
Fardels, 12
Farmers, 9, 70
Fascinators, 109
Fashion, 106, 108, 112, 120,
125-126, 128, 131-148
Fatima, 34
Feasts, 26, 63
Felt, 81
Ferdinand & Isabella, 19, 132
Filament, 18
Flanders, Flemings, 23, 36,
41, 52, 59, 65, 68, 70,100,
Flashmen, 126,
Florence, 23-27, 41,44,48-49,
52-53, 61, 85, 100,

Floss, 69
Flowers , 4, 87
Foreigners, 6
France, 44, 47, 52,60, 63, 66-
67, 73, French, 14-15, 17-
18,28-29,36, 65-68,75-77, 93,
100, 106, 138,141,146
French Revolution, 104, 147,
Frankfurt, 43,
Furnishings, 3-4, 18, 23,51,
66, 81, 120, 134-138, 145-146
Furs, 3, 47

G

Galli, 48
Galleys, 18. 23, 37-38
Gall nuts, 62
Garments, 4,10,23,34,55, 58,127
Garthwaite, Anna Maria, 75
Gems, 4, 48
Geneva, 44
Genoa ,9, 11, 22-26, 33-36,
38, 41, 43, 47,52,87, 94, 103,
108, 132
Germany, 40-41, 49, 62, 72,
79, 84, 87, 92
Gifts, 8,18,28, 145
Gloucester, 96
Gloves, 42, 54, 84-86, 93,
110, 127, Mittens, 111
Goblein, 70
Gold, 2-3,6-7,9, 18, 22,25,29,
33, 43-44, 51-56, 67-68, 70,
94, 101, 103,107, 132, 135,
139, 141
Gold lace, 54, 100, 107
thread, 55, 141
Goldsmiths, 51, 55
Government, 10
Granada, 19, 47
Great Palace, 2-3
Great Wardrobe, 135-136
Greece, 1,7,9, 22,33,57
Griffins, 4
Guilds, 3-5, 19-21, 25,31, 39,
72-73, 87, 93, 115, 124, 127,

Haberdashers, 87
Mercers, 133, Silkwomen, 30
Spinners, 13, Tailors
Guildsmen, 4-5, 21, 31

H
Haberdashery, 38, 42
Half silks, 10,24
Hanseatic League, 39
Harems, 13
Hargreaves, James, 120
Haute-Loire, 105-106
Headdress 42, 108, 134, 146,
Bonnets, 132, 140
Gable, 133-135, Hairnets,
head, 103
Heathcote, John, 111,
Henry of Navarre, 68,
Heraldry, 52
Holland, 14-15, 60, 63, 72
Holy Family, 83
Honiton, 110
Home, 131-148
Hose, Hosiers, 25,111, 116,
132, 134,
Hormuz, 11
Huguenots, 53, 59, 65-79,
124, 148

I
Illegal goods, 6
Immigrants 23, 66, 78
Imperial silks, 2,5
Imperial workshops, 2-4
Imports & Exports, 4,10,12,
14,18, 25,49,79, 118,
Incroyables, 147
India, 2,11-12,103,
Indigo, 42, 58-59, 62
Industry, 20-24, 29, 35-36,69,
78, 110, 119
Inquisition, 19
Invention, 117-120,
Iran, 10-13
Islam 28, law,10,
Italy,9,12,14, 17,23-25, 28-

29,34-35,37-38,40-42, 47-48,
52, 61,67, 74, 81,84-85, 94,
100, 108, 116-117, 132

J
Jacquard, 78, 128
Jewels, gems,7,
Jews,9-10, 23,44, 59-60,
Journeymen, 122
Justinian, 1-2

K
Kay, John 120,
Kekolymena, 4
Kermes, 22,29, 34, 36, 58, 60, 63
King Charles I, 63, 95, 127,
132, 141, Charles, II, 73, 95,
102, 142, Charles V, 20
Charles VIII, 29, Edward 1,
124, Edward III 45, Edward
IV, 86, Erik XIV, 91, George
II, 78, 145, Francis I, 29, 53,
Henry II, 86, 100, 138, Henry
III, 138, Henry IV 69,90,
Henry VII, 52-53, Henry
VIII, 53-54, 75, 86, 134-136,
James I, 55, 69-70, 101, 140,
Johan III, 91, Louis VI, 40,
Louis IX, 44, Louis XI, 29
Louis XIV, 72, 141, Louis XV,
104, 110, 144, Louis XVI ,
104, Roger 1, 9, Roger II,10,
22, 58, William 1, 22,
Knotless netting, 82,
Knights, 132,
Knitters, 30,school, 88-91
Knitting, 79,81-97,109,111,116
Kommerciarioi , 5
Kommerkion, 6
Koran, 17,22,34

L
Labour, 21
Lac, 60
Lace, 53, 71, 99-113, 115,
122, 140-142, 145, Tambour,

103, 110, chemical 113,
Lace Machines, 108-110,
Bobbin 100, net, 113, Levers,
112, Pushers, 112-113,
Landlords, 11
Las Hueglas, 84
Latin, 11, 34
Leadenhall, 78
Leather,10
Lee, William, & James, 88-91, 95
Leek, 96 , 124-126
Legislation, 72, 78-79,
Le Puy, 105-106
Levant, 15,26,35,38, 42-43,
46, 124,
Leveuse 105,
Lichens, Roccella 60-61
Lille, 65
Lincoln, 90
Linen, 52, 68, 102, 136
Liturgical, 84
Livery, 55, 135
Loans, 10,43-44
Lombards, 45
Lombe, 116-118
London, 38, 55-56, 59,61,65,
68-70 74-75, 78-79, 87, 91,
95, 97, 115-119, 124-127,
144,148
London Weaver's Company, 90
Looms,12, 18, 20-21,70, 79,
120, 127, 141
Low Countries, 65,102,
Lucca, 23, 27, 29, 41-41, 48,
52, 103, 116
Lyons, 26, 29, 44, 65, 72-73,
92 , 110, 113, 138,148.

M
Macclesfield, 118, 125-126
Macedonia, 7,
Madder, 58, 60-63
Madonna knitting, 82-84
Madrid, 21,
Magazines, 148
Maidstone 66, 125

Malta, Maltese, 108-109
Manchester, 79
Mantillas, 108
Mantua, 48
Manufacturing 29, 45, 49, 108, 115, 118, 141,
Markets,3,5,8,10,13,15, 21, 45, 48 , 126, 128, 148
Marriage, 5
Marseilles, 14, 38, 46
Massacre of St Bartholomew, 67
Master, 25,74, 79,111, 122,
Masterpiece, 87
Mawata caps, hankerchiefs
Medici , 45-46, 88, 90, 100, 138
Mehmet II, 12,
Meister Bertram of Minden, 84
Merchants, 4,10-15,18-20,22-26,29, 31, 34,36,38, 41,45, 47-48,52 , 60,76, 78, 94, 106, 112, 120-122
Mesopotamia, 6,
Messina, 22
Midlands, 79,
Milan, 22-24, 29, 48, 87, 94-95, 103 , 132
Military, 10
Mills, 27, 92, 102,115-119, 123, 125,
Mirrors, 77, 148
Modon, 38
Monastries, 5,
Money, coinage, 9,11,14,20, 44
Montague, 88, 100
Montpellier, 29, 41, 46, 59, 138
Moors, 17, Morisco, 19
Mordant, 59
Moscow, 12
Mourning, cloth, 67, 75,148
Muhammad, 33,
Muhtesib,10
Mulberry Trees, 2, 8, 11, 15, 17, 22.26-27, 29, 69-70
Murex, brandaris, 56-58, principalis, 56,
Muslims, 19, 33-35

N
Nalbinding, 85
Naples, 9, 26,48, 70, 87,
Narrow ware, 52, 125
Neckwear, Collars, 102 138, 141, Cravats, 101, Fichu, 107, neckerchiefs, 110, Ruffs, 100,
Needles, 82-83, 90-91, 99
Netherlands, 66, 92, 100,
Nets, 99,103,109-112
Niccolo di Buonaccorso, 84,
Nimes ,28-29,72,74,84,92,138,
New College Cambridge, 85
Nobles, 9,
Noil , 66
Non-Imperial guilds, 3-4
Norfolk, 79
Normandy, 72, 87, 107,
Norwich, 65-66, 70-71, 77, 87, 89, 125
Nottingham, 95-96, 109, 111
Nuremburg, 51

O
Opus Anglicanum, 52
Orchil, 58
Ottoman, Empire, 10-11,35
Outworkers, 20, 31, 117

P
Padua, 117,
Paleologs, 58
Palermo, 22,27, 58
Palestine, 9
Panier, 144,
Papal Bull, 85 States, 61
Papyrus Holmiensis, 58
Parasols, 107, 139, 142,
Paris, 38-39, 72, 86, 92, 95, 103-104, 110, 144
Parliament, 63
Passementerie, 115, 125, 127
Pasteur, Louis, 113
Patches, 146
Patras, 7, 35,
Patronage, 90, 107,

Patent, 117-119
Pattern Books, 100, 104, Paul, Lewis, 120
Pax Mongolica, 11
Peasants, 38
Peek District, 95
Pegolotti, Francesco Balducci, 36
Peasants, 11,18,
Pebrine, 113,
Peddlars, 38, 126
Peloponnese, 7-9, 22, 43,
Pepys, Samuel, 142-143
Persecution, 19, 65, 72-73,
Pescia, 27, 48
Perfumes, 137, 146,
Persia, Persians, 2,17,24,42,
Petticoat Lane, 75, 79,
Phoenicia, 56
Picardy, 60-62
Piedmont, 74, 116-118,
Pilgrims, 36, pilgrimages,
Pirates, 36, 49
Pisa, 34, 48
Poland, 87, 92
Politics, 72
Pope, 46, Paul II, Urban II, 34, Innocent IV, 85
Pomegranates, 25
Pompadour, Mme, 145
Por Santa Maria, 17, 25,
Portugal, 60, 79,
Ports,10, 15,18, 22,33,38,79
Poverty, 20, 30
Power, 7,10, 46 , 63
Prefect, eparch, 2-5
Princess Charlotte, 112
Privileges, 74
Procopius, 2
Profit, 5-6,10,15,37, 45,118,
Prostitution, 20, 30, 43
Protestants, 65-72, 90
Puritans, 142
Purl, 84, 91, 128
Purple, 4,57-58, 60, 136,

Q

Quakers, 109, 128
Queen Anne, 140, Caroline, 145, Catherine of Aragon, 54, 134, Catherine of Braganza, 142, Catherine de Medici, Eleanor, Elizabeth I, 54, 67-68, 86,88-90, 100, 135-136, Elizabeth of York, 53, 133, 135, Isabella, Henrietta, 142, Margaret of Scotland, Marie Antoinette, 146-147, Mary Stuart, 138
Quet, Jean, 74,

R

Rabbi, 8
Ravenna, 58
Raw goods, 34
Raw silk, 2 ,9,11-12, 14, 17-18, 20, 22-29,31, 34, 36-37,
Reeling, 14, 27, 79,115,119, 122,
Relic bags, 81-85
Ribbons, ribands, bows, 26, 42-43, 56, 63, 106, 112, 115, 124, 127-128, 131, 141-142,
Rome, 23,26, 46, 132,
Rouen, 90
Ruff, 100, 132, 139, 141,
Russia, 14, 92, 129

S

Sacque, 144,
Safflower, 61
Saffron, 63
Saints, Catherine, 83, Lucy, 87 Ursula, 87, Brigid, 91
San Vitale, Ravenna 58,
Scarf , 107, 126
Scarlet, 59-60
Schools, 108
Scotland, 138-139
Seals, 6
Secondhand clothes, 42, 148
Selim1, 12
Sericulture, 2, 6-7,11, 15, 17-19,69, 84,

Setaiuoli Minuti, 25
Seville, 19-20, 36,43,85,
Shawls, 71, 107,
Ships, Shipping, 11, 33,
Shoes, 88, 144
Shops, 4, 46, 48, 76,148
Shuttles, 120
Sicily, 17, 19, 22-23
Silk Fabrics, 4, 8-9, 14, 22, Alamodes, 75, 148, Baldachin, 23, Bombazine, 66, Bourette, 66, Brocade, 1, 6, 11, 18, 23, 25-26 ,48, 51, 74-75, 94, 138, Brocatelle, 68, Caffa, 67, Camlets, 69, Chambleys, 70, Chenille, 120 Cocculario, 9, Corduroy, 29, Crapes, 71, 110, Damask, 23, 29, 34,68, 72, 74-75, 120, 132, Druggets, 70, Ferradines, 70, Filoselle, 69, 94 Flowered silks, 68, 74 ,Fustinadoes ,68, Gauze 68, 71, 99, Grenadine, 104, Grosgains, 69-70, 74, Lampas, 12, Lustring, 143, Mockadoes, 66 Mosulin, 146, Odoratoes, 71, Paduasoys, 70, 74, Piccadillies, 71, Plush, 70, 68, Rashes, 67 Samite, 9, 23, Satin, 25, 29, 63, 67-69, 74, 134, 138, 142, 145, Sayes, 67, 71, 131, Sendal, 8-9, 23, Shot silk, 67, Sidonia,8, Stamins, 67, Stuffs, 66, 120, Tabby, 9,24, 68, Tamarines, 70, Tiffanies, 68, Tufftaffeta, Taffeta, 21,23, 25, 29, 63, 69-75, 120, 141, 147, Tissues, 69, Tulle, 99, 103, 110, twill, 12, 34, Velours,29, 68
Silk Fibres, Floss, 18, 104
Silk Threads, tram, 121,
Silk Wars, 12
Silkwork, 30, 72,
Silkworms,6, 15,27, 69-70, 113,
Silkworm eggs, 2, 15, 27,

Silver, 25, 49, 53, 67-68, 70, 94 100, 132, 144, Silver-gilt
Skeins, Skeining 121
Slaves, 2,5,8,13, 33
Sliver, 29, 51
Smuggling,6, 10, 12, 56, 95
Smyrna, 15
Southampton, 77,79,
Spain, 1,10,17-20, 22, 29, 41, 43, 47, 60, 81, 84, 87-88, 92-94, 100, 108, 113, 132, 134, 138, 141,
Spindles,13, 119,
Spinning, Spinners, 4, 12, 21, 23, 25,30-31, 119-120, 123
Spinning wheel, 24,119,
Spitalfields, 65-79, 91, 94, 115, 118
Spun silk, 10, 18
Statutes, 31, 132,
Stays, 138
Steam power, 112, 128
Stepney, 71, 78
Stockings, 84-88, 92-95, 111, 115, 137-138
Stockholm, 58
Stolen silk, 96, 148.
Stow, John, 75,
Strangers, 66-69, 77,
Strutt, Jedediah, 109
Sudac, 34
Sudbury, 118, 125
Suffolk, 79,
Suleyman I, 13
Sumptuary Laws, 86, 88, 131-132,
Switzerland, 72, 85, 87
Syria, 6, 9,14-15,35,42

T

Tabriz, 11-12
Tapestry, 22,70,131, 135,
Tarrifs, 72
Tassles, 115
Taxes, 6,9-10, 14-15,21, 29, 31, 34,43, 66,77,
Textiles, 17-19,28, 37, 53, 133
Thames, 78,

Thebes, 8-9,
Theophanes, 2
Throwsters Throwing, 23, 27, 29, 72, 79, 115-118, 122-123,
Tiraz, 17-18,
Timken Museum, 84,
Tokat, 10-11,14,
Toledo, 20, 87
Tombs, 85
Tommaso da Modena, 82
Tournai, 66
Tours, 29, 65,67, 72-73, 138,
Trade routes, 11
Trade Traders,10,20, 33-34, 42, 44, 141,
Transport,11, 35, 37, 53, 55
Treasure, 7
Treasury, 34
Troyes, 41
Truck system, 31,
Tudor, 54,133,
Turin, 94-95
Tunisia, 18
Turkey, 27
Tuscany, 23, 27, 48
Tyre, 6, 34, 56

U
Unwinding

V
Vagabonds, 21
Veil, 23, 39,
Velvets, 6.12, 23-24, 26, 29, 52, 66 69, 72, 74-75, 120, 135-136, 141-146, cisele, 24, velluti ad inferriata, 24 alto-e-basso, 24 Allucciolatura, alla vincizani, 24
Venice, 10, 14, 23, 26, 33-36, 38, 43, 48, 52, 54, 94,132,
Vestments, 3, 9, 23, 26, 28
Veit Stoss, 84
Villages, 10
Virgin Mary, 82-84
Vitale degli Equi, 83

W
Wages, 30, 102, 106, 115,122
Walloons, 65-68
Wapping, 77
War, 49, 73,131,
Warehouses, 39, 76, 120, 148,
Warp, 67, 115,
Warsaw, 49
Waste silk,18,66, 94
Water power, 23, 27, 116-117, 120,
Watteau, Antoine, 144
Wealth, 53-54, 63, 78, 104, 120, 141
Weavers, 4,8, 19-20, 22-23, 25, 47, 56, 65, 70, 75, 77, 115, 121-122, 128, 148
Weaving, 2, 17-18, 21, 23, 37, 53, 116
Weld, 62
Weights & Measures, 22, 40, 121, demi-aune, 42, 105
Westminster, 69-70, 148
Whalebone, 137
Whitechapel, 75
Widows, 19-20, 79, 139,
Wig, 110, 141-1423
William of Wyckham, 85
Wills, 9
Winders, 79, 115 121-122,
Woad, 58, 60-62
Women, 19, 21, 27, 29-30 51, 58-59,79, 106, 110, 118, 127, 132, 145, 148
Wool, 42, 52, 59, 66, 81-83, 87-88, 95
Workshop, 7, 18, 21, 25-26, 35, 49, 122
Wright, Phoebe, 75

Y
York, 70, 89, 95

Z
Zonca, 117,
Zurich, 100

Picture Credits: